MAGDALENA

MAGDALENA

INTERNATIONAL WOMEN'S EXPERIMENTAL THEATRE

Compiled and Introduced by
SUSAN BASSNETT

BERG PUBLISHERS LTD.
Oxford / New York / Munich
Distributed exclusively in the US and Canada by
St. Martin's Press, New York

First published in 1989 by
Berg Publishers Limited
Editorial Offices:
77 Morrell Avenue, Oxford OX4 1NQ, UK
165 Taber Avenue, Providence, RI 02906, USA
Westermühlstraße 26, 8000 München 5, FRG

British Library Cataloguing in Publication Data

Magdalena : international women's experimental theatre.
1. Women's experimental theatre
I. Bassnett, Susan
792'.022

ISBN 0–85496–016–3

Library in Congress Cataloging-in-Publication Data

Magdalena : international women's experimental theatre / compiled
and introduced by Susan Bassnett.
p.   cm.
      Bibliography: p.
      Includes index.
      ISBN 0–85496–016–3 : $22.50 (est.)
      1. Magdalena Project. 2. Feminist theater. 3. Experimental
theater. 4. Drama festivals.
PN1590. W64M34   1989
792'.082—dc20

89–31863

Printed in Great Britain by
T.J. Press (Padstow) Ltd, Padstow, Cornwall.

For Jill Greenhalgh

Contents

Illustrations

Photo credits: 1, 2, 3, 4, 5, 10, 12, 14, 15, 16, 17, 20, 24, 25 by Mary Giles of Cardiff. 9 by Jan Pieniazek of Warsaw, Poland. 11 by Inge Fjelldalen of Grenland Friteater, Porsgrunn, Norway. 18 reproduced by permission of the *New Theatre Quarterly*. 26 reproduced by permission of the *New York Drama Review*. 23 by Vladislav Vanak of Brno, Czechoslovakia. 27, 28 by Philippe Gabel of Paris. 29, 30, 31, 32 by Douglas Cape of London.

Acknowledgements

A large number of people have helped to make this book possible. Magdalena '86 came into being with financial assistance from the Welsh Arts Council and the Calouste Gulbenkian Foundation and with practical assistance from a whole team of people, all of whom contributed a great deal. Special thanks are due to all those women who took the time and trouble to write about their experiences of Magdalena, often at some length, and to suggest ways of moving the project forward. Jill Greenhalgh worked tirelessly at collecting and coordinating material. Aileen Christodoulou interviewed participants at Magdalena '86 and thanks are due for her work and for her enthusiasm. The book would have been far less interesting without the fine photographs, taken by Mary Giles, Douglas Cape, Philippe Gabel, Inge Fjelldalen, Jan Pieniazek and Vladislav Vanak.

The manuscript was typed with her usual care and skill by Irene Pearson Renshaw, to whom grateful thanks. Finally, as always, thanks to those who make it possible for me to have the material time in which to write, my friends, my husband, my mother and Lucy, Vanessa and Rosie, my daughters.

Introduction

In normal scientific practice, experiments are conducted, and then the findings are documented and written up in a proper form. The experiment is thus perceived with hindsight, and the results can be assessed from a discreet distance and, if necessary, compared with other similar experiments undertaken elsewhere.

This book is an account of an experiment, but contrary to normal scientific practice, it has been written while the experiment is still in progress. The results are not yet known and are unlikely to be clearly assessable in any case. For the Magdalena Project, as the experiment has come to be known, is a complex network of ongoing research initiatives into that most understudied and underdeveloped area: women's theatre.

In the past twenty years or so, since the rebirth of international women's movements in the 1960s, thousands of women writers, artists, film-makers, theatre practitioners and other creative artists have emerged into the public gaze. A new methodology, loosely termed feminist criticism, has compelled us all to rethink our notion of the great Canon, the list of great works deemed worthy of respect, a list which has traditionally excluded or marginalised women.

Vast numbers of previously unknown and forgotten women have been recovered from the past and are now being read and recognised. The dominance of women playwrights in the late seventeenth and early eighteenth-century English theatre has at last been noted; the long list of women poets and novelists writing under their own names, with no male pseudonyms required, has amazed us all. Art historians have uncovered a lost history of women painters and sculptors; historians of science have brought back the names of women whose contribution to knowledge was as great as that of any

1

man. And this process of rediscovery has been matched by a flowering of creativity by women in the latter part of the twentieth century. Suddenly, women are everywhere as creative artists, and perhaps for the first time, questions have been raised about the existence of a women's culture in its own right, something different from that made by men, something new and reflective of the new status that women are just beginning to feel they can have.

In 1949, when Simone de Beauvoir published her book, *The Second Sex*, which was to be such a fundamental text for future generations of feminists, she too was still subscribing to the notion that women's art is necessarily inferior to that of men because of the restricted socio-economic conditions in which women have existed for centuries. Women have been confined to the home, married young, frequently unhappily, forced to bear and rear children and have often lived the lives of slaves to their husbands. Such circumstances, the argument runs, seriously hamper the production of great novels or great paintings, for the world that inspires their art is so restricted. Simone de Beauvoir notes regretfully that there has never been a female Tolstoy and argues that this is because he, as a man, had access to the whole wide world, to battlefields and parliamentary chambers, to the corridors of power and the inner circles of economic shaping, whilst women were nursing babies and tending gardens or, at most, participating in village or community life in some small way.

One of the most exciting ideas to emerge from the new feminist criticism is a conception of women's creativity that challenges the view of Simone de Beauvoir, founder feminist though she may have been. The alternative vision suggests that the breadth and range of life experiences has little or nothing to do with producing great art, and that the core of the problem lies not with the restrictions women have so obviously suffered but with the arbiters of taste and greatness, those persons who determine what is and is not great art and who have always been men.

Adrienne Rich sums up the problem in a nutshell:

in pretending to stand for 'the human', masculine subjectivity tries to force us to name our truths in an alien language, to dilute them; we are constantly told that the 'real' problems . . . are those men have defined, that the problems we need to examine are trivial, unscholarly, non-existent . . . Any woman who has moved from the playing fields of male discourse into

the realm where women are developing our own descriptions of
the world knows the extraordinary sense of shedding . . .
someone else's baggage.[1]

The image of 'shedding', of losing the burden of a borrowed skin,
a borrowed language, has been prominent in the work of numerous
feminist creators. Verena Stefan, in her book entitled *Shedding*
(*Häutungen*), depicts a new woman, a new being emerging from the
weight of the past by asking questions and listening to her own inner
feelings for the first time:

> We constantly
>   come up against
> limits in our explorations. The limits
> of our own strength of available time of
> economic resources, of our careers and
> our longings. When can we
> clarify what longings really are? How can we make
> room for our sensual life? The new
> emerges but slowly, shedding the old, patchwork.[2]

Both Adrienne Rich and Verena Stefan, American and European,
two roughly contemporary women writing independently of one
another on either side of the Atlantic Ocean, reject a view of the
world that seeks to place women's creative achievements in a lower
position, and in doing so they reject the concept of the great Canon of
literature, the process of evaluation that has gone on for so long, and
call for a new aesthetic, a women's aesthetic. Quite what that may be
they do not say, only that if it comes, it will come from within
women, from a recognition of what it means to be a woman.

This great difference in attitude separates Simone de Beauvoir from
her successors. For Rich and Stefan offer an alternative to the frightening statement in *The Second Sex* that 'as long as [woman] has to
struggle to become a human being, she cannot become a creator.'[3]
They suggest that what has to evolve is a new process, an alternative
form of creativity. The starting point, the only starting point, has to
be within the consciousness of the individual woman, and the question of whether what she produces will be great art or not is entirely
irrelevant; that is a male question posed in male terms. The notion of a
woman's creativity is not new; there are many examples of women

who have reflected on the idea of an alternative art, one that would be truly feminine and not derived from male traditions. Writing to Virginia Woolf in 1935 Victoria Ocampo, the Argentinian writer, says:

> My sole ambition is to one day write more or less well, more or less badly, but like a *woman*. If I could have a magic lamp like Aladdin and, by rubbing it, could have the power to write like Shakespeare, Dante, Goethe, Cervantes, or Dostoyevsky, I truly would not take advantage of it. Because I believe that a woman cannot unburden herself of her thoughts and feelings in a man's style, just as she cannot speak with a man's voice.[4]

Forty years later the French feminist writer, Hélène Cixous, echoed Victoria Ocampo's desire for something new, for something truly belonging to women. In an essay entitled 'Le rire de la meduse' (The Laugh of the Medusa), she tries to describe the frustrations of wanting to create, of beginning to be in touch with something deep and personal and new but of not quite managing to let it out:

> Time and again, I, too, have felt so full of luminous torrents that I could burst – burst with forms much more beautiful than those which are put up in frames and sold for a stinking fortune. And I, too, said nothing, showed nothing; I didn't open my mouth, I didn't repaint my half of the world. I was ashamed. I was afraid, and I swallowed my shame and my fear. I said to myself: You are mad. What's the meaning of these waves, these floods, these outbursts?[5]

In asking herself such questions, Cixous maintains that like so many other women, she argues herself out of creativity. How many women have been ashamed of their own strength, she asks, or have been horrified by the violence of their energy, having been led to believe that women ought always to be calm and composed and self-effacing? 'Who, feeling a funny desire stirring inside her (to sing, to write, to dare to speak, in short, to bring out something new), hasn't thought she was sick?'[6]

Feminist thinking has opened up these issues. Like the box that Pandora is supposed to have opened, releasing sin into the world, feminism has subverted our traditional notions of art and aesthetic judgement. There are new forces unleashed in the world; old skins are being shed every day.

1. *The Magdalena '86 team at the Potato Factory*

The Magdalena Project, from its beginning, has been an attempt to slough off old preconceptions about women in theatre and make new statements that can lead into new areas. Originally conceived as a one-off festival, the Project has mushroomed into a series of workshops, conferences and performances, often very different from each other, but all trying to explore ways forward for women working in the theatre. From its origins in Cardiff in 1986 it has spread across Europe and over the Atlantic to North and South America, and in the process of growth it has also shifted focus, from experimental theatre in the first instance to all forms of theatre in which women are involved.

Although it is still far too early to form any critical assessment of the Magdalena Project, some of its more obvious successes and failures can be seen, and this book looks at what has taken place so far and what is planned for the future. The voices of many women involved in Magdalena can be heard, some enthusiastic and some very negative – the quotations are taken from original letters, tapes and recorded statements. The vision of Jill Greenhalgh, the original founder of Magdalena, involves a belief in the uniqueness of women's creativity, although she admits that as yet she cannot articulate what it is that she is striving for. Some women share her vision, but others have been more critical, rejecting what they perceive as woolly idealism in favour of a theatre practice that has its roots in social need and real experience. The Magdalena Project is therefore a forum for debate among women, and although participants may share a common belief in the value of women's work in theatre, they often share very little else. The violence and energy described by Hélène Cixous as part of woman's struggle to release her own creative potential has been a constant feature of the Magdalena encounters. As the Magdalena Project extends its programme of events forward through the 1990s, the struggle seems likely to go on and on.

Notes

1. Adrienne Rich, 'Conditions for Work: The Common World of Women,' *Heresies*, 3 (1977), pp. 53–4.

2. Verena Stefan, *Shedding*, trans. Johanna Moore and Beth Weckmüller (London, The Women's Press, 1978), p. 108.

3. Simone de Beauvoir, *The Second Sex* (Harmondsworth, Penguin, 1974).

4. Victoria Ocampo, 'Carta a Virginia Woolf,' in D. Meyer, *Victoria Ocampo* (New York, Braziller, 1979), p. 127.

5. Hélène Cixous, 'The Laugh of the Medusa,' in Elaine Marks and Isabelle de Courtivron, eds, *New French Feminisms* (Brighton, Harvester, 1981), pp. 245–64.

6. Ibid.

I
The Birth of Magdalena

Women's Theatre Past and Present

Despite the large amount of work published on women's creativity in general and women's writing in particular, the theatre has received little attention. This seems curious at first glance, given the long history of women's involvement with theatre and the public attention focused on female performers, but it is nevertheless true. Not only has contemporary work by women in theatre received scant attention, but very little has been written on women's theatre history, a fact which leads to the continuance of all kinds of misconceptions and wrong assumptions about that history, principal of which is the belief that actresses were a late arrival to the scene, in the seventeenth century, and that there have rarely, if ever, been any women involved in management and production. In 1931 Rosamond Gilder published *Enter the Actress. The First Women in the Theatre*,[1] and despite the publication of studies of individual aspects of women's theatre history, her book is still the only one we have that tackles the question on a large scale. Yet without an awareness of history, it is impossible to discover the origins of prejudices still operating against women, the best defence against which must surely be adequate information and knowledge.

The role of women in theatre management, for example, is an important one and deserves to be fully explored, but the role of woman as actress also needs reassessment. Contrary to popular belief, women players were an integral part of theatrical performances for centuries. When Isabella Andreini, the Italian *commedia dell'arte* player (who also wrote texts), died in 1604 aged forty-two, pregnant and still touring with the company in Lyons, the whole city attended her majestic funeral. Yet across the Channel in Shakespeare's London, women's roles were being played by young men, it being deemed offensive for women to appear on a stage. The history of theatre has remembered the prohibition of women from the London stages; it has forgotten the European-wide success of actresses in the *commedia* companies.

Scholars generally agree that the earliest dramatic dialogue in Western theatre history after the decline of the Roman Empire is the *Quem Quaeritis* trope which dates from the latter part of the tenth century. Theatre, we are told, vanished with the collapse of the Roman tradition and appeared again in churches through the dramatisation of crucially significant moments in the Mass. But in the late fifteenth century a German scholar discovered a manuscript of plays, religious comedies in the manner of the Roman playwright Terence, written at the same time as the *Quem Quaeritis*. What perplexed him, and has perplexed scholars ever since, is that the plays were written by a woman named Hrostvitha, a nun in the prestigious convent of Gandersheim in Saxony. Controversy has continued to rage about Hrostvitha's plays: could they really have been written by a nun, in view of the often scurrilous sense of humour and wit displayed in them, and if they were written by her, who performed them? Could nuns in a tenth-century German convent have performed plays? And if they did, for whom did they perform, and most problematic of all, if one convent was engaged in the writing and production of plays, how did this come to be? Was it an aberration, or was there a tradition of similar activity, something that centuries of scholarship managed to overlook, because it was always looking for theatre produced by men, never for theatre made by women?

Many of the apparent inconsistencies in women's theatre history can be explained by the poor state of scholarship in theatre studies, which is itself, after all, a fairly new discipline. Much work in theatre studies has tended to focus on the text, on the actual script of the play that was performed by the actors, and this is perhaps understandable, since theatre is an ephemeral art, and the written text is often all that remains. But emphasis on the written text creates an imbalance; in the history of performance prior to the Renaissance, for example, it is very clear that the actor, performing a scenario or play, was one of a much wider group of dancers, singers, musicians, jugglers and artistes of all kinds. The act of 1572 for the punishment of vagabonds, passed during the reign of Elizabeth I in England, divided performers into categories. Those who belonged to a formally constituted company and had a legal patron were acceptable to the law. Those

*2. Brigitte Cirla
discussing her
training session at
Magdalena '86*

who could 'gyve no reckninge how hee or shee dothe lawfullye get his or her Lyving' were to 'bee taken adjudged and deemed Roges Vacaboundes and Sturdy Beggers'.[2] Into this category came fencers, bear-keepers, common players in interludes, minstrels, jugglers, ped-lars, tinkers and travelling salesmen or chapmen. The theatre world was divided into the acceptable and the outsiders, and women per-formers were well and truly outside the homophilic courtly circles of Elizabethan theatre.

In Italy, the process of commercialisation of the *commedia* companies also led to radical changes in structure and resulted in a less prominent place for female performers. But more seriously, at the same time as theatre was being established on a commercial basis in sixteenth-century Europe, there was also a radical shift in ideology and in perception. The Reformation had spread throughout Northern Europe and was being met head on by the conservatism of the Counter-Reformation. In both these world views, the role of women was circumscribed and determined by a rigid moral code. The literary women of the High Renaissance and the age of Humanism vanished and were not replaced. The emergent middle classes saw little reason to educate their daughters, unlike the Renaissance barons and theologians. And in the new moral climate, women exposing themselves to public gaze became synonymous with whores. The actress, reintroduced into England in the licentious ambiance of the court of Charles II, was an object of male desire, a prey, a thing to be bought and sold. She was also, of course, good box-office material, and female sexuality was there for the exploitation. The pit, former home of Shakespeare's groundlings, became the best place in the house and consequently the most expensive, once it was realised that the occupants of front row seats could look directly up the actresses' skirts in an age when they wore no knickers.

The process of rediscovering the history of women in the theatre has barely begun, but as it starts to happen it is bound to affect present work. Certainly, from the 1960s onwards women throughout the world have felt a need to create something they could define as 'women's theatre', and since traditions and history appeared to be absent, women have set about creating that theatre on their own terms. Describing her work with the Women's Experimental Theatre in New York, Roberta Sklar, one of the artistic directors, tries to explain some of the problems of finding a voice in the theatre for women:

> I was interested in developing a theatre, a method and a theory. How do you act as a performer and a person when you have been taught not to ACT, not to do, not to take action? The performer is taking an action. The study of acting is an analysis of human behaviour and a projection of that analysis. Once I realized that, I knew that I had to rediscover or reanalyze even the things I had been part of inventing at the Open Theatre, because these inventions were made from a male-identified perspective. Now I needed other voices.[3]

Wrestling with these problems in the late 1960s, Roberta Sklar claims that she began to see a way forward after first watching a feminist company, the It's Alright to be A Woman Theatre, perform in 1971. Though theatrically naive, the performance provided an example of a new role for theatre, one in which performers and audience could act in partnership and share in consciousness.

Early feminist theatre in the late 1960s and early 1970s was, as Roberta Sklar suggests, exciting, new and very simplistic. Essentially agit-prop theatre, small companies toured shows through Britain, North America and Europe, drawing attention to the new demands being made by women for improved working conditions and equal pay, freedom from violence, abortion and child-care facilities, divorce, equal rights and equal status with men. The terminology of Women's Liberation united both performers and audiences, and this kind of theatre had a clear function as both consciousness-raising and supportive. In Rome the first women's theatre was established, La Maddalena, coincidentally drawing on the same name that would be used fifteen years later when the Magdalena Project was devised.

In her book, *Carry on, Understudies* (1986), Michelene Wandor discusses the way in which women's theatre in Britain developed over two decades. She divides the work into several phases: phase one is the street-theatre phase, when feminist theatre was essentially a political theatre, a theatre of the barricades, which she locates between 1969 and 1973. The second phase, a more complex organisational phase, she locates between 1973 and 1977, and during this period she sees feminist theatre as becoming more complex and theatrically more sophisticated. The third phase, from 1977 to the early 1980s, is the period in which a small but increasing number of women began to move into mainstream theatre, into positions as directors, managers and playwrights:

> The vivid visual imagery of the early street theatre, with its
> spontaneity and its attack on stereotypical 'feminine' imagery
> gave way in the mid-1970s to a period of consolidation and the
> development of a theatre of argument, a theatre which explored
> what it would mean to reclaim the experience of women and
> gays from the militant sexual–political perspective of the
> period. . . . The third phase towards the end of the 1970s
> showed a return to some of the early spontaneity, but now in a
> different context . . . the new spontaneity revolved around an
> examination of the way the theatrical forms themselves work to
> represent sexuality.[4]

Though applied to the British theatre only, Michelene Wandor's divisions into phases roughly correspond to the stages of development in women's theatre elsewhere. The first period was clearly more of a

naive, propagandist phase for the women's cause, characterised by great energy and enthusiasm. The second phase, which occurred rather later in Britain (it had already begun to happen some four or five years earlier in North America, for example) saw women beginning to deal with the historical problem of their exclusion from the power machinery of theatre production, and therefore moved beyond the straightforward depiction of stage images of women's condition. In this second, organisational phase, all kinds of issues were addressed: the marginalisation of women from positions in management, the need for genuinely cooperative company structures that did not place the technical work in a lower category, the question of whether a director was necessary in a cooperative structure and if so, what the role of a woman director with an alternative notion of power hierarchies might be, the problem faced by women (in touring companies particularly) of child care and the collective responsibilities of the company for the provision of that child care. These issues were among the many that began to enter into the discussions surrounding the development of a specifically 'women's theatre'.

The movement of women into mainstream theatre, though obviously significant, marks one of the ways in which feminism has changed with the changing times. Although it is important for women to work in national theatre companies and to direct large-scale, prestigious companies, such work does not fall within the scope of this book, nor does the increasing amount of work being produced by women playwrights, particularly in Britain, since this kind of theatre work, interesting and valuable though it may be, is rarely experimental. The presence of one or two women directors in the Royal Shakespeare Company, for example, does not radically alter the kind of theatre produced by that company, and certainly does not take women's theatre very far forward, even though all women working within the theatre will note with a small degree of satisfaction the breaching of yet another bastion of male culture. The Magdalena Project starts with a different kind of theatre, a theatre that stands in relation to contemporary National Theatres in much the same way as the jugglers, minstrels and sturdy beggars stood in relation to the liveried players of courtly companies in the sixteenth century.

Third Theatre – The Women's Story

Michelene Wandor's second phase of the British feminist theatre ends in 1977, and that year was also significant in other countries. In Italy, where there had been a huge ferment of alternative theatre companies and feminist creative work since the early 1970s, 1977 marked a watershed year in national politics. It was the year of the 'historic compromise', the accord between the parties of the centre-right and the Communist Party, traditionally the largest communist party outside Eastern Europe. The 'historic compromise' was seen by many as a great betrayal on the part of the Italian Left, and repercussions were felt immediately in the world of theatre and writing. With the Left prepared publicly to do business with the old forces of opposition, the role of an alternative theatre became more questionable, particularly since subsidies for small companies had come primarily from parties on the Left. The historic compromise caused a crisis of confidence.

In Britain, that crisis was becoming daily more evident and resulted in a shift to the right in 1979 with the first of three successive Conservative election victories. In France, the rise of the far right and the Neo-Nazis, with all the paraphernalia of male militaristic ritual, brought all kinds of skeletons out of the cupboard, and in West Germany a similar process was under way. The latter part of the 1970s throughout Europe and North America, which saw Ronald Reagan elected to power in 1980, was characterised by a move to the right, and the cultural policies of right-wing governments firmly exclude small, alternative theatre companies, which do not have international status or appeal and which all too often tend to be sharply critical of society.

It would not be unfair, therefore, to see 1977 as the end of the Age of Alternative Theatre that had lasted some fifteen years and provided such vital stimulus to the development of a new women's theatre. But even as that age came to an end, other things were happening that offered a more hopeful prospect for the future. The Jamaican women's theatre collective, Sistren, was founded in 1977, a group of working-class women on a government-sponsored emergency employment programme. Women's alternative theatre may have been in trouble in the industrialised world, but in the Third World it was just beginning, and increasingly the theatre work that was taking place outside Europe and North America came to be a source of energy and inspiration for theatre practitioners who felt constrained by the cultural backwardness of the new right.

In Belgrade in 1976 the first encounter of Third Theatre was held, and Eugenio Barba, founder of the Odin Theatre which has been a powerful force in helping to shape the work of many alternative theatre practitioners in the 1970s, wrote a short document that later came to be seen as a Manifesto for Third Theatre. In this document he

4. *Kozana Lucca demonstrating Beauty's voice at Magdalena '86*

tried to explain the choice of the term 'Third Theatre' and to explain what it was that characterised this kind of work. On the one hand, he argued, was the official, subsidised, institutionalised theatre, and on the other hand the theatre of the avant-garde, always searching for new ways forward. Somewhere between the two exists a vast, amorphous group of people who spend their lives trying to make theatre, often with no formal qualifications other than their own enthusiasm and determination:

> The Third Theatre lives on the fringe, often outside or on the outskirts of the centers and capitals of culture. It is a theatre created by people who define themselves as actors, directors, theatre workers, although they have seldom undergone a traditional theatrical education and are therefore not recognized as professionals. But they are not amateurs. Their entire day is filled with theatrical experience, sometimes by what they call training, or by the preparation of performances for which they must fight to find an audience . . . Like islands without contact between themselves, young people in Europe, North and South America, Australia and Japan gather to form theatre groups, determined to survive.[5]

Eugenio Barba's list of islands has since expanded to include India, Africa, the Caribbean and the South Pacific, but the initial principle is clear. He had identified a new phenomenon, one for which he chose the appropriate metaphor of floating islands, that of a collective turning to theatre not as a profession but as a way of life.

The great hopes of the 1960s had turned sour a decade later, with the growing power of reactionary forces, and the generation that had devised picket-line theatre, guerrilla theatre, and the Happening began to change direction and to look for new modes of expression. The expansion of feminism, in the meantime, with its emphasis on alternative social structures and alternative modes of perception, meant that women were in the vanguard of the search for new forms of theatre.

By the end of the 1970s, therefore, there were three distinct lines of development in women's theatre work: propagandist theatre still continued, but in a very diminished form and with little artistic potential; women were moving in substantial numbers into main-stream theatre and into television especially, and finally, in the floating islands of theatre communities, women were beginning to come to the fore, devising all-women shows, taking major organis-ational roles and, above all, testing the power and potential of women for a future, as yet unknown, theatre.

Mary Magdalene – The Archetypal Performer

Travelling round Europe, working in different Third Theatre companies, Jill Greenhalgh, the woman who devised the Magdalena Project in the first place, was struck by the energy of many of the women she encountered in contrast to their male counterparts. The general sense of disquiet at the narrowing of the political spectrum was experienced by both sexes, but it was in the work of women that Jill Greenhalgh found a greater sense of hopefulness and determination. The idea began to germinate for a meeting point that would bring together women from a wide variety of theatre backgrounds and many different cultures to share their experiences and compare notes. The history of individual women would also, she felt, have an impact on other women, and they would be able to compare notes on how they had dealt with discrimination, how they collaborated with their companies, how their work was received. Most significantly, they would be able to share their practical work, through training sessions and demonstrations. The idea for a festival of women's experimental theatre began to germinate, and the first stage of the Magdalena Project was under way.

Jill Greenhalgh describes how that first phase took place:

Magdalena '86 – International Festival of Women in
Experimental Theatre was born at a cafe table by Lake Bracciano
near Rome at the international theatre festival *Il Segreto di Alice* in
1984. This festival brought over 100 practitioners from the Third
Theatre family together to perform their shows and make special
events. It was a lovely sunny crazy gathering. The village was
delighted to have us, and we celebrated our knowing of each
other. There were many reunions, love affairs, much eating and
drinking together and an enormous amount of work. The events
we made were huge joyful occasions enjoyed over 10 days by
thousands of Italians. However, underlying this apparent
strength and energy was the feeling of being at some kind of
fantastic wake.

Many of the independent theatre groups that had grown up
through the 70s and early 80s had reached a crossroads and were
unconfident about which road to take next. It was as though
there was a drought and the search for fresh water had its effect
in a certain amount of disillusionment. In many cases it was

apparent that individuals were leaving the companies they had worked with for many years. This disintegration clearly indicated the need for change and the digging of new wells of inspiration . . .

In the cafe we thought how fine it could be if all the women from the groups could come together to meet and to work for a while . . . what an extraordinary energy that would create . . . and the drinking and dancing continued. Then the festival ended. The groups went on their separate tours with their separate work.[6]

One of the reasons why feminism had made so much progress in such a short time is that the ideas in circulation within the differently developing women's movements were shared by so many women from so many different societies. The remarkable advances of feminist thought in a brief twenty-year period certainly suggest that such a phenomenon as *Zeitgeist*, the spirit of an age, exists. Jill Greenhalgh's idea for bringing together women in theatre to share their experiences coincided with similar ideas already in circulation, and consequently an organisational committee came together very quickly, based in the Cardiff Laboratory Theatre.

Working with an ensemble company in the Cardiff Laboratory Theatre, Jill Greenhalgh had been involved in a performance called *The Heart of the Mirror*. The performance was difficult to create and painful for the performers, since it involved them in dealing with traumatic issues concerning the oppression of women, the abuse of women through pornography and the destructive force of patriarchal morals and ethics. The performance was, for many of those involved, a watershed, and for Jill Greenhalgh and Helen Chadwick especially, it was a further testament to the need for an articulation of women's culture, since in devising the production they had been shocked by the history of silence that surrounds women. As Jill Greenhalgh put it, 'I stayed with the Cardiff Lab determined to use our resources to create a situation in which women could find a voice, to tell of a female experience. A voice that would be heard . . . a place where feminine culture could be celebrated and where women's distinctive creativity would be recognized.'[7] The idea of a festival returned.

The initial support group, intent on creating the means whereby a women's theatre festival could take place, changed several times in the early stages due to pressures of work that meant moving from the

Cardiff base, but plans began to materialise, and in 1985 a small-scale project was devised that would serve as a pilot for the much larger festival planned for 1986.

At some stage in the deliberations the name 'Magdalena' emerged. No one is quite certain who first thought of it, or when, but the name appealed and was accepted by the group. Nobody knew that it was also the name chosen earlier by the Rome women's theatre; coincidentally two entirely separate ventures involving women in theatre had chosen the same symbolic name, that of Mary Magdalene.

According to tradition, Mary Magdalene was a performer, a woman whose body was her greatest talent. The old equation of performer–whore has as its archetype the figure of Mary Magdalene, the fallen woman who danced and sang in exchange for money, until converted and redeemed by the coming of Christ. Mary Magdalene has been depicted by generations of male artists, always beautiful, with long flowing hair and graceful limbs but without the diabolic quality that appears so often in representations of that other archetypal performer, Salome. Feminist representations of Mary Magdalene, however, have presented a different image. Marguerite Yourcenar, in her story of the betrayal of Mary Magdalene by her husband, John the Baptist (the same man whose death was the price of Salome's performance), depicts her as a victim of the male God, denied happiness and fulfilment and condemned to serve a patriarchal plan.[8] Other representations stress the independent spirit of Mary Magdalene, the woman alone surviving in a man's world, a very different image from that of the languid repentant sinner, offering herself on her knees to her saviour. Because of the ambiguities surrounding the image of Mary Magdalene, because of her history as a performer, because of the ambiguities surrounding the image of woman as performer in general, the name Magdalene seemed appropriate and was adopted.

The Captive Waves

In July 1985 Cardiff Laboratory Theatre supported a pilot project for the Magdalena Festival. The Captive Waves project brought together six professional women theatre practitioners and musicians from different backgrounds, with the aim of exploring new working methods without the pressure of touring commitments or producing a final product. It was to be an experimental collaborative project concerned with uncovering hidden symbols of feminine culture. It was not concerned with creating narrative but rather with creating a resonant atmosphere that might touch on the subconscious of an audience.

Sandra Salmaso, an Italian actress, Ali Robinson and Charlotte Buchanan, both classical musicians, Kari Furre, a well-established theatre designer and Jill Greenhalgh as director made up the company. (Claire Hughes, an English actress, was involved in the early stages but due to a serious illness was unable to complete the project.) There were only five weeks in which to complete the project, and as the group was completely new and one member spoke no English, it was a challenge to remain constant to fundamental concerns and not return to known theatrical formats.

The process embarked upon was eclectic. There was no fixed theme and no predetermined direction. It was irrational in the extreme, seeking only to follow an instinctive path. The six members of the company proposed ideas, presented personal material, books were passed around, themes developed, dances and songs were improvised, visual materials were shared. Step by step solid material was created but never with any conscious aim in mind. Common thoughts and images began to emerge, and these became the signposts of the work.

The final piece, therefore, was the result of the collective imagination of two musicians, two actresses, an artist and a director, who facilitated the work and wove together the threads of material. The performance was a fragmented evocation of a young woman's fall into her own conscience. Through a series of dances, songs and sculptural animations she confronts her deep fears and tries to dissect them. The piece spoke of the lies that are inherited and accepted from one's foremothers about who women are and how they should be, and how generation after generation of these lies has formed a protective layer shielding woman from knowledge of herself.

Sandra Salmaso's strong solo performance gave the impression of a woman–child beginning to hack away at these layers in her search for the answers to the plaguing question of her identity. The soundscape was composed and performed by the two musicians on a grand piano, cello, violin, conga drums and various other metallic objects used for percussion purposes. It used special effect amplification causing distortion and echo. The texts, chosen from Sylvia Plath, Phyllis Chestler and Susan Griffin, were both sung and spoken. Kari Furre's set design gave the effect of a cave-like labyrinth, in which

5. *Graciella Serra's
workshop on
Sense Perception
at Magdalena '86*

painted faces and figures of women appeared to ooze from the
hanging walls, being revealed and disappearing as the lighting
changed. The primary objects were a white bed, a rocking chair, a
grossly ugly doll, a typewriter, many red-bound diaries, a pitcher
and shattered mirror pieces suggesting a waterfall.

The work was shown over three nights, once to all women, once to all men and then to a mixed audience. Discussions that sought immediate reactions and feelings rather than opinions followed each performance. The audience of women spoke of feeling a recognition but were unwilling to articulate that feeling. That discussion was short but encouraging. The all-male audience shocked the performers by indulging in a two-hour series of dogmatic arguments among themselves, that bore little or no relation to the work they had seen, which eventually resulted in two or three men making angry recriminations against their own sex and the inability, in this forum, to genuinely speak of the work they had been shown. The mixed audience took the opportunity to question each other and analyse their collective reaction. The three types of audience therefore produced three *very* different reactions, and this fact in itself deserves further attention in similar future experiments.

The Captive Waves was an important pilot experiment for the Magdalena Project, since the sources that it revealed inspired much of the thinking behind the construction of the larger festival project. The aim remained that of looking for a process that might uncover and theatrically present signs that had some common female meaning, rather than distorting what was seen as the truth of woman's experience to fit the existent symbolism of male culture. It was a simple theatrical experiment allowing for a practical rather than a theoretical exploration. As Nor Hall in her book *The Moon and the Virgin* puts it:

> Essential to the task of finding out for oneself is the willingness to engage in, or be engaged by, a process of reflection and fabrication – of seeing and making. . . . The woman who can bend enough to go from reflecting to fabricating will be the one who can make up for something that is missing in the world. She is the one who can give shape to things lying beneath the surface . . .[9]

Belief in the shapeless but potentially powerful force of women's creativity was therefore fundamental to the Captive Waves project, as it would be later to the first Magdalena meetings. Reactions among the participants of Captive Waves were positive, with the women struggling to articulate what they felt had happened to them. In all their comments there is a sense of bewilderment, combined with a sense of excitement about what has begun to take shape.

FLOW: A word that has been on my mind, for, after three days, I began to feel a strange energy in the air – a sensorial current of creative energy.

How was it possible to work without knowing anyone or speaking the language common to all – English? The degrees of perception, reception, understanding and of 'listening' to one another was absolutely new to me, strong . . . strangely tangible . . . even to the degree of divergent opinions.

And what was behind all this? Was it because we were all women, with strength in a group, or was it the combination of personalities which got along together so well? I think, but I am still unsure, that it was our disposition, the attitude we all came here with. Open, responsible, ready to take risks . . . perhaps it was our dialectical attitude? It has been the 'first time' for each of us.

Sandra Salmaso (translation Katy Dymoke)

Theatre design is an interpretive art concerned usually with presenting the writer's and director's visions. An artist, however, has a responsibility to comment and respond to her own vision. The working process for Captive Waves has attempted to present a collective vision.

As designer, I have experienced no 'power struggle' problems with the director, the problem being rather to avoid imposing *my* will on the performers.

Working on a project for women has not allowed me to take refuge in 'known' and 'safe' methods of work – rather I was able and free to express self-doubt and inadequacy without being judged. I have functioned as an artist but with shared responsibility for the vision and, ideally, should like to work in this way again.

Kari Furre

The relationship of sister to sister is a unique and complex mixture of intense competitiveness, irritation, even hatred, coupled with deep understanding. Indiscriminately calling our women friends our sisters belittles the intensity of these emotions and the repercussions they have in our adult relationships.

If we six really were sisters, we mightn't have made this piece.

Ali Robinson

We shared in a process which opened to question any conceptions of sisterhood we have had. The ups and downs brought out 'captive waves' in all of us. From the outside I feel we have touched on a universal female consciousness that is sadly so soon silenced, clouded or denied in a male-dominated profession and world. The showing of the work so far shows the strength and potentialities of an alternative process. We can only go forward.

Katy Dymoke[10]

The voices are optimistic, but guarded. What seems clear is that all believed in the possibility of discovering an authentic women's voice, and they shared a further belief in the existence of some kind of transcultural female consciousness. This conviction inspired them to continue with the larger, more ambitious Magdalena Festival a year later.

Notes

1. Rosamond Gilder, *Enter the Actress. The First Women in the Theatre* (London, Harrap, 1931).

2. Quoted in Andrew Gurr, *The Shakespearean Stage 1574–1642* (Cambridge, Cambridge University Press, 1970), p. 19.

3. Roberta Sklar, quoted in Cornelia Brunner, 'Roberta Sklar: Toward Creating a Women's Theatre,' *The Drama Review*, Vol. 24, No. 2 (June 1980), pp. 23–41.

4. Michelene Wandor, *Carry On, Understudies* (London, Routledge, 1986), p. 87.

5. Eugenio Barba, *Beyond the Floating Islands* (New York, PAJ Publications, 1985), p. 193.

6. Jill Greenhalgh, letter to the author, undated.

7. Ibid.

8. Marguerite Yourcenar, 'Marie-Madeleine ou le Salut,' in *Feux* (Paris, Gallimard, 1974), pp. 113–35.

9. Nor Hall, *The Moon and the Virgin* (London, The Women's Press, 1981).

10. All quotations are from the report on Captive Waves, a privately circulated document addressed to Jill Greenhalgh.

II
Magdalena '86: The First Meeting

Planning the Festival

In August 1986, the first international festival of women in experimental theatre, known as Magdalena '86, took place in Cardiff, supported by the Cardiff Laboratory Theatre, the Welsh Arts Council and the Calouste Gulbenkian Foundation. The festival lasted for three weeks, from 11 to 30 August, with a programme of training workshops, performances, discussions and a concluding collaborative performance staged in an old factory down by the docks on two consecutive nights.

From the outset, the organisers of Magdalena were acutely aware that mounting an international festival of the work of women in experimental theatre carried huge responsibilities. They wanted the festival to be big, in order to make a significant impact on the theatre world, and they wanted to show a quality cross-section of exciting new work by women. This required complex, professional organisation and a high degree of personal commitment. Facing up to the realities of the situation, the organisers accepted that to find funding to support such a huge experiment seemed an unrealistic possibility with the limited resources and experience of the committee. So from the outset, it was accepted that the first festival was likely to be both underfunded and time-consuming, requiring the unremunerated, committed energy of all those involved in the process of making Magdalena '86 viable.

Magdalena '86 was the first festival of its kind in Europe. As a project of the Cardiff Laboratory Theatre it continued to promote their policy of exposing the work of foreign artists and groups to audiences in Wales, and was the first multi-cultural event hosted by the 12-year-old company. It was also their first major all-women project.

The budget was minimal. Grants of £9000 from the Welsh Arts Council and £6000 from the Calouste Gulbenkian Foundation supported the essential skeleton of the organisation, allowing basic wages for the small team of organisers, funds for a publicity campaign, administration and documentation costs. The aim was also to keep the charges for admission to performances and workshops during the first week as low as possible, to give the maximum opportunity for as many people as possible to attend.

Food, accommodation and travel within the United Kingdom was offered to all the visiting artists. The women from countries with restricted currencies received a small daily allowance to cover their personal needs. All children were supported in the same way, and in some cases accompanying colleagues were accommodated.

None of the visiting artists, however, were paid a fee for their performances or workshops, nor did they receive money for international travel. The task of raising essential personal money was the responsibility of each practitioner. In many cases, the Magdalena organisation assisted practitioners by lobbying the cultural funding bodies within their respective countries or by applying to foundations representing those countries in Britain. Some performers were supported by the British Council; Netta Plotsky received a travel grant from the Israeli Ministry of Culture and Education; Zofia Kalinska and the Akne Company were funded by Krakow House of Culture, Poland. In some cases, women continued to draw salaries from their respective companies. The director of the 1986 Coventry Festival, Maggie Russell, offered to stage four of the performances for that Festival immediately prior to the start of Magdalena, and the money earned from that source enabled the Argentinians, Graciella Serra and Kozana Lucca, to attend and also assisted other performers.

In some cases, women arranged to take time off to coincide with the dates of Magdalena, in order not to interrupt the touring commitments of their own companies for the rest of the year. In the main, most supported themselves through savings or taking loans. The full complexities of the financial arrangements cannot fully be dealt with here, but attempts were made by the organising committee to evaluate each case according to the personal situation of the practitioner and to respond with whatever financial or administrative support the limited resources could muster.

The decision to go ahead with organising the festival without financial security was perceived critically by some women. Review-

6. *Daria Anfelli and Michelle Kramers of Osmega Dnia giving a demonstration of their work at Magdalena '86*

ing Magdalena '86 in *Performance* magazine, Mina Kaylan remarked that:

> it seemed ironic that in the process of giving professional recognition to women artists, Magdalena had to ask them to work on less than (financially) professional terms. Many of us who paid for performances and/or workshops were oblivious of this political irony. Had we known, we could have had a tangible example of the notion that 'the process as well as form and content determines the politics of a piece of work'.[1]

This is an important point, though it should be set against the feeling of the organising committee that large-scale funding by public money might well have imposed unacceptable working conditions upon the whole project. Crucial to the festival, they felt, was the need for artistic freedom, for a space in which to allow things to happen. The small amount of funding that the project received already carried with it one constraint – that of the final performance, the public demonstration of the work that was undertaken by the group in residence for the full three weeks of Magdalena '86. As will be discussed later, there were feelings voiced that this kind of constraint was already unacceptable, since it meant that for the last few days of the project all attention had to be directed towards shaping that performance, and much of the work barely begun was left by the wayside. Nevertheless, the festival was underfunded, and it remains an unfortunate fact that many of the participants were under severe financial pressures right from the start, and in some cases the financial difficulties proved an insurmountable barrier.

The Shape of the Festival

Magdalena '86 was divided into two distinct phases. Phase I, which ran for one week, was open to the public, and some 150 people took part in workshops and discussion groups. During this first phase, individual performers presented shows they had brought with them, either already in repertoire or specially devised for the festival, and altogether there were twelve performances, all playing to packed houses. Phase II was the most complex part of the festival, the least planned and therefore potentially the most dangerous. For a two-week period, 38 women lived together and, out of their daily exchange of training methods and ideas, devised the final performance, which was again open to the public. The performance was to be the climax of the festival, a demonstration of the possibility of collaborative theatre work among women from so many different backgrounds and with such varied experience and skills. In her letter to the participants, Jill Greenhalgh attempted to explain what she hoped might develop from the collaboration. Noting that with so many women (and with such a short time in which to work) a polished performance would of necessity be impossible, she stressed her feelings that, with the collective resources that were to be made available, something extraordinary would certainly be produced:

> From the outset of this project it has been of paramount
> importance to try to define clearly a working process for this
> complex experiment. A female process. Do any of us know
> what that is? As director of the project I have been battling with
> this concept since the beginning and have been loathe to commit
> myself on paper. . . . I feel that this is a *work to be woven*. This
> piece will be made from material belonging to 35 individuals.

7. *Cinzia Mascherin and Sandra Salmaso in* No Man's Land

The task of making a whole from all the different input is something that each one of us will be responsible for, but we must be clear in our role and be able to let go of an over-personal attachment to any one direction.

Through sharing and developing our original ideas with each other, some common themes or threads will emerge and become

a natural direction, while others will have to be discarded. . . .
We imagine that groups may develop. It may also seem
appropriate to ask some people to lead work for the whole
company. It may be that there will be moments of working in
isolation.

Although we will of course be sharing all the work, the
overall musical co-ordination will be the final responsibility of
the three musicians. The performance environment and the
overall visual impact of the piece will be created and designed by
the team of artists. The performance *material* will come from the
actors and the whole will be *woven* together by two or more
weavers.[2]

The working method of the second phase was therefore completely
open, and the success or failure of the project depended entirely on
the ability of the group to find a means of working productively
together. For some, the experience of working without a director
was entirely unknown; for others the experience of improvising in
large groups was quite new, and for all the participants the experience
of running vast training sessions had never been encountered before.
Performers, administrators, technicians, artists – all came together in
training sessions, regardless of physical or vocal skills, and tried out
whatever was being offered. In this way, all kinds of barriers began to
break down – barriers between clearly defined roles in the theatre,
barriers between hierarchies and barriers of language. Most important-
antly, individuals began to let down their own private barriers, to let
other women pass through and begin to make contact in a new way.

A Magdalena Manifesto

Just before the Festival, Jill Greenhalgh issued a manifesto of what she
hoped would happen:

An international Festival of the work of women in
experimental theatre is taking place in Cardiff, Wales, in
August. . . . . YESSSS it's the same time as the Edinburgh
Festival!

It has been initiated and organised by Cardiff Laboratory
Theatre who, in recent years, has been committed to themes
Female.

Around 30 experienced women theatre practitioners are gathering from 15 different countries, together with anyone else who's interested and decides to make their way; and pay their way here.

Actresses, directors, designers, artists, musicians, technicians, administrators and academics from Czechoslovakia, Italy, N. America, Israel, Poland, Belgium, Spain, Japan, Norway, France, Argentina, Denmark, Wales, Scotland, Ireland and England have been invited to take part.

All are passionately enthused by the chance to expose their work in an all female forum and are looking forward to intelligent and unprejudiced feedback. The opportunity to share work not only with a foreign public but also with colleagues is rare and always welcome.

For the first week (August 11–17) the invited practitioners will be conducting public events; staging performances, teaching workshops and leading a number of seminars relating to women's role in contemporary theatre. They will be talking about their work, watching others work and making new work. It will be a time for a lot of women to exchange ideas, share some doubts, try to answer a few questions, attempt to establish some definitions and perhaps even initiate some new vocabulary. We plan to ask a lot of questions on the essence and nature of female creativity. There will be a lot of work on show, a lot of talk and probably a lot of singing.

No, the events are *not* closed to men. There will be something going on for anyone with an interest in which direction the female contribution to contemporary theatre is taking. It will encourage an intellectual and practical debate about New Theatre – at least there should be a good chance.

In the second two weeks the invited women will all be involved in a collaboration that will result in a piece '*The Magdalena Performance*' being publically shown on the 29th and 30th August. . . . We shall not be working in a theatre . . . we don't know what the piece will be about. . . . . we do know it won't be led by a single creative vision but will attempt a collective piece woven from strands made by the individual women during the process of work here in Wales. It will be a piece that we might study once it has been mounted, and then try to understand what it has to tell us. . . . . We do know that

35

8. *Jolanta Krukowska*
in A Dance
About . . .

we are taking a risk. The alternative, of imposing predetermined structures or even a process, seems somewhat
contradictory to the spirit and reason of the festival.

The spirit and reason??. . . . . to wait and see what happens
when you bring women, from a number of different cultures,
together to make theatre.

. . . . . ah. . . . . I was asked to write a polemic article about
why *Magdalena '86* . . . I looked up the word 'polemic'; 'a
wordy warfare' it said, among other things. So I'm sitting here
wondering what wordy warfare I should be waging and how it
should relate to the reasons for organising this festival.

Perhaps I should take the line that attacks our culture's art
which, in my humble opinion, is still hugely dominated by
masculist energy, imagery, ideology, symbology, iconography
and pornography, but which, even in our most progressive

circles, justifies itself as a true reflection of modernist society . . .
but why should I make enemies?

Or perhaps a wordy warfare that might viciously reveal the
hollow apathy of some contemporary critics who seem to whine
their way through comfy salaries and add little or nothing that's
dynamic, to the growth of theatre . . . but that's been done
before.

Or . . . maybe we could examine the repetitive pattern that
many women in theatre fall into, as a designer friend put it,
playing nursemaid to men's visions.

Or I could put myself on the line and try to talk honestly about
a deep feeling and fear of never being heard, of feeling you've
been silenced, that somehow the work that you can feel lining
your stomach wall, that you can't quite see because it's in
shadow, has got no place. There isn't a language invented to
cover or to search for it. And because there isn't this language
it's as though the feeling doesn't exist. That's frightening when
you know it's not true. It's a funny feeling not being able to
explain yourself . . . especially when there's a knowing that
there is something new and vital and female that is lying latent
and untapped, trapped under thousands of years of patriarchal art
and you just can't quite grasp it. Perhaps it has something to do
with shape, colour, atmosphere and secrets . . . perhaps it is
how music weaves with an image and an action to reveal
something you never felt before. But mainly it's about not
knowing yet and I, for one, am not ready to write polemic
articles about this feeling.

You have to admit that it's not easy when what exists is a
rigid and imaginatively infertile approach to devising new
material, and that the work that is held up for us to praise as the
brave new theatre is. . . . . well. . . . . why can't we get around
to admitting that a hell of a lot of it is just plain boring . . .
dull . . . manically egotistical and archaic? When did you last see
something that moved you? When did you last get really excited
about a piece of contemporary theatre? When did you last feel
that you were in the midst of a serious, interesting dialogue
about the finer points of theatre form? More often than not,
these days, the discussion centres around the financial and
administrative promotional coups that are achieved.

It's a fun game, some might say an essential one, but shall we stop kidding that it's got anything to do with a real passionate caring about the state of the art and the things it needs to speak of. There seems to be an insistence that there's all this interesting work around . . . but there isn't, is there? Of course there are one or two companies with some real guts whose theatre is genuinely evocative and important and some of that has been shamelessly plagiarized.

I don't want to sound all negative . . . it's just that I cannot understand why there is such a fear – in artists as well as the surrounding personnel who push the work out – to come clean and say 'that piece hasn't made it . . . it's close but . . .' At which point one could extract the genuine steps forward that have been taken, put them in an overall context and learn something. What is getting in the way of this kind of development? What's stopping this more honest approach that would ultimately benefit us all? We could be constantly opening new doors, seeking fresh influences and we could be listening instead of constantly having something to say. If you've got the courage to share your work, rather than jealously guarding it, it has a far better chance of growth. We're not too keen on sharing in this country though. An idea becomes the property of the person who thinks they thought of it rather than something which has simply been revealed. It's extraordinary the arrogance and selfishness of British theatre art. And what is it really saying these days? – half of it seems to be involved in trite, visually interesting, psychological arty thrillers, while the other half makes banal (and sometimes not particularly accomplished cabaret. *And* there must be another way to end a show than with yet another stunning apocalyptic vision of man's potential for self-destruction . . . with over-loud music.

I should be writing an article on 'Why Magdalena'. . . . . why a women's experimental theatre festival?

I've often wondered why the British are so stuffy when it comes to the term festival.

The French, Italian and Spanish theatre festival admits to the importance of sitting down and eating and drinking together. Talking, shouting and laughing about all the work that's on show could be the most important element of any reason behind organising a Festival. It's a very important way to feed the work. And I think we all need to show our work to our peers and we need to whinge and dream about it in the company of those we know are likewise struggling to get it right. And mostly failing.

This Festival is about bringing a whole load of strong, talented women theatre artists together and seeing what happens. And it's done with love to theatre and a caring about its future.

Jill Greenhalgh[3]
Director, Magdalena '86

The Practitioners

MANAGEMENT TEAM

The organising team of Magdalena '86 consisted of the following people:

Gilly Adams	*Advisory group*
Susan Bassnett	*Documentation*
Pam Blackwood	*Production manager*
Peter Brooks	*Catering*
Sally Broughton	*Press consultant*
Yvonne Cheale	*Advisory group*
Aileen Christodoulou	*Documentation*
Judie Christie	*Administration. Front of house*
Ken Coburn	*Front of house*
Katy Dymoke	*Fundraising. Welfare*
Becky Fawcett	*Technical assistant*
Jane Fitzgerald	*Video documentation*
Mary Giles	*Photography*
Kari Furre	*Visual coordinator*
Jill Greenhalgh	*Festival director*
Richard Gough	*Artistic director of Cardiff Laboratory Theatre*
Kate Long	*Box office*
Joan Mills	*Advisory group*
Kay Stopforth	*Video documentation*
Sian Thomas	*Workshop coordinator. Translation*
Sally Thompson	*Information*
Mandy White	*Publicity Officer*
Faith Wilson	*Press consultant*
Tricia Webb	*Technical coordinator*

THE INVITED PRACTITIONERS

For the second stage of Magdalena '86, Jill Greenhalgh convened a group of some 35 invited women. In the event, this number varied slightly, and the final figure was closer to 40, hence the apparent discrepancy of the figure quoted in some of the documentation. Originally it had been hoped to include women from Europe, North and South America, Africa and Asia, and to have a combination of women whose experience of theatre was extremely varied. For reasons that have already been discussed, the final membership was somewhat different than the list originally proposed, but there was nevertheless a wide range of nationalities represented, and a wide range of practitioners with different working styles and methods.

In order to provide readers with some idea of the variety of skills represented, short biographical details of the performers, artists and directors are given below:

Alena (Atka) Ambrova
Born 24.12.1955 in Brno, Czechoslovakia.
Studied ballet at the State Conservatory, Brno, then acting at the Janacek Academy, Brno. In 1977 she joined Divadlo na Provazku (Theatre on a String) as an actress. Since its earliest beginnings in 1967, Divadlo na Provazku has come to be seen as Czechoslovakia's leading experimental theatre company. Despite its growth both in terms of size and variety of productions, and despite the move from amateur status to full professional status in 1972, Divadlo na Provazku has maintained a highly individualistic performance style. Since joining the company, Atka Ambrova has taken part in all the company's productions, contributing her own highly skilled anarchistic sense of comedy. Her solo performances with the company include: *Pas de Deux* (1980), *Concertina* (1982), *Old Woman* (1985).

She is also a writer and has choreographed several shows for the company. She is married to Vladimir Sedivy, the anthropologist, and has one daughter born in 1984.

Mistress of ceremonies in the final *Magdalena Performance*.

Helen Chadwick
Born 25.6.1955 in Cambridge, England.
Studied at Dartington College of Arts, then moved on to become a founder member of Dr Foster's Travelling Theatre Company in 1979, now one of the leading community theatre groups in south-west England.

In 1982 she joined the Cardiff Laboratory Theatre, moving on a year later to take the Advanced Diploma in Voice Studies at the Central School of Drama. Having decided that her principal interest lay in developing voice work, she has gone on to teach freelance in this area and is currently working part-time at the National Theatre. In 1983 she created her first solo performance, *A Gift for Burning*, a celebration of the work of six women poets. She is currently devising a new solo performance on women and fathers, and is working on a project on women and ageism. *A Gift for Burning* was presented at Magdalena, and Helen also ran a workshop on Voice, Improvisation and Song.

Brigitte Cirla
Born 3.6.1956 in Montagne au Perche, France.
She first performed in the French Cabarets in Rome, singing and playing the accordion, then in 1979 joined Zero de Conduite company. In 1981 she created her first performance for children, *Le Voyage en Plastique*. Since founding the La Colline Compagnie in 1982 with her husband Dominique Collignon Maurin, she has increasingly special-ised in theatre work with children and adolescents. Faced with what she perceives as the difficulties adolescents encounter with short attention spans, she has developed a series of physical exercises designed to build up confidence and develop creativity. Her theatre work is closely linked to work in therapy. Besides this, she performs as actress and singer. Recent productions include *Medea Malum* (1985), *Jeux de Roles* (1986) both with La Colline and *Electre* (1987) with the Théâtre du Lierre, Paris. She has one son.

At Magdalena she ran a workshop for teenagers aged between 13 and 17 which led up to an open-air performance in the Hayes shopping centre in Cardiff.

Maria Consagra
Born 15.4.1954 in Rome, Italy.
Studied Theatre Arts at Sarah Lawrence College, New York, gradu-ating in 1976. From 1977 to 1980 she worked with the Teatro del Sole in Milan, then joined Farfa under the direction of Iben Nagel Ras-mussen from the Odin Teatret. Whilst with Farfa she appeared in a one-woman performance, *La Canzone di Rose* (1984) and with the company in *Heridos por el Viento*. She began her work as director with the Teatro del Sole, and in 1985 studied directing with Lee Breuer of

Mabou Mines. In 1987 she directed and performed in a children's show with the Teatro del Sole, *Uffa!* Besides her work as director and performer, she has been teaching theatre techniques since 1977. From 1984 to 1986 she taught acting and improvisation in the Dept. of Experimental Theatre in the Tisch School of Arts at New York University.

Maria ran workshops at Magdalena and made a street-theatre performance.

Grenland Friteater – Geddy Aniksdal, Anne Erichsen, Elin Lindberg

Geddy Aniksdal
Born 20.8.1955 in Vigrestad, Norway.
Presented two performances at Magdalena – *Les Miserables*, with Anne Erichsen and Elin Lindberg, which was first performed in Porsgrunn in 1985 and *The Stars are no Nearer*, her own one-woman show based on the life and work of Sylvia Plath. She also ran an improvisation workshop, using highly energised physical training techniques which have become a hallmark of the Grenland company work.

Geddy Aniksdal is married and has two children.

Anne Erichsen
Born 14.4.1957 in Copenhagen, Denmark.
She began working in political street theatre in Oslo in 1978. Then in 1981 she took part in a workshop run by Ingemar Lindh and entered into a period of intense learning, during which she worked with Odin Teatret, Riszard Cieslak and studied at the Institut for Scenkonst. In 1983 she joined Grenland Friteater.

Elin Lindberg
Born 10.12.1963 in Melay, Norway.
She joined Grenland Friteater as a pupil in 1983, and worked with Geddy Aniksdal and Anne Erichsen on the creation of *Les Miserables*.

All three performers perceive their work with the Company as central to their development as actresses and musicians. Grenland Friteater was established in 1976 in Porsgrunn, an industrial town to the south of Oslo. The Company work principally in the Porsgrunn area, though they have also toured extensively abroad. They regard it as important to attract visiting performers and companies to Norway, in an effort to widen the horizons of Norwegian theatre. Grenland Friteater helped to start Norway's first theatrical journal, *Spillerom*. In addition to their productions, Grenland Friteater offer seminars based on their physical and voice training methods. The Company has developed an extensive physical vocabulary which has come to characterise their work.

Lis Hughes Jones

Born 4.10.1954 in Swansea, Wales, native language Welsh.
Studied English at Exeter University, graduating in 1977. As a result of meeting Mike Pearson she began working with Cardiff Laboratory Theatre as a costume maker. During her beginnings at Cardiff, she took part in a seminar on Kathakali and Balinese dance and a training workshop by Tom Fjordefalk of Odin Teatret, both of which gave her the basis of a physical vocabulary. Two women performers were also important influences – Sian Thomas and Iben Nagel Rasmussen. In 1981 Lis and Mike Pearson left Cardiff to form Brith Gof, in an attempt to found a theatre that reflected contemporary Wales. Since then, Brith Gof have created and performed more than twenty productions, and Lis has sung in almost all of them. At Magdalena '86 she presented her one-woman show, *8961 – Caneuon Galar a Gobaith (8961 – Songs of Grief and Hope)*. She has travelled and worked extensively in South America and performed *8961* in Buenos Aires to a group of Mothers of the Plaza de Mayo.

Zofia Kalinska

Born 17.1.1931 in Horochow, Poland.
She studied at the Actor's School in Crakow and then worked for three years with Powszechny Theatre in Łodz. She was invited by Jerzy Grotowski to join his Laboratory Theatre but found it impossible to leave her small daughter and move to Wroclaw. Then in 1959 she met Tadeusz Kantor and joined his Cricot 2. Her collaboration with Kantor lasted for twenty years, during which time she created such roles as the Water Hen and the Street Walker in *Dead Class*. In 1984 she organised her own company, Akne Theatre, the first all-woman theatre group in Poland. Her aim is to create a new kind of theatre, based on psychodrama and trance, that concentrates on the psychology of women and explores female archetypes. Akne's first production, a new version of Genet's *The Maids*, received great

critical acclaim in Poland and abroad. In 1988 she directed the first Magdalena production, *Nominatae Filiae*, which was awarded the Lublin Festival Prize in October 1988 after a successful European tour.

Zofia Kalinska has one daughter and one granddaughter.

The Maids was performed at Magdalena '86 with Jolanta Biele Jelzmyk and Jolanta Gadaczek, and Zofia Kalinska also ran a two-day workshop on the Daemonic Woman.

Brigitte Kaquet
Born 7.2.1952, Liège, Belgium.
Studied at the University of Liège, then in 1975 worked on actor training methods at Odin Teatret, Denmark. In 1977 she co-founded Cirques Divers, a multi-media performance arts centre, and in the same year set up Théâtre de la Marmite, an all-women company in Liège. In 1979 she created the Cirques Divers Atelier de Récherches Théâtrales (A.R.T.). As one of the directors of this research centre she has organised a number of international theatre seminars with teachers from many parts of the world. She has worked with Jerzy Grotowski and Riszard Cieslak in Italy and has also maintained a strong interest in Oriental dance theatre. In 1983 she studied Balinese dance at the Seni Tari Academy in Indonesia. Between 1983 and 1986 she worked on the creation and performance of *Hésitations*, a multi-media experimental theatre sequence. This was followed by *Une Nuit ou l'autre*, which was first presented at Lille in 1987. At Magdalena Brigitte Kaquet presented *Hésitations 3 – La Présence d'esprit*.

Ida Kelarova
Born 10.2.1956, Bruntal, Czechoslovakia.
The daughter of Koloman Bitto, a well-known traditional Gypsy musician, she began at the age of seven to study music at the Opava Drama–Music School in Moravia. She went on to study classical piano, cello, voice and theatre at the Janacek Academy, Brno, and although offered a position in the Janacek National Theatre, she decided to join Divadlo na Provazku. She stayed with the company for eight years, during which time she became musical director, in addition to her work as actress, singer, composer and teacher. Since leaving Divadlo na Provazku she has lived in Britain and is currently living and working in Denmark.

She has two children.

Her current concert performance, *Gypsy Celebration*, was performed at Magdalena. Ida Kelarova also ran a day-long workshop on Halecacky singing, which culminated in an impromptu late-night mass concert outside the Chapter Arts Centre in Cardiff.

Stacy Klein
Born 16.11.1955 in Baltimore, USA.
Studied at the Universities of Tel-Aviv, Wroclaw and Boston, culminating in a Ph.D. on theatre history and criticism at Tufts University. She has done a vast amount of work in education on all levels, ranging from university lecturing to teaching drama in primary schools. Her publications include a handbook on teaching children's theatre. She began her professional directing work with Little Flags Theatre, Boston, a political theatre committed to the production of original musical theatre for working-class and minority communities. In 1980 she founded the Feminist American Theatre, Boston, and produced the 1980 and 1981 Boston Women's Theatre Festivals, the first festivals of this kind in the USA. In 1982 she founded Double Edge Theatre and has worked as resident director with this company since then. She won awards for staging one of the ten best Boston productions in 1982, 1983 and 1984. Stacy Klein's work has evolved through the exploration of extensive physical and psycho-physical techniques. Double Edge feel they have progressed as a company from experimental feminist theatre work to a stage which they describe as a Theatre of Question.

Together with Stacy Klein, Andrea Dishy and Lorien Corbelletti ran a two-day workshop at Magdalena, entitled Touching the Core.

Jolanta Krukowska
Born 15.5.1950 in Warsaw, Poland.
Jolanta Krukowska is a founder member of Akademia Ruchu ('The Academy of Movement'), which was established in 1973 under the artistic direction of her husband, Wojciech Krukowski. Akademia Ruchu grew out of student theatre activity in the early 1970s and has developed a method of working based on intensive collective improvisation, seeking to transform signs of the usual into images of the unexpected. Besides their carefully structured indoor performances, the company set great store by their collective outdoor work. They have presented over 90 street performances and over 100 street events which are designed to reflect some of the absurdities of contemporary

urban living. Until December 1981 the company organised the programme of the Cultural Centre of Grochow, the working-class district of Warsaw. The work of the company is now widely recognised internationally and has been well received at major European festivals of theatre.

Jolanta Krukowska has one son.

At Magdalena she premiered the performance of *A Dance About . . .*

Anna Lica
Born 9.6.1957 at Aarhus, Denmark.
Studied at the Aarhus Theatre Academy, then in 1981 joined the Theatre Marquez. She stayed with the Company for five years, working closely with Else Marie Laukvik of Odin Teatret, who encouraged her to create her own piece. In 1985 she premiered her solo performance, *Madame Bovary – Downtown*, directed by Tage Larsen. After performing for a season with the Aarhus Theatre, she began working on a Shakespeare performance together with Tage Larsen, continuing to tour with *Madame Bovary – Downtown*.

At Magdalena she presented *Madame Bovary – Downtown* and made an appearance in Netta Plotsky's performance *The Happiness of the Pre-Form*.

Kozana Lucca
Born 18.3.1940 in Cordoba, Argentina.
After extensive travelling, she met Roy Hart in London and joined his company in 1972. She has remained with the Roy Hart Theatre ever since. The Roy Hart Theatre is a company whose work is based on the study of the human voice and extension of the vocal range. Since 1974 the Company's centre has been in the Cevennes in southern France. The Company comprises forty members, who live communally and continue to develop the work begun by Roy Hart and his teacher, Alfred Wolfson. Kozana Lucca works principally between South America and France, teaching voice and leading explorations into techniques of bio-dance. She is also an accomplished visual artist. After miraculously surviving a terrible car accident in 1985, she has turned increasingly to work on myths and archtypes, concentrating on positive life energy and affirming the harmony of human existence. She created *Piantos* in 1981 and in 1985 devised *Biting Life*.

At Magdalena she ran a specialist workshop on the Human Voice and led the seminar on Private and Public – Women's Spaces through Theatre. In the second phase of Magdalena, she created an autobiographical exhibition using as a metaphor the image of women's hair. Her book, *Madame Chevelure*, appeared in 1987, published by Editions Arbres de Vie, Malérargues.

Cinzia Mascherin
Born 29.12.1955 in Treviso, Italy.
Interested in theatre design and sculpture, her first full-scale project was with the Centro teatrale San Geminiano in Modena in 1985 where she devised a scenic sculpture for *Brevi Amori di Tartarughe*, directed by Alessandro Tognon, who also directed the 1986 Magdalena show *No Man's Land*. In 1987 she designed a production of *Waiting For Godot*, directed by Carmen Jakobi and performed in Cardiff.

At Magdalena she performed in *No Man's Land* and devised sculptures in wood, cloth and papier mache.

Sandra Salmaso
Born 5.5.1958 in Padua, Italy.
Studied at the University of Bologna, then took a series of courses on modern dance and attended Ingemar Lind's workshop on Delcroux. In 1983 she worked in France and Spain as joint organiser of theatre festivals, and from 1978 to 1982 was a performer with the Teatrocontinuo group in Padua. Between 1980 and 1986 she worked with several directors, including Alessandro Tognon, and was one of the members of the Captive Waves project, the pilot for Magdalena '86 that took place in Cardiff in 1985.

At Magdalena she performed in *No Man's Land* with Cinzia Mascherin.

Netta Plotsky
Born 4.7.1944 in Russia, she emigrated to Israel at the age of 13.
She studied at the Nissan Nativ Acting Studio and at the University of Tel-Aviv. She performed with Khan Theatre in Jerusalem, playing leading conventional roles, then followed a period of work with the International School of Theatre Anthropology in Italy in 1980. She went for a time to Odin Teatret, exploring various modes of theatrical expression. She had developed an interest in the Oriental theatre,

47

and studied Buto in Japan with Kazuo Ohno and Nihon Buyo with Katzuko Azuma. Her teaching and performance work fuse Western and Oriental theatre traditions.

At Magdalena she performed *The Happiness of the Pre-Form*, a three-part improvised demonstration of her work in progress. She also acted as interpreter, facilitating communication between East and West, and ran a workshop entitled Every Moment Different Moment.

Graciella Serra

Born 4.4.1952 in Buenos Aires, Argentina.
Studied at the Primera Escuela Argentine de Expresion Corporal, specialising in the teaching of movement. In 1978 with her husband, Eduardo Hall, she founded Inyaj Teatro. Both continued to teach while beginning to work on popular Argentine mythology. In 1980 they toured *Las Andanzas del Sapo* and in 1981, a year of intensive international exchange work, they began their exploration of *Facundina Miranda, una Historia de Vida*, by the anthropologist Manuel Rocca. The first performance of Graciella Serra's solo performance *Facundina* was in 1983, and after receiving major critical acclaim in Argentina, *Facundina* was chosen to represent Argentinian theatre work at the Festival of Theatre of the Americas in Montreal in 1985, where it won the award for best production. Besides her performance work, Graciella Serra has developed her teaching in schools and universities. Since 1985 the company has been based in Valencia in Spain.

Graciella and Eduardo have one son.

At Magdalena, Graciella presented *Facundina* and ran a workshop on Sense Perception. She also led a seminar on Women in Latin American Theatre.

Osmega Dnia (Theatre of the Eighth Day) – Daria Anfelli, Michelle Kramers

Daria Anfelli

Born 1959 in Italy.
Studied at the University of Bologna. In 1978 she began working with the La Ciotola group in Verona, that was closely linked to Libre Teatro Libre. In the early 1980s she worked under the direction of Isabel Soto and Graciella Ferrari. In 1984 she met up with Teatr Osmega Dnia and began her association with the Company. Having

returned from Poland to Italy with some members of the Company, she began work with Michelle Kramers on a street performance, *If One Day in a Happy City* . . . early in 1986.

Michelle Kramers
Born 25.10.1952 in Djakarta, Indonesia. Nationality Dutch and Swiss.
After completing her formal education, she worked for some time in publishing and was actively involved in leftist politics. In 1981 she returned to her initial passion for theatre, taking courses in Wroclaw, Paris and Zurich. In 1983 she travelled to Poland with her first performance, a clown street show, and met up with the Teatr Osmega Dnia. She is currently working with Daria Anfelli and Barbara Theobaldt on *If One Day in a Happy City* . . . and has just completed work on a joint German-Seneghalese performance project, *Forgotten Elements*.

Daria and Michelle came to Magdalena as observers and stayed to participate for the full three-week period, being especially appreciated for their translation work.

Julia Varley
Born 20.7.1954 in London, England.
Educated in Italy. During a period of intense political activity, she began working with Teatro del Drago, and took part in several tours before moving to Holstebro in 1976 to begin a period of training and study with Odin Teatret. In 1978 she entered the Company and since then has toured throughout the world in *Anabasis, J.S. Bach, Millionen, Brecht's Ashes* and *Oxyrhincus Evangeliet*. She has also worked in film as assistant director and producer and has extensive experience of running workshops. She has been involved in group projects in Wales, Spain, Canada and Scandinavia.

Julia Varley collaborated closely on the organisation of Magdalena from its beginnings.

ARTISTS

Gerd Christiansen
Born 5.2.1955 in Silkeborg, Denmark.
From the age of 14 she has worked with different aspects of the image – sculpture, painting, masks, environmental art, etc. She became involved in theatre when she was 20 and since then has worked

towards achieving a union between images and movement. She has also worked as a performer. In 1983 she moved to live in a small village in the South of France, having decided she no longer wanted to live in large international cities. In the village she is part of an artists' collective, *Totem*, working on theatre images and music. Her most recent work, *Dreams*, a project that attempts to cross the boundaries between artist and actor, is currently in progress.

At Magdalena she was one of the team of artists responsible for the visual impact of Phase II. Together with Rona Lee she designed and constructed the River Room.

Amanda Dike
Born 1960 in England.
Degree in Creative Arts from Alsager College. Co-founded a multi-arts co-operative, the Front, based in Lancaster. Among her projects with the Front are the multi-media performance event, *Mooring Big Ships in Tidal Waters* (1986), a film, *War Widows* (1983), and projections in support of the Lancaster miners and the anti-apartheid movement in 1985. Since 1985 she has also worked on set construction for the Duke's Playhouse, Lancaster. In 1984 she co-founded the Lancaster Women's Art Group.

Amanda Dike made a short film of Magdalena and was one of the team of four women who technically managed the performances in Phase I.

Kari Furre
Born 29.1.1950 in England.
Studied at Rose Bruford College. After working with the Young Vic and the Derby Playhouse, she settled in Lincoln and from 1976 to 1981 was Resident Designer with the Great Eastern Stage. Since then she has worked extensively as a freelance theatre designer in Coventry, Hull, Liverpool, Barcelona, etc. In 1983 she was commissioned to design the huge Christmas crib for Lincoln Cathedral, and in the same year she became artist in residence at St John's and St George's Hospitals in Lincoln, working on sculpture projects with patients. In 1985 she worked on the Magdalena pilot project, Captive Waves, with the Cardiff Laboratory Theatre.

Karri Furre has one son.

At Magdalena her role was to coordinate visual art work.

Hilary Hughes
Born 5.5.1949 in England.
Between 1967 and 1970 she studied at the Bingley College of Education, specialising in Art and Drama. After leaving college, she worked as a freelance silk-screen printer and designer and ran a shop specialising in arts and crafts. Between 1974 and 1976 she worked with Rat Theatre as technician and performer touring in Britain and Europe. She worked for a time as performing arts technician at Crewe and Alsager College, then from 1980 to 1983 as freelance designer and maker. In 1983 she began working again with Rat Theatre as performer, designer and stage manager, and took part in the Theatre Guild of Greece Festival of Women in Athens. In 1985 she became a founder member of Beavers, a company based in Newcastle, Staffordshire. She has taught stage management at Newcastle Polytechnic and performed at numerous community theatre events. In 1987 Beavers were actively involved in the Arts for Labour campaign.

Rona Lee
Born 29.3.1957 in England.
Studied at Goldsmith's College and Sherman Theatre, Cardiff. Since 1980 she has worked as a freelance designer and maker with Cardiff Laboratory Theatre, Horse and Bamboo, Theatre Alibi and large-scale community arts projects in south-west England, Wales and Northern Ireland. Her work includes fire sculpture, mask making, processional events and costume design. In 1985 she devised a performance art piece entitled *The Spear Side.*

At Magdalena she was one of the six visual artists and with Gerd Christiansen she designed the River Room. She also coordinated the Magdalena exhibition.

Jenny Spiers
Born 1963 in Edinburgh, Scotland.
Was accepted for the National Youth Theatre and from the age of fourteen worked in alternative theatre and explored natural history. In 1981 she began a foundation course in art at York College of Fine Arts and Technology, then moved on to Newcastle Upon Tyne Polytechnic, where she graduated in 1985 in Fine Art. Whilst still a student, she met Ian Hamilton Finlay and began to learn about gardening. In 1984 she exhibited at Northern Lights, a group show

by five artists of contemporary approaches to Northern European landscape, at the Edinburgh Festival fringe.

In 1985 she became a founder member of the Greenhaus Artists group in Newcastle. During Magdalena '86 she worked closely with Zofia Kalinska's Magic Circle, producing sculptures using natural objects.

Performances, Discussions, Workshops

Twelve performances took place in the first week of the Festival; three of them were world premieres and one, *No Man's Land*, was created specially for Magdalena by Cinzia Mascherin and Sandra Salmaso.

The five-woman technical crew worked flat out for the first seven days and were remarkably efficient. All the performances went off without a hitch and played to full houses. Reviews of the performances were generally good, though on the whole the Festival received very little media attention. The *Guardian* (21 August 1986) mentioned only three shows, by Zofia Kalinska, Lis Hughes Jones and Jolanta Krukowska in a tiny review that served more as an advertisement than a critical assessment. It is tempting to jump to certain conclusions about the lack of media interest in the Festival, and certainly many women participating in Magdalena felt strongly that the idea of an all-women event was antipathetic to the predominantly male reviewers and theatre critics. The organising committee had appointed a press officer and hoped for a much wider response to the Festival, in view of its uniqueness and in view of the large number of internationally known practitioners working together and showing their work, but this did not happen.

The performances varied enormously and revealed a wide spectrum of theatre work. In general terms, they can be categorised into performances structured around visual objects (*A Dance About . . .* , *No Man's Land*, *Hésitations 3 – La Présence d'Esprit*), performances based on the life histories of other women (*The Stars are no Nearer*, *Facundina*, *A Gift for Burning*, *Madame Bovary – Downtown*), musical performances (*Les Miserables*, *Song of Celebration*), performances reaching across cultural boundaries in terms of content and technique (*Life among Forms* and *8961 – Caneuon Galar a Gobaith*). There was also one production of a classic text, Zofia Kalinska's version of Jean Genet's *The Maids*.

9. *Jolanta Krukowska in* A Dance About . . .

Workshops also tended to fall into categories, with some focusing on voice work, particularly the ones led by Helen Chadwick, Ida Kelarova, Kozana Lucca of the Roy Hart Theatre and Brigitte Cirla of La Colline Company who ran a workshop especially for young actors. Other workshops took up the work on objects, as in the case of Maria Consagra's, whilst others stressed physical techniques (Netta Plotsky's workshop, and the one run by the performers from the Grenland Friteater). The levels of competence required in each workshop also varied, and some leaders chose to run their sessions throughout the week, while others preferred a weekend, and still others opted for a single day.

This variety of approaches and methods enabled a large number of participants with very different degrees of physical and vocal competence to work without feeling inhibited by their lack of experience or by the lack of experience of others. Clear indications were given by the workshop leaders as to what would be required of the participants. In some cases, the experience of taking part led to a strong sense of bonding between participants. This was very much the case for those women who took part in Graciella Serra's workshop on 'Sense Perception', for those who joined Zofia Kalinska's sessions on the 'Daemonic Woman' and for those who took part in the weekend workshop run by Stacy Klein and Andrea Dishy of Double Edge Theatre, 'Touching the Core'.

Working with Objects

The emphasis on objects involved for some a process of seeing as creativity. Sandra Salmaso and Cinzia Mascherin, both from Italy, devised *No Man's Land*, described by Cinzia as 'an empty space, without border, beyond quiet'. The performance itself was structured around elements of dance and sculpture and hinged on images of fluidity and stillness. Inspired by Pina Bausch's *Bluebeard's Castle*, the two women constructed a performance with the intention, as Cinzia put it:

> of introducing a 'light', almost rarified environment in a landscape that I imagine as a lunar one, where there is a feeling of exasperated tension in the lives of the characters. In a second stage a feeling of calm develops with the passing of time. A desert landscape, where everyday objects take on a different meaning from the past and hung rope ladders are the place for forgotten memories.[4]

Both Sandra Salmaso and Cinzia Mascherin, in devising their performance especially for Magdalena '86, were concerned with trying to understand and make understood their process of working. In this respect, their performance typified much of what Magdalena '86 was about, of women groping for understanding, with half-formed ideas and a lot of energy, but never quite clear as to where that energy would lead them. Sandra attempted to sum up her feelings in a verse statement, written in August 1986:

> My eyes are curious and uncertain.
> Everything is out there in the world, so I have to refine my powers of observation, my seeing.
> I have to learn to see. Everything is out there in the world, you can imagine things that you don't actually live through or maybe your imagination really lives in its own right somewhere else.

I think that from seeing with the eyes we can move to intuition.
Intuition is knowing, guessing, seeing beyond.
The act of creating seems to me to be the instant of really
seeing:
CREATIVITY IS SEEING.[5]

The problem for these performers was to find a means of representing the intuitive, of shaping in some form the process of movement and change that flickered across their awareness. Theatre, Sandra Salmaso argues, being on the borderline between dreams and reality, is the place where the fog can be allowed to lift, where fantasy can be shaped and made into concrete images.

Cinzia Mascherin, principally a sculptor, used a combination of natural and manufactured materials, combining the two in a series of explorations of kinetic art. The motif of the web recurs through her work, as does the motif of the labyrinth, the forest and the cave, archetypal symbolic images represented in wood, wire and plastic. Describing her working method, she suggests that the theatre is the natural habitat of varied materials, and that actors' bodies are one further source of sculptural material:

10. *Brigitte Kaquet
in* Hésitations
3 – La Présence
d'esprit

Theatre is space, which offers me possibilities for filling it, but it can also be a void, though always something in motion. Theatre is also time, and this devours you and inspires you. I realize that my colours are those of the seabed, both natural and fantastic: blue, green, violet, gold. My materials are: cloth, animal skins, copper, brass, clay, stones, rocks from the sea, shells, seaweed, moss. I think that when a woman creates it is as though she were submerged in water, through a finely suspended spider's web. Men work on dry land. Women are consoled by what they make. Men console the things they do make.
Women seem more magical to me.[6]

The emphasis on objects, on seeing as a form of creativity, recurred in the striking use of object-centred images in the final performance and was present also in other performances. Jolanta Krukowska's performance, *A Dance About . . .* relied on a combination of the solo performer's extraordinary technical skills as a dancer and the effect created by minimalist objects – stones scattered about the floor, old potatoes, a pair of high heeled sandals into which she tried unsteadily to climb. Above her head hung a plastic bag, and during the dance she steadily filled the bag to bursting point with the objects from the ground, naming each one as she put them in – 'my work', 'my marriage' and so forth. The simplicity of her performance high-lighted the size of what she was saying – through the device of the stones, potatoes and plastic bags, she offered an image of her own life and, by association, of women's lives in general – a balancing act, an attempt to combine the impossible opposites of heavy stones and air, a growing sense of oppression as the bag of problems hung ever lower over her head and the final act of rebellion, desperation or explosion as the stones fell to the ground and the dance began again.

In the workshops, Maria Consagra from the United States pro-duced some fascinating results from her technique of inviting actors to channel energy through the use of an object. Elin Lindberg's improvisation with a suitcase, begun during the workshop and continued in the final performance, was a virtuoso display of physical and imaginative skills, as she transformed the battered brown suitcase into a living creature, a Pandora's box, a tightrope, a confessional, a screen and a whole range of other living and dead things.

Brigitte Kaquet (Belgium) in her *Hésitations 3 – La Présence d'Esprit* relied instead on painting as a source of inspiration, using as its starting point Magritte's surrealist *La Présence d'Esprit*, in which a man, a bird and a fish are represented rising enigmatically out of a landscape. For Brigitte Kaquet, the painting raises fundamental philosophical questions about human evolution, and her dance–drama similarly asks fundamental questions about the nature of theatre. *Hésitations 3* was part of an ongoing work in progress, of which two previous

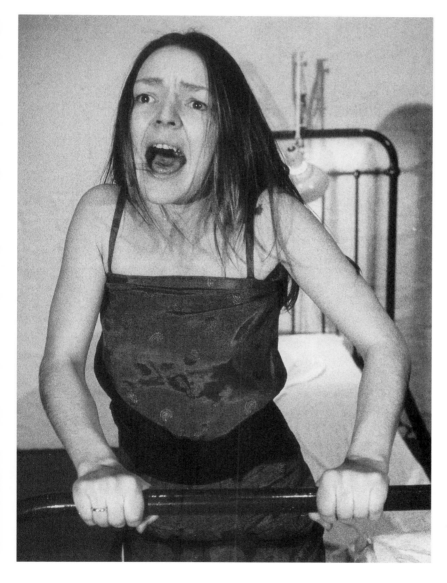

11. *Geddy Aniksdal
    as Sylvia Plath
    in* The Stars
    are No Nearer

stages had already been presented elsewhere, that tried to explore the processes of an actress's creativity through visual images. Directed by Michel Antaki, *Hésitations 3* was an exploration of feminine archetypes, such as Ophelia and Faust's Marguerite, and this theme also emerged strongly in the final performance, fed by related work on archetypal figures by many of the other performers. *Hésitations 3* used texts by Shakespeare, Dostoevsky, Gertrude Stein and Marguerite Duras, and in her choice of written and visual points of departure, Brigitte Kaquet's show developed the idea of continuity through art, of women in contact with archetypal images of themselves across the ages.

ReCreating Women

Geddy Aniksdal's show, *The Stars are no Nearer*, directed by Tor Arne Ursen, was her first solo performance and was based on five poems by Sylvia Plath. In this piece Aniksdal explored the narrow divide between motherhood and madness, giving and devouring, that the imagery of the poems suggests.

Helen Chadwick's show, *A Gift for Burning*, also used texts by Sylvia Plath, along with others by Frances Bellerby, Stevie Smith, Ann Sexton, Marina Tsvetayeva, H.D., Susan Griffin and herself. Georgiana Berry, from the Performing Arts School of Worcester, Massachussetts, who took part in the first week of the Festival, had this comment to make about Helen Chadwick's work:

> For me this was disturbingly thoughtful work . . . the set
> seemed right for the texts chosen; the lamps were supportive of
> the theme of *A Gift for Burning*, and the combination of original
> songs sung, often in a hauntingly modal style, set a tone that for
> me combined the moods . . . it was a work that was artistically
> executed in a style that spoke the times, emotions, nightmares
> and wove them into a setting that reminded me for an hour of
> some of the writers and how they speak across time . . .[7]

Both Helen Chadwick and Geddy Aniksdal constructed their performances in similar ways, using poetic texts but extending beyond the verbal to create a series of very physical images. Helen Chadwick's set, with a piano, chairs and lamps, was more naturalistic than Geddy Aniksdal's minimalist set with just a bedstead, but both performers created a powerful atmosphere by relying primarily on the strength of their own voices and, in Geddy Aniksdal's case, her physical agility.

Another show derived from a literary text was Anna Lica's performance of *Madame Bovary – Downtown*, directed by Tage Larsen of the Odin Teatret. In this performance, a woman in the big city, Sally, shares the sense of oppression and entrapment experienced by Flaubert's Emma Bovary. Both women yearn for an ideal fulfilment of their dreams, but Sally's illusions, like her literary predecessor's, end ultimately in her own self-destruction. This performance used a number of different elements to create effects of power and disturbance – verbal texts were extended by the use of taped songs; lighting changes cut across the dance routines, and Anna Lica managed to generate an extraordinary energy, which made the final cutting off of that source of power all the more poignant.

Geddy Aniksdal's portrayal of Sylvia Plath and Anna Lica's *Madame Bovary – Downtown* introduced a theme that was controversial: the woman as victim, the woman whose suffering has no hope of escape and whose death becomes an inevitable last stage. Helen Chadwick's choice of material, though not avoiding the victim theme, nor the deeply disturbing question of violence, especially sexual violence against women, was nevertheless built around the idea of struggle for survival, rather than of conceding to despair. The woman as victim was noticeably absent from the final performance, almost as if there had been some tacit agreement amongst the practitioners to work on more positive aspects of women's experience. Even Brigitte Kaquet's portrayal of Ophelia in the final performance offered the image of an Ophelia striving for awareness and understanding, not of a woman giving way to madness and helplessness.

The triumph of a woman against all the odds was the theme of Graciella Serra's show, *Facundina*. The true story of a Chinquana Indian woman who lived to the age of 110, the performance, directed by Eduardo Hall, was played with a bare minimum of props and no scenic effects, and relied exclusively on Graciella's capacity to win over spectators, who could not understand the language she was using, by her powerful physical language. Her technique was to dissolve the invisible barrier between actors and audience by generating enormous emotional energy, an energy that seemed indeed to be rooted in the earth and in time. In her workshop on sense perception, she focused on the mechanisms by which a deep body awareness can

12. Helen Chadwick in A Gift for Burning

be reached, exploring a process of reaching within the self in order to offer oneself as an actor more completely to an audience.

All these performances in their different ways used the lives of other women as texts, and as the stories unfolded, they began to acquire a universality beyond their individual characteristics. So Geddy Aniksdal, a heavily pregnant Norwegian actress, playing Sylvia Plath, and Graciella Serra, an Argentinian actress of great

13. *Anna Lica in Madame Bovary – Downtown*

beauty playing an old Indian woman, both appeared to be perform-ing at the same time as themselves, as their characters and as arche-typal female figures that belonged to all times and all places.

Netta Plotsky's show, *The Happiness of the Pre-Form*, created three universal images of woman: the mad woman in the first part, an Ophelia as she might have been if conceived by Samuel Beckett, an old Polish Jewish woman in the second part, and a young woman in the third part, in which Netta Plotsky demonstrated her Buto training and explored work with masks. Diane Speakman, who took part in the first week of Magdalena '86 and afterwards wrote a detailed article of what took place, commented that: 'Netta Plotsky from Israel gave a performance remarkable for its inventiveness, visually, its generosity. She was the only performer to establish an explicit relationship with the audience: she started playing among us, eating an apple, tearing our tickets, making noises, evoking laughter. . . . She believes that . . . there can be no creativity without sexuality . . .'[8]

Music and the Voice

Some of the most successful workshops and performances in the first
week developed aspects of voice work. Ida Kelarova ran a huge
workshop on traditional Eastern European mountain singing, which
culminated in a late-night, outdoor concert by all the workshop
participants, and she also performed *Song of Celebration* to one of the
biggest audiences of the Festival. In an open letter after the event, Ida
Kelarova pointed out that this was the first time she had performed
alone in front of an audience, and she believed that the workshop had
overcome completely all possible communication difficulties due to
the various languages spoken by the participants: 'I opened my heart,

*14. Graciella Serra
in* Facundina

my everything, energie [sic], confidence completely – and I believe I gave a strong message.'

Kozana Lucca's workshop, 'Beauty and the Beast', developed some of the techniques on bio-voice on which she works with the Roy Hart Theatre. Kozana's work is based on the notion that voice work should be conceived holistically and that body awareness is an essential component of vocal training. This method differs from other forms of voice work which often focus on sound itself rather than on sound as a function of a larger organism, the body as a whole. Kozana's distinction between 'beauties' and 'beasts' was not only designed to explore the higher and lower vocal ranges, but also to enable women to play two completely different roles and so investigate two opposing facets of themselves. This was another extremely popular workshop, which allowed a lot of energy to circulate and which participants found very rewarding. The final performance at the end of the three-week period contained very little voice work, and this was in marked contrast to the amount of work in this area throughout the whole period. Helen Chadwick and Lis Hughes Jones led group singing sessions that everyone enjoyed, but in the final resort voice work gave way to the creation of visual images, which many participants felt was a great pity.

One of the most enjoyable shows of the Festival was the three-woman performance by Geddy Aniksdal, Elin Lindberg and Anne Erichsen, *Les Misérables*. Dressed as three boorish men in dark suits and dark glasses (interestingly, this was one of the rare moments of transvestism in the whole Festival), the three performers sang jazz, country-and-western and rock-and-roll pieces, creating an atmosphere of comedy and celebration.

The celebratory quality of the voice work was very obvious in the first week. Participants in the workshops seemed to emerge with the will to share and continue the work begun. Ida Kelarova fused her performance work with her workshop by inviting the members of her workshop to sing with her, and Kozana Lucca's massive session, in which the high sounds produced by Beauties struggled with the deep sounds produced by Beasts, was one of the memorable moments for all concerned. In contrast, those people who took part in some of the more physical or psychophysical workshops found it difficult to describe their experiences, and small separate groupings tended to develop as a result of the intensity shared inside the sessions.

Politics and Plays

The most overtly political show, and one of the most highly acclaimed, was Lis Hughes Jones' solo performance, *8961 – Caneuon Galar a Gobaith* (*Songs of Grief and Hope*). Directed by Mike Pearson, who, along with Lis, is a founder member of the Welsh language company, Brith Gof, the performance created the portrait of a woman whose loved ones are *desaparecidos*, kidnapped, murdered and tortured in Latin America, using texts by Pablo Neruda and Victor Jara. The 8961 of the title represents the number of people missing in one country, Argentina, in the 1970s during the period of repressive military dictatorship, and shortly after Magdalena '86, Lis Hughes Jones toured with the show in Argentina and gave a special performance for the Mothers of the Plaza de Mayo, all relatives of the disappeared.

Describing her working method, Lis Hughes Jones has said:

> I try to capture in performance the appearance and experience of women, often in a historical context or within a foreign culture. . . . My characters are rural or recently urbanized, and my voice is their voice. It is strong, often mistaken for a man's, but it is recognized as that of a woman by those who have heard a similar voice in another time or place. . . . Perhaps it is my voice which I feel is most my own, together with the songs I have written for several shows. And perhaps it is those songs which best convey my 'mothertongue'.[9]

The powerful political message of Lis Hughes Jones' work aroused a lot of discussion, and there was a separate session on Latin American women and theatre, where the question of the relationship between the Third World experience and the more distanced First World was heatedly discussed. But *8961* was not only about Latin America; it was also a universal statement about oppression and suffering and about the role of women left behind with their pain and little else for comfort.

If *8961* stood out as a uniquely political piece of theatre, Zofia Kalinska's production of *The Maids* stood out as a unique example of the performance of a classic text. This production, like her workshop sessions, relied on the psychophysical skills of performers in their relationship to one another. Trained for years with Tadeusz Kantor in

Poland, Zofia Kalinska broke away to create her own all-female company, Akne. Her working method is a lengthy one; performers gradually construct, destroy, deconstruct, and remake relationships within a group, stripping away layers of superficiality as they do so. *The Maids*, Genet's play about the power struggle between a mistress and her servants, was given another dimension in Kalinska's production. Madame, as portrayed by Kalinska herself, was a terrifying figure whose heavy footsteps could be heard even when she was not an actual presence on stage and whose white-painted face leered cruelly out of the semi-darkness, thwarting whatever pretensions to freedom the maids might try to develop. The source of the maids' fear and loathing of their mistress was skilfully transformed, and in addition to the class conflict that is embedded in the play, the production also explored the archetype of the devilish mother, the anti-carer, the destroyer.

Significantly, *The Maids*, written by a man (though a man defined by at least one feminist writer as an ideal example of 'the feminine'),[10] offered insights into another aspect of women that was barely touched upon elsewhere. Whilst some performances tended to show woman as victim, a fact which aroused a lot of critical comment, Zofia Kalinska's work showed women as capable of destructive power, as bearers of daemonic energy. It was an image that held strong appeal for some, and during the second phase of Magdalena '86, a group emerged that worked exclusively with Zofia Kalinska, her Magic Circle, as it came to be called, and in the final performance the group presented some of its work in progress. It is also noteworthy that of all the varieties of work that were shown and tested at Magdalena '86, only Zofia Kalinska's work resulted in the formation of a new, separate all-woman company, which came together in January 1988 to begin work on a new production, *Nominatae Filiae*.

The Second Phase

At the end of the first week of Magdalena '86, the mood was euphoric. The practice of eating together in the large kitchen was taken a stage further, and a great celebratory party concluded the public phase of the work. Thereafter, those involved were limited to the invited practitioners, who had agreed to remain and push the work onto its second phase, and the participants who had come to Cardiff for the first phase departed once again, though many returned for the final performances to see whether they could detect what kind of changes had taken place in the intervening two-week period.

Diane Speakman, who did just that, leaving at the end of week one to return at the end of the month, summarised some of the questions that had arisen during the first stage of the Festival:

What is the nature of women's inspiration and creativity? Does it differ from men's? Is there a separate style of acting and directing that can be described as belonging to women?

Why are there no influential women theoreticians in the theatre, equivalent to Barba or Grotowski?

Can child-bearing, which many women feel is a creative experience, be combined with artistic work in a process of cross-fertilisation? What is theatre? What takes place between spectator and actor? What is experimental theatre?

Have we, as spectators, the right to say a performance is not theatre? Do there have to be professional standards of singing, dancing, acting, before theatre can take place?

Do we have to understand a performance for it to be valid? Does it matter to the creators that people see different meanings and significance in the same performance?

Are collages, fragments, episodes, cycles, natural structures for women? How can women go public, gain more confidence as artists in a patriarchal world?

Do women speak a different language at work? Have we learned to speak in two modes? Can we develop our own language?[11]

Diane Speakman's list of questions, put together as a result of listening to the main issues discussed formally and informally throughout the week, cover a lot of ground and can be divided into various categories: those concerning theatre and its definition and policies, those concerning the problem of women's creativity on a more abstract level and those concerning the socio-economic status of women and the way in which this relates to theatre work.

The problem of the absence of women in theatre as theoreticians, directors, managers, etc. has historical roots, and although the Magdalena Festival was a forum in which to raise this and similar problems, the principal function of the event had always been to explore the possibility of women's artistic work. In this respect,

Magdalena '86 occupied an ambiguous position *vis-à-vis* feminist thinking about theatre, and significantly perhaps, there were relatively few women present whose work was principally in feminist theatre. However, several disconcerting questions were asked by feminists, particularly in relation to the representation of women as victims, which some women felt was offensive, and to the fact that so many of the performances had been directed by men. In a truly women's theatre, it was argued, the role of director, which is ultimately a very powerful one, should not be undertaken by a man. The counter-argument, also hotly defended, suggested that a concept of theatre which attributes all the power to the director is one which undervalues the performer and that experimental theatre is all about restoring the performer to a position of authority, despite the existence (or not) of a director. But what also emerged from the discussions was, perhaps predictably, an age difference that carried at least as much significance as other differences. Many of the performers were women in their thirties or older, who felt that they had already lived through their phase 'at the barricades of feminist ideology', as one person put it, and that the time had come to move on to other, wider things. In this discussion there were also marked differences between British women and women from other cultures; for the Eastern Europeans, for example, the feminist question was non-existent, whilst many others were surprised by the British insistence on class, accessibility of performance style and overt feminist statement as important ingredients in performance work.

One of the most important and vocal protests was led by one of the participants during the first week, Margaretta D'Arcy, Irish playwright and Marxist feminist of long-standing reputation, who attacked much of the work as elitist. She argued that most of the performances had set up barriers between performers and audiences, that the performer appeared on stage like 'a princess'. She also felt strongly that the tendency to emphasise the visual and not the verbal was potentially dangerous, since images can often avoid censorship, whilst a verbal text becomes a statement that, once made, has to be dealt with by the forces of authority. This view aroused considerable sympathy, especially since Margaretta's own clashes with censorship in Northern Ireland had resulted in her being held in prison, but her suggestion that much of the Polish experimental theatre work she had seen was quintessentially reactionary and anti-Marxist was more doubtful.

Margaretta d'Arcy's protest was important because she summed up the disquiet felt by a number of women present, particularly with regard to the type of theatre work that was being shown. Diane Speakman's resume of questions also raises the matter of what constitutes theatre, of whether 'understanding' is necessary for a spectator to be able to share fully in the experience, of whether aesthetic criteria also count. The ideological divide between 'showing' on the one hand, offering a series of suggestive words and images and leaving the spectator to develop those as she thinks fit, and 'telling', on the other, with a clear narrative line and strong textual component, came to be defined in class terms.

On the one hand, the 'showing' type of theatre was perceived as elitist, and the 'telling' version was suggested as engaging genuinely with the needs and possibilities available to working-class women. The counter-argument to this line of reasoning proposed that a narrative theatre, working from simple, accessible themes and structures, was aesthetically uninteresting and part of the heritage of traditional theatre work that many wanted to shake off. The question of being patronising to those women whom it was felt would be unable to cope with complex, abstract structures in theatre was also taken up, but the gap remained unbridged and probably unbridgeable.

The problems that emerged during the first phase highlighted the wider problems of the social contexts within which women were working. One issue that recurred several times in reviews (*Spare Rib* took up this point, for example) was the small number of women of colour who took part in the proceedings. Jill Greenhalgh was questioned about why there were no African women performers, and although she explained that African women had been invited but had been unable to accept the invitation, charges of racial prejudice remained on the table. On the night of the final performance one woman, who had taken part in Phase 1, staged a protest about the absence of women of colour, suggesting that this had been deliberate policy rather than accidental.

Besides the controversial issues of race, class, age and ideology that came to light during the public debates in the first week, other significant issues also started to emerge. For whilst there was a group that could be designated as 'feminist' in the widest sense of the term, there was also another group of women, many of whom were actively involved in peace camps, whose starting point was an absolute belief in a separate female/feminine creative process. This group, which tended to exalt the image of woman as mother, as human incarnation of the Great Mother, the Ultimate Creator of all things, often stood at the opposite pole to the feminists. So, for example, in a discussion on what kind of images should be presented in a women's theatre, one group wanted to glorify and develop images of domesticity and caring, whilst the other group wanted to reject all such images as typifying the history of women's confinement to the home and oppression in the world outside it. Likewise, whereas one group looked to images based on cyclical movements, on phases of the moon and menstrual rhythms, the other group rejected these as symbolic of the biological constraints that restrict the free movement of women in the world.

By the end of the first week it was clear that no agreement was possible. A very large number of women had come together, had shared their work and explored new areas with one another, crossing barriers of all kinds in the process. But beneath all the solidarity and sense of sharing, there were strong undercurrents of difference, an awareness of varied points of origin and very different goals and intentions.

Magdalena Voices

The women who remained to work together for the next two weeks were aware of the problems that had begun to emerge but were immediately faced with other, more practical problems. The principal questions were organisational: the disused potato factory that was to become the performance space had to be prepared; strategies of daily work had to be developed; the vexed question of directorial control and responsibility had to be taken on board; the relationship between performers, technicians and visual artists had to be worked out. In an open letter, written some months prior to Magdalena '86, Kari Furre warned about the possible difficulties that awaited them:

> During discussions about Magdalena '86 I have found myself
> retreating from and rejecting innocent comments about the
> design and feeling alienated from the project and not really sure
> why I was reacting so badly. I think that this is because there is
> no history (that I know) of visual artists working independently
> within a theatre structure. . . . Visual artists clearly cannot

become performers, but no more must they be there to refine the visual contents of the performance. There is such a strong element of illustration in theatre visuals which would be so easy to take refuge in, indeed difficult to avoid, that I feel Magdalena '86 needs to take a sideways look at the way the visual content is achieved.[12]

In the event, Kari Furre's reservations proved only too true. She herself left in the second week, because she no longer felt able to work in an environment that she felt was draining rather than energising. The other visual artists remained, but for all of them, except for Jennie Spiers, who worked closely with the small, separate Magic Circle group, there were serious problems. Cinzia Mascherin found herself increasingly isolated, in part because of her lack of English, and spent some time transforming areas of space on the margins of the main playing areas, outside the building and in a room that served as a kind of antechamber. That she felt constrained to work on the margins speaks for itself.

Gerd Christiansen and Rona Lee worked on devising the River Room, a long empty space with pillars reminiscent of a Roman arcade, which they covered with pallets and sand and then filled a central strip with water to create the impression of a river. Because of the size of the River Room, which was not only the largest physical space used but also required the most preparation, that space came to dominate the other areas, and perhaps because of this Gerd Christiansen, along with Geddy Aniksdal, who elected to do so by choice, came to take on directorial roles. This assumption of the role of directors of the final performance came to be seen as problematic for many of the participants, and the hostility generated on some occasions shows the extent to which the vexed question of power structures within theatre failed to be solved by the women in Magdalena '86.

Rona Lee's final assessment of what happened is representative of the negative feelings shared by some of the visual artists:

I now feel it to have been a failure, victim of its own arrogance and naivety. The underlying premise of the collaborative section of the work was: 'that there is a uniquely female expression' and that it could best be explored by dispensing with defined structures. I do not doubt the existence of a store of female expression nor its value; the danger is however that in a situation such as Magdalena '86, it becomes exploitable, the prerogative of the few rather than the many.

The notion that structures can be dispensed with is wrong; all that happens is that they become covert and consequently open to abuse. Freed from some of the constraints of patriarchy, did we really question existing hierarchies? I think not. However sound the intention, it is not in itself enough. Agents of change

15. *Ida Kelarova performing at Magdalena '86*

must be both pragmatic and rigorously self-questioning in order to avoid becoming zealots. Sentimental notions of sisterhood and the mystification of art do both feminism and theatre a disservice. The unwillingness to address oneself to process and content can be irresponsible, allowing room for the misuse of power. Overly concerned that there should be harmony, some took it upon themselves to edit the opinions of others. Those who expressed fear, anger, dissent, were made to feel, both publicly and in private, that their feelings were gauche, disruptive and insensitive. Thus, beneath the hugging and singing, there lay a sense of fear which, fuelled by insecurity over the public presentation, created an increasingly ruthless atmosphere of individualism and competitiveness.

It is not that either of the latter are themselves unhealthy. Indeed, self-responsibility and interest are an important part of independence. Nor was there a lack of individuals prepared to be generous and supportive. The problem was that the body politic lacked the means to protect itself from prejudicial practice and the oppression of minorities. However tacitly, Magdalena '86 subscribed to a system of values which were racist, ageist and artistically elitist. Those who suffered most were the least confident, least established and least articulate. Also marginalised were those whose concerns were deemed to be non-artistic: administrators, technicians, the production team.

Another casualty of this situation was the content of the work. Throughout the Festival individuals shared work which was powerful, witty, intelligent and socially and politically aware. The group work, however, was clichéd, sentimental and indulgent. Hardly surprising when the group forum raising issues such as the non-involvement of black women was throwing stones in a glass house.[13]

The problem of power was also keenly felt by some of the technical staff and particularly by the younger women. Mandy White, who had served as publicity officer, wrote to Jill Greenhalgh some months after Magdalena '86 (all participants had been invited to write in with their comments) and expressed her feelings about a sense of having been marginalised and made to feel less important than 'the performers'. She also questioned the different experiences she had felt in the first week and in the second two weeks of the project, saying that:

In hindsight, my feeling about the work (cruelly) is disappointing. The audiences accepted poor work. Having been in a workshop all day, 'high' and 'buzzing', really anything could be shown. And that first week was such a wow. For the performers to be asked in the second two weeks to disregard the structure of the first week and get on with working together – of course they were inflated by this and quite tempted by the traditional hierarchic theatre structure – made them nervous, frightened. The first week had proved so successful. What a pressure.[14]

Mandy's point was that the performers were being asked to readjust not only their method of working, i.e. to move into a large collective structure, but also to rethink their traditional notions about the roles of technicians, performers and directors in the theatre, and that this was bound to fail. As a technician, and hoping for an alternative relationship with the performers, she was disappointed when that change did not happen. She also pointed out, significantly, that many of the technical staff were considerably younger than some of the performers, and again the question of age and experience emerged as a point of contention.

Katy Dymoke, one of the organisers, wrote:

Magdalena '86 fell into the bracket of elitist international festivals despite itself. Performers were given precedence over the service women – technicians, designers, crèche workers, etc. – if only through no better motivation than an honest attempt to make up for their lack of comfort and to acknowledge their efforts to come. It remains true though that we did fail to escape from the patrilinear tradition; we were all supposed to do our work and be considered equally creative whether holding a hammer, a light or the stage.

The apparatus didn't change – the performances were in the box, with the technicians hidden from view; there were no curtain calls for them, etc. There was also no discussion about the possible implication of a feminine model. So, many women were excluded from feeling any more affinity with the work than they would have in a mixed group. There was nothing 'new' offered.

Sadly, in the discussions, precedence was given to the practitioners, or known names, and this suppressed the voices of

16. Grenland Friteater: Geddy Aniksdal, Elin Lindberg and Anne Erichsen as Les Miserables

many who expected to find an opportunity to speak in an environment that offered support, in the hope of discovering new ways forward. We rarely got beyond statements, and discussing titles and the known. It seems phase one was much about projection and very little about exploration. Something we could have learnt to help phase two would have been to avoid the precedence given to age and experience – listen and learn, yes, but for a truly organic collaboration to occur, let all be heard.[15]

The work in the second phase quickly developed into a pattern. In the mornings, different women would run training sessions in the gym at the Chapter Arts Centre, open to everyone. In the afternoon, the women moved down to the factory and divided into groups to carry out different kinds of work. Zofia Kalinska's group gradually emerged as a team of eight, meeting daily and working on improvisation techniques within the circle they created, and another group collected around Anna Lica and Atka Ambrova of Czechoslovakia, who eventually took on the difficult role of becoming mistress of ceremonies in the final performance. For Katy Dymoke, this fragmentation into smaller working groups, however, represented a failure of the collective ideal:

> There was, consequently, no common vision, no binding to hold the work together. We deceived ourselves by believing the collaboration would unearth the 'darkness' stirring inside women today; it was possible only until there was a choice to work in groups, with Zofia on Trance, or with Anna on another entrancing piece, or with Geddy and Gerd in the River Room. This choice was an abdication of the idea of collective spectacle, resulting from a process of collaborative work with the space, with artists and with technicians, to try a new way/new ways which would break down these divisions.
>
> Surely a woman director in Magdalena would consciously avoid the label 'director', and try to be a 'Weaver', if aware of the silencing we had all hoped to escape. What happened was that the weavers had status, status attained by the experience of years working with *masters* in the Experimental world. There were differences? There was deception, self-deception; Michelle cried when she realised she had capitulated, in a piece that was suppressing her creative energy, to the vision of the weaver who she trusted because of the fascination surrounding her work, the daemonic woman. Zofia's group constantly collided with one another and reached a level to be expected in any project that involves peripheral listening and watching and yet total absorption/entrancement, till the darker forces are unleashed, carried on over ten days. However, the process was, we hear – and we all tried it – fascinating.[16]

If the responses of some women were negative, however, others found the experience of working together an enlightening one. The following quotes, taken from letters of several women describing what Magdalena '86 had meant to them, suggest that the impact of the Festival had far-reaching consequences, both in personal and professional terms:

> I have had to rethink my position/role as a feminist theatre woman both in terms of work and the community. Maybe the

conclusions both of us reach are different, but I think the confrontation with certain questions is ultimately more important than the answers.

Stacy Klein

Normally I work in a company with five actors, and it was amazing to feel the energy of being so many. To me, there was some kind of gap in energy and concentration between the morning training at Chapter and the performance work at the factory. The most important to me was the work with Zofia's group. When I realized that it would be impossible to create the show all together at the potato factory (it took me some time because I was really hoping for it) I decided to work with a smaller group and go fully into that instead. Here, I found something specifically female in the essence of what we improvised. Some of us could, in this situation with no men, even do some research on our stronger, more 'masculine' sides that seldom show up when there are men.

Anne Erichsen

Elin Lindberg, one of the youngest practitioners, tried to describe what had happened to her in terms of images:

Wales and the rain – the first night: thunder and lightening and Jill was standing on a chair wishing us all welcome. 'She looks like a kind of witch', I thought, and I looked around at all the other women – 'hm, is this some sort of witch-congress? Daemonic women?' I looked around again and I felt fine.

The women's suitcases were well filled with performances and knowledge. I saw all the performances and I became impressed – so many ways of being an actress.

The working sessions in the mornings were very important to me – tastes of different ways to work.

It was a moving festival in many ways, but I didn't really understand the richness until I came home and suddenly was standing still – still – still; I had to start walking on my own legs again.

Elin Lindberg

Julia Varley wrote at length on Magdalena '86, describing her reactions on arriving at the Festival (she came later than the other practitioners, due to professional commitments), and her document again shows the way in which so many of the women present struggled for an adequate language through which to articulate what had taken place:

It was not easy to be always questioning while going against the rules our professional experience had taught us. Wisdom was immersed in chaos and obviously very emotional.

Jill was choosing to be responsible by being irresponsible, to be the director of the project by not directing.

We worked without a director, without a theme, without scenes; we worked as much as possible all together, 38 women, without a title, following all possible threads.

Magdalena . . . Magdalena? Magdalena! became the title, nearly an anthem, during what was called 'the' performance, a collective improvisation developed from the morning work session of Jolanta, which half of us were lucky enough to see and the other half to experience. A 'performance' for no outside spectators, which could not be repeated. Just the first, tentative and insufficient step of theatre.

When I arrived, two things surprised me: that smaller groups had not automatically formed to propose and fix performance material and that so many hours were still spent in the gym.

Looking back, Zofia's work, the potato song, the bed scene, the River Room, Atka, the final offering were smaller groups, were fixing material, were using the chosen spaces of the potato factory, but at the time everything and everyone criss-crossed to an indistinguishable extent, so it did not in any way resemble or feel like groups and scenes. It looked like theatre work being developed by people following chaotic inclinations.

Why the river? why were tons of sand shovelled into a room? why the bed? why pulled by strings in opposite directions? why the table? the drop of water? why the magic circle? I don't know. A few answers could come from those who first proposed those items, if they remember. But I did not ask myself those questions.

I heard Kozana wanted a boat of voices; I joined. Going through a text in the early morning to keep up my personal

17. *Lis Hughes Jones in* 8961 – Caneuon Galar a Gobaith

voice training and finding it had a different meaning in that context, I took it to the river together with Helen and her baskets. Cinzia asked me to throw my hair over the railing, and I did. Netta wanted to see my childish face, and I showed her. Whenever it could my obsession with the manifestation of opposites found its space, commenting on the work I saw.

I looked at Jolanta dig a hole in the sand, take some in her hand, cover the hole, walk to another place, dig another hole, put the sand from her hand in it and cover the hole, then walk

78

away, smiling. The questions I *was* asking myself were others. Why is this different? what is different about working just with women? what, how, when is this experience helping each of us to go forward in our profession, to define our language, contributing even more strongly to the theatre groups we come from? what is particular to a woman? to an actress? to her way of perceiving and expressing reality? what is her special secret? An answer came to me from Eugenio during the Ista congress of September 1986 in Holstebro. He was talking of the arrogance of knowledge, which had mined the curiosity of exploring to assert positions, avoiding the meeting points to exchange and keeping the clash with no development. I looked back to Magdalena and understood clearly that there it had been different. *Because* it was only women, the need to discover, to question was overwhelming. It created a common solidarity which used the big differences in experience, style, character, colour, to go deeper into the questions. There could not be a winning statement, because no one was interested in hearing or uttering it.

Julia Varley

Maria Consagra, director, performer and academic, also tried to describe her feelings and to provide insights into the significance of Madalena '86 for women's performance as a whole:

My first reaction to the idea of Magdalena was a bit sceptical; I felt that the women chosen to participate were not from a wide enough range of theatre styles, of theatre worlds. They all belonged to the Odin Family – most did. The idea of creating something to show – a piece – in two weeks, while sharing each other's background, seemed terribly difficult. Zofia's group was formed for the most conventional reasons and in the most conventional (almost) way. Zofia's work was admired extremely by all of us; we wanted to learn from her; we wanted her to lead us. It seems natural that, when something wants to get done, individuals bring out these competencies, and natural leaders emerge. It seems logical that the magic circle had the least problems. And the frustrations of some women make me think that they focused too much on product. Magdalena is passion

79

that has not found a structure. Magdalena changes its meaning as I change, as my change meets other women changing, for *Magdalena is us*. We can understand the shape of Magdalena only after it has happened; you cannot see the shape of something as it is happening. Magdalena is not a Festival; Magdalena is not a workshop; Magdalena is Jill; Magdalena is Susan; Magdalena is Brigitte C.; Magdalena is Brigitte K.; Magdalena is Julia; Magdalena is Anna; Magdalena is Anne; Magdalena is Jolanta; Magdalena is Jolanta's show. . . . OK, I'll stop.

Jolanta's show. It is the most FEMALE show that I have ever seen, the show that most made me realize, reaffirm, that women do have a different poetic of expression than men do – and let me add that I think it is strictly connected to the work structure of the group – the poetics of theatrical expression. (I should think about it more actually, but not now. I'll keep that affirmation, none the less.) Jolanta was Jolanta in front of that specific audience that night, by which I mean she was speaking to us, picking up at times, ever so delicately, on our reactions. She spoke about herself in theatrical metaphor. She was completely present to that room, to that space and to us. She had no fourth wall. The show she did the last night was completely different than the one she did the first night. She was not a *personaggio*. She was shy, and we saw it; she was embarrassed, and we saw it; she did not have a structure of *personaggio* through which to mediate and focus those feelings. Why do I think all this is more female work than Pina Bausch, let's say – when Pina does use a fourth wall – I suppose it is because the primary difference for me between men and women is how they relate to others, to life, to themselves. They interact differently with others, and others in theatre is not only others on stage with you but the audience.

My workshops – the ones I gave the first week – were very rewarding, or should I say the second was very rewarding, for I worked with only three people, and they were older and already *really* professional, and thus I tried out many things. The workshop was on creating a small theatrical piece with an object. The objects used were suitcases, umbrellas, pots (heavy). The object becomes a channel–obstacle through which energy and imagination must move, deal with. At the beginning one creates actual physical tasks – balancing the object on head, throwing it and catching it, allowing the energy exerted to carry you into new dynamic ways of dealing with the object's weight solely; it helps you discover new actions/movements; part of the interest for me was to discover the different approaches that each person had to the object – after the first indication of moving with the (weight of) the object.

Maria Consagra

Some of the impressions were expressed with great clarity; others seemed vaguer and more confused, but from all the testimonies came the sense of an active attempt to articulate the unspoken and not only to describe an enriching personal experience but also to establish some notion of what a women's theatre might be. All those who wrote about Magdalena '86 were aware of the additional difficulty posed by the absence of an adequate terminology through which to describe what had occurred. The problem of defining a women's theatre without a language in which to speak about it came to the fore and has since provided a central area of investigation in later Magdalena conferences and workshops.

18. Jolanta Biele Jelzmyk and Jolanta Gadaczek as Claire and Solange in Zofia Kalinska's production of The Maids

The Magdalena Performance

The final performance took place on the last two evenings in August
and was open to the public free of charge. The performance had
always been perceived as an integral part of the Magdalena Festival,
but during the second phase some disquiet had been expressed about
the constraints posed on the daily working routine by the need to
create a performance. It was argued that in barely two weeks,
anything presented to the public would be inadequate, but at the
same time it was important to open up the work and show what had
been going on. The daily routine of morning training sessions,
followed by afternoon work in separate groups, became more focused, and energies were directed towards the creation of a performance. In this process of creating a public demonstration of the work,
choices were made, and again the way in which those choices took
place caused a lot of controversy. The two women in the directorial
role accepted and rejected work offered, and the performance spaces
became localised in two areas, the River Room and the large, square
space in which Anna Lica had placed a double bed. Early ideas for
developing a labyrinth, which Cinzia Mascherin had wanted, or for
the inclusion of group singing were abandoned. The final performance consisted of a sequence of improvisation work performed by
Zofia Kalinska's Magic Circle, Anna Lica's group work with the
brass bedstead in the square space, a brief improvisation outside the
building beside the canal, a short weaving sequence in the anteroom
which Cinzia Mascherin had decorated with her sculptures and which
Kari Furre had used to paint a savage, bloody mural, expressive of
her feelings of frustration and pent-up anger, and a series of individual improvisations in the River Room. Diane Speakman, who saw
the performance on both nights, describes what she saw:

> I saw the work-in-progress (for which the public was not
> charged) on both nights, and this proved to be essential, for
> spectators were split up and saw different things each night. I
> hadn't known this the first evening and had interesting if
> bemusing discussions with other spectators afterwards.
> The area outside and the whole ground floor of the factory
> were given over to a promenade production in twelve scenes.
> The structure, particularly the first night, resembled a patchwork
> of different pieces of material woven – an image floated by

19. *Kari Furre at work*

Greenhalgh to practitioners at planning stage – into a loose whole. There were changes to the content the second night, with the result that the place cohered much more, and was seen to be a time piece – no one actually took an alarm clock apart, but we had to wade through a sea of them on the way out. . . .

Several sequences did work or did begin to work, for me. The

83

opening was haunting. Set in an industrial urban wasteland fit for washer-queens, and to bell-peal and gulls' cries, Hughes Jones and Krukowska shared a work song (if not the work), as Hughes Jones thwacked and washed and hung out sheets by the canal. Lica walked perilously along a parapet, in her potent slipper-satin dress, lunatic, and beat the water with the long strait-jacket sleeves before rescuing a baby from the water (Moses! the Divine Child of Eleusis?), while the other women whispered together and looked righteously askance . . .

Then, inside, the group of six daemonic women working with Kalinska, who want to continue their collaboration, in symbolic white, black and red evening dresses, circled around a clock face, looking, as women have had to, through another medium – here, a bandaged mirror/window – into worlds within and without, playing with ritual objects and fighting, loving, despairing, hating, to climax and reprieve, as Kalinska tightened one thread – 'Remember the circle' – and Susan Bassnett the other, with her improvised archetypal narrative.

The next sequence built up a lot of tension but went on too long. To the rhythmic striking, by Lica, of rock on rock, four women wound and unwound, but stayed attached to, the bed-rock of existence (childbed, marriage-bed, deathbed), the earth, Gaea. Simultaneously, Krukowska darted across the playing area and Hughes Jones and Chadwick sang, in counterpoint, a composition by Chadwick about our mother: 'it is a silent song . . . sing it, sing it; it is a hidden thing . . . bind it, bind it; it is a bleeding wound . . . love it, love it'.

Another sequence, woven by Atka Ambrova from Theatre on a String, Czechoslovakia, provided a rare and welcome note of surreal humour and fun. In dream-time, several diners, sitting on non-existent chairs, fenced with knives and tried to eat objects (dream hamburgers, for instance) which arrived – or not – via the roof from which they were all suspended, their flight controlled by Ambrova.

Passing quickly by the Triple Goddess Fates (first night) spinning from a suspended mermaid-like figure (of the White Goddess, Aphrodite, creator–goddess, Eurynome, Tiamat of Sumerian myth?) we were in the room of time and the river, facing sands of time. Here, on this bank and shoal of time I thought I saw a butterfly (Hughes Jones) jump . . . certainly several performers played the fool with time and poked fun at Magdalena and themselves – for instance, Rona Lee, visual artist, blind and dressed in a ballet skirt of Magdalena leaflets. Lindberg was, as usual, very funny physically, demanding to know where the fish was (*Hésitations 3*) and then starting to swim on top of a box.

I was very shocked and moved, the first night, by Kaquet's appearance, naked, as the mad Ophelia with weeds entangled in her hair and flowing down her (and our) beautiful and vulnerable female body. She slowly advanced along the sand, writhed, turned, and retreated, to a speech pre-recorded: 'I always thought that I loved you so much, Daddy, but sometimes I have to beg your pardon because I am so happy without you; I am so happy because you are dead.'

After a tender and farcical meeting, mid-stream, between an ageing Mary (Ambrova) and a heavily-pregnant Joseph (Aniksdal), presented as Andy Capp at the seaside, we were ushered back into the first arena for the final re-enactment: The Last Supper. Hughes Jones sang us out, the second night, simply, fittingly, in Welsh.[17]

20. *Discussion between visual artists – Kari Furre, Gerd Christiansen and Cinzia Mascherin at Magdalena '86*

Strength, Silence and Unresolved Doubts

On the final day of Magdalena '86 a general discussion took place, during which everyone who had been in any way involved in the second phase, including one man, Richard Gough, artistic director of the Cardiff Laboratory Theatre, made a short statement. Even those whose later reassessments of what had happened were more negative offered positive feedback in that discussion. There was a great deal of emotion, and some very strong feelings were expressed. Two recurrent images kept appearing in the statements of very varied length made by all the participants – imagery and terminology of *strength* and of *voicelessness and silence*. References were frequently made to the 'strength' of the joint work, to the 'strength' of the feelings of friendship and solidarity that had developed during the three weeks, to the 'strength' of women that was finally allowed to appear in the absence of men. But equally, there were many references to women's silence, to the way in which some appeared never to have found a voice, the way in which some women had effectively silenced others even within an all-woman context.

This double imagery of strength and silence links the Magdalena work to the ongoing debates on feminine aesthetics, and it is interesting to see how this polarity came clearly to the surface. Hélène Cixous, describing women both as stormy and turbulent and as repressed and gagged, argues that women have never had their turn to speak. She goes on to add:

> It is impossible to *define* a feminine practice of writing, and this is an impossibility that will remain, for this practice can never be theorized, enclosed, coded – which doesn't mean that it doesn't exist. But it will always surpass the discourse that regulates the phallocentric system; it does and will take place in areas other than those subordinated to philosophico-theoretical domination. It will be conceived of only by subjects who are breakers of automatisms, by peripheral figures that no authority can ever subjugate.[18]

Significantly, since she wrote those words in 1975, Hélène Cixous has turned to theatre as a mode of expression, working closely with the director Adriane Mnouchkine in Paris. Theatre, for all the problems of shaping that it imposes, nevertheless seems to offer some of

Magdalena '86

21. Jennie Spiers at
work in the
Potato Factory

22. Rona Lee in
the final
performance,
Magdalena '86

the possibilities of breaking into new ground that Cixous believes are essential for women.

The final Magdalena discussion revealed another aspect of the whole question of women's creative language. Without exception, the feeling was voiced that the final performance had been disappointing. Looking at it from the point of view of a member of the audience, Richard Gough commented:

> I came away last night disappointed. I wanted to see something
> that was struggling to say something . . . I went in open to
> listen, but I didn't hear anything. I don't think that's just because
> I'm a man. The central metaphor of the performance was the
> search for a voice. What was disturbing was that I saw the
> movement of the jaws, but I didn't hear that voice at all.[19]

Those who had taken part in the performance offered various suggestions as to why it had seemed such an anti-climax – there had not been enough time to prepare anything really worthwhile; it had been difficult to establish a comfortable working method, with so many women involved; there had been no serious attempt on the part of the collective to decide on the content of the performance, so it was assembled out of many disparate bits and pieces; the pressure of having to show something distorted the work of the last week and unbalanced it. Jenny Spiers stated simply that 'the performance was the least rich thing we did'. But in contrast to these negative assessments of the performance work, again and again the women stressed how much they had gained both personally and professionally from the work in progress during the whole Festival. In other words, whilst the final product was generally held to be inadequate, the process of creating work together was regarded as a uniquely enriching experience.

In her very useful essay, 'Is there a Feminine Aesthetic?', Silvia Bovenschen, the West German feminist theorist, makes some important suggestions:

> I believe that feminine artistic production takes place by means
> of a complicated process involving conquering and reclaiming,
> appropriating and formulating, as well as forgetting and
> subverting. . . . If women have different assumptions with
> regard to their sensory approach, their relationship to matter and

material, their perception, their experience, their means of
processing tactile, visual and accoustic stimuli, their spatial
orientation and temporal rhythm – and all these things are what
aesthetics meant at one time, according to its original definition
as a theory of sensory perception – then one could logically
expect to find these things expressed in special forms of mimetic
transformation. But it will be nearly impossible to find
categorical evidence for this changed relationship: reality is not
that logical and there is no female cosmology either.[20]

Silvia Bovenschen cites Lucy Lippard, whose discussion of feminine
art forms raises the question of how best to express feminine sensi-
tivity, whether through fragmented forms or unity, through particular shapes or types of texture. Lippard notes that the images
created by women are superficial indicators of more fundamental
differences between the sexes, but again the problem here is that the

23. *Atka Ambrova
as the old
woman who
became Mistress of
Ceremonies in
the final
performance,
Magdalena '86*

difference is undefined and unspoken, hinted at by the work but impossible to define in concrete terms. The contrast between the Magdalena discussion of the working process and its final product bears out precisely Lucy Lippard's dichotomy between the instinctively felt and the actual result of trying to express that feeling in imagery. Silvia Bovenschen sums up the situation:

> Is there a feminine aesthetic? Certainly, there is, if one is talking about *aesthetic awareness* and *modes of sensory perception*. Certainly not, if one is talking about an unusual variant of artistic production or about a painstakingly constructed theory of art. Women's break with the formal, intrinsic laws of a given medium, the release of their imagination – these are unpredictable for an art with feminist intentions.[21]

Magdalena '86 ended with nothing resolved. As an experiment, it was magnificent, attempting to do something completely new and explore new ground. In doing this, all kinds of problems appeared. It was very clear that the problem of power structuring, even in an all-woman situation, remained unsolved. The performers, whether consciously aware of what happened or not, came to the fore and found ways of speaking that were not available in the same way to visual artists and technicians. Despite all the good intentions, traditional theatre hierarchies prevailed. Moreover, the fact that many of the performers were more experienced than some of the younger women involved in creating the environment for the Festival caused another form of hierarchy to be established. The criteria of the outside world, which some had perhaps idealistically believed could be abandoned for three weeks, constantly crept back in. And yet, at the same time, despite the clashes between idealism and harsh practical necessity, strong bonds of friendship developed between many of the women, and some felt sufficiently supported to take greater risks with their own personal work.

Notes

1. Mina Kaylan, 'Magdalena '86,' *Performance*, No. 44/45 (Nov.–Dec. 1986), 44–5.

2. Jill Greenhalgh, document sent to participants of Magdalena '86.

3. Jill Greenhalgh, 'Magdalena,' *Performance*, No. 42 (July – Aug. 1986), pp. 32–3.

4. Cinzia Mascherin, private statement for Magdalena '86, Aug. 1986.

5. Sandra Salmaso, private statement for Magdalena '86, Aug. 1986.

6. See note 4 above.

7. Georgiana Berry, private letter to Magdalena, 29 Aug. 1986.

8. Diane Speakman, 'The Next Stage: Devaluation, Revaluation and After' in *Themes in Drama*, No. 11 (*Women in Theatre*) (Cambridge, Cambridge University Press, 1989).

9. Lis Hughes Jones, private statement for Magdalena, Aug. 1986.

10. Hélène Cixous, from *La jeune née*, in Elaine Marks and Isabelle de Courtivron, eds, *New French Feminisms* (Brighton, Harvester, 1981), pp. 90–8.

11. Diane Speakman, 'The Next Stage: Devaluation, Revaluation and After.'

12. Kari Furre, open letter to Magdalena organisers, 12 Jan. 1986.

13. Rona Lee, letter to the author, undated, 1987.

14. Mandy White, letter to Jill Greenhalgh, 23 Nov. 1986.

15. Katy Dymoke, letter to Jill Greenhalgh, 12 Nov. 1987.

16. Ibid.

17. All quotations taken from reports on Magdalena '86 sent to Jill Greenhalgh and the author.

18. Hélène Cixous, 'The Laugh of the Medusa', in Elaine Marks and Isabelle de Courtivron, eds, *New French Feminisms* (Brighton, Harvester, 1981), pp. 245–64.

19. Richard Gough, author's transcript of the final Magdalena discussion, August 1986.

20. Silvia Bovenschen, 'Is There a Feminine Aesthetic?', in Gisela Escher, ed., *Feminist Aesthetics* (London, The Women's Press, 1985), pp. 23–51.

21. Ibid.

III
The Magdalena Project

The Search for New Directions

Reactions to Magdalena '86 were mixed. Press coverage, though slow at first, increased as major international theatre journals carried articles examining the work of the Festival, which rapidly came to be known simply as 'the first Magdalena'.[1] Many of the participants did not write immediately to the organisers but held back for a period of reflection, and significantly, some of the more negative assessments were written once the period of immediate enthusiasm had died down. As with any intense working experience in which a restricted group of people is in close contact for a limited time, excluded from the outside world, it was difficult to explain adequately to others what had taken place. Accusations that the whole event had been simply a kind of self-indulgent encounter-group session began to surface, along with the suggestion that the whole Festival had been wrongly conceived, along elitist lines, and that the vast majority of women working in theatre had not been affected in any way.

The decision to transform the whole enterprise into a permanent Project had therefore two distinct points of departure. On the one hand, the organising committee felt that the initial venture had been a great success, and the response of funding bodies to the final reports seemed to them to bear this out. On the other hand, the accusations of racism and elitism and the inadequacy of the final performance made it more urgent to extend the range of women involved in Magdalena and to attempt alternative forms of meeting. In September 1987, at a three-day conference on the subject of 'A Women's Language in Theatre?', the Magdalena Project was established on a permanent basis in Wales at Chapter, Cardiff.

The need for a more broadly based structure and for clearer objectives had become apparent during the summer of 1987, when a

small-scale Magdalena meeting was held at the Nordiskteaterlabora-
torium in Holstebro, Denmark. A group consisting principally of
women who had taken part in Magdalena '86 and a few others
interested in finding out about the work came together for a short
period. What emerged straight away was a difference in discourse
between the women who had been part of the first Magdalena and the
others. This was especially clear with regard to Zofia Kalinska's
work. In Cardiff, the Magic Circle group had become an auton-
omous unit, and already by July 1987 plans were well under way for
the formation of an *ad hoc* company that would continue to work
together and create a performance. But in Holstebro, with a combination of women who had already started work with Kalinska and
women who had never worked with her before, it was obvious that
the two groups could not combine forces. Magdalena had started
with an idealistic, some would say utopian, belief in the capacity of
women to come together and share their lives and work. Differences
of culture, language, race, class, age and sexual propensity would, in
this idealistic vision, be subordinate to the commonality of women's
experience and the assumption that a group of women together
would create a sympathetic environment, rather than a destructive
one. Julia Varley, organiser of the Danish workshop, described her
hopes for what would come out of the meeting in the following
terms:

'What was most important was the morning work sessions
together. I can imagine a next Magdalena meeting developing
from them, with each participant leading a session in turn and
creating a starting point for the next, without having to start
from the idea of the end, the performance, but from the
beginning, our own need to explore in darkness.' This is how I
concluded an article written after the experience of the
'Magdalena Festival of Women in Experimental Theatre' of
August 1986.
     The words spoken during the last day of the Festival, in
meetings, speeches and personal conversations, expressed a need
to continue what had started, but also a need for time to
understand. Time to just let the very strong, exciting and
confusing outcomes of those days settle, in order to clarify the
new steps to be taken in view of meeting again.
     It was suggested that encounters at a less official level,

involving fewer women, could be organised, to continue asking the questions and give deeper outlines to the many themes which had emerged, before confronting them again all together.

Why and how women working in theatre can contribute even more strongly and differently to new directions in their field of work and give form and light to the hidden world of women's expression in theatre are basic issues that 'The Magdalena Project' is continuing to deal with in all its different initiatives which have flowered from last year's Festival.

And these questions are also at the base of the aspects on which I would like to concentrate during the two periods of practical work I propose.

The two aspects being: (1) the creative process itself, or in other words, 'work on the way of working', and (2) elements of performance production.[2]

The first Holstebro workshop in July 1987, though enjoyable for many, did not appear to have moved on at all from the work of the first Magdalena. Rather it exposed a flaw in the idealistic thinking that became even more apparent in the first of the two Cardiff workshop conferences which asked the question 'A Women's Language in Theatre?'. It is significant that this title was posed as a question in the first place, rather than as a statement. At the first Magdalena there had been a separate session on Women's Theatre Language, as though it were a given fact rather than a controversial suggestion.

The Cardiff conference in September 1987 was structured very straightforwardly. Four women led working sessions, and there were general meetings and discussion groups. At the final plenary session, a whole range of problems came to the surface, many of which had been apparent all along. From transcripts of the discussions, it is possible to distinguish some recurring difficulties that many women were experiencing: the problem of exclusion from what was perceived to be an elitist inner Magdalena group consisting of those who had taken part in previous meetings, the problem of power relationships between performers and their director, the problem of talking about 'women's theatre' with its implications of common ground as opposed to 'feminist' theatre which implies a basic commitment to a political programme or specific causes, the problem of a theatre of the image as opposed to a theatre of the word and image. Once again, the question of why so few coloured women were present was raised, and there was a heated argument about the decision of the organisers to open the workshop to men. It was pointed out that all the Magdalena meetings had been open to both sexes and that few men ever chose to attend, but many women felt that they should be excluded altogether. The tone of the discussions was extraordinarily old-fashioned, and many women commented afterwards that they felt that they were still caught up in consciousness-raising sessions of twenty years earlier. The question of whether there might or might not be a women's language in theatre was barely addressed at all.

With hindsight, it is not difficult to see why this should have happened. Central to Magdalena is the idea of unity, of bringing together women with a common interest in theatre work, regardless of age or experience. In the first Magdalena, boundaries had been drawn from the outset between the invited group of practitioners and the other women, many of whom were also experienced practitioners, who took part in the workshops during the first week. At the 1987 workshop conference, however, the boundaries were less clear, and furthermore, expectations were very high. What happened was that women of very mixed abilities and experience met and found difficulties, that might well have been easy to predict, in working closely together. While everyone, regardless of their background, was able to take part in sessions and learn from them, there was nevertheless a substantial difference between some of those who had years of professional training and experience behind them and some of those with no experience of working in theatre at all. The result was a difference in focus: some women were concerned with developing their own work and exploring ways of extending their range of technical skills, while others wanted to experience group work with other women often for the first time. In the closing debate, it became clear that many of those present did not understand the concept of theatre as a way of life, one of the fundamental presuppositions of the Third Theatre world. In the clash of opinions, the traditional theatre of the play, with its fixed rehearsal periods and its focus on public performance, met head on with the experimental theatre world of daily training sessions and incidental performances. With such major differences, the question of whether there might be a women's theatre language could not even begin to be aired.

The September 1987 conference was planned from the beginning as the first of two meetings, and the second encounter in December of the same year was very different in organisation, tone and results.

24. *Zofia Kalinska's Magic Circle group*

Benefitting from the problems that had arisen the first time round, the organisers decided to rethink some of the initial presuppositions. Large group discussions were ruled out, and instead participants were organised in small groups, each with their own nominated spokesperson who was to report back to the plenary meeting in a final session. Group reports were coordinated by Mara De Witt, who also established a series of specific topics for discussion and briefed the spokespersons on how to record the essential points made in each of the groups. The result of this organisation was a positive step forward: much of the vague arguing that had characterised the first conference was eliminated, and participants worked with a greater sense of purpose. Jill Greenhalgh set out the revised aims of the December conference in a publicity document sent to all participants:

> We avoid an academic approach to this huge question. We aren't expecting answers; we're using the question as a vehicle for research.
>
> An important aim this year is also to encourage a greater

dialogue between those working in the mainstream and those in alternative or experimental work. Through looking at existing work by women, by sharing methodologies, by examining form as well as content or by making new material, we are trying, practically, to reveal recurrent themes and images. Perhaps we can begin to identify some vocabulary that has some universal resonance for women – perhaps not. The work of this project is to find out. In brief, the aims are to set up opportunities for women to explore new approaches to theatre-making that more profoundly reflect their own experience rather than that of men.[3]

The programme of the second conference reflected the organisers' awareness of the changing needs of the participants. Each of the three days was carefully timetabled, and great effort was made to keep within those time limits. Participants were able to take part in different types of activity: Iben Nagel Rasmussen from the Odin Teatret gave a performance–demonstration of her work on the first day, and Cora Herrendorf and Nicoletta Zabini from the Teatro Nucleo of Ferrara gave a second performance–demonstration on the last day. Vanya Constant of 'Pauper's Carnival', Jane Bassett and Louise Rennison of 'Etheldreda' and Tanya Myers and Tamsin Griffin of 'Meeting Ground' gave short performances of their work in progress, and the South African women's company, the Vusiwe Players, presented their show *You Strike the Woman, You Strike the Rock*. In the mornings, at 8 o'clock, voice and physical warm-up sessions were run by Helen Chadwick, Claire Hughes, Ruth Posner and Mala Sikka.

The second day of the conference followed a slightly different pattern. Five all-day optional workshops were offered, and partici-pants chose which one they wanted to follow. Lis Hughes Jones of Brith Gof offered a workshop entitled 'Women and War: Finding a Voice'. Based on her own current work in progress, *Disasters of War*, her workshop was structured around a series of questions, outlined in her programme note:

What do women have to say about war?
What has their voice been in past wars?
Is our fate always to be the grievers?
Can the voice of our resistance be strong, confident, powerful?[4]

Also central to the workshop was the use of images taken from etchings by Goya and photographic material of women in wartime situations.

Beatriz Camargo of the Colombian Teatro Itinerante del Sol entitled her workshop 'The Rose of Winds' and declared that the task of the participants was to 'discover the voiced and dance of the eight elements in the body'. The most intensive of all the workshops, Beatriz's group worked without a pause for seven hours. Interestingly, she chose not to focus on women alone in her workshop nor to start from any preconceived notions of 'the female' or 'the feminine'.

Jude Alderson, founder of the Sadista Sisters, ran a workshop on 'Women and Ensemble Theatre'. Her programme declaration began with an autobiographical statement about how she had come to work together with other women after years in what she termed 'male-orientated theatre' and had begun as a result 'to explore the female psyche and concentrate on classic themes that preoccupied women'. She proposed to work with masks and to enter into areas of unconscious possession, with a view to creating 'Epic scenes that are specifically female'.

The fourth workshop, run by Julia Pascal, was entitled 'Risk, Bravery, Fear, Confidence, Danger' and in her programme note she directly addressed the issue of a women's language in theatre: 'Are women confined to a secondary role because they have no language of their own? Is all language "men's language"?'[5] Participants were invited to bring along a piece of text and encouraged also to use languages other than English. Also text-based was the fifth workshop, a day split into two parts and run by Susan Bassnett and Deborah Levy on topics entitled respectively 'Archetype and Autobiography' and 'Writing for Performance'. This workshop aimed at enabling the participants to create pieces of text and to look at some of the problems involved in writing for performance.

The Conference was therefore a major departure from previous Magdalena meetings, in that physical work was not given prominence over voice work and work with texts, but instead there was a greater sense of integration. Moreover, just as there was an attempt to address the need to be expressed as well in the September 1987 conference for work with 'the play', so also was there an attempt to bring in more women working in mainstream theatre. Central to the first day was Phyllida Lloyd's workshop demonstration with actress Rosie Powell on 'Interpreting the Female Role in Shakespeare'.

Setting out to explore some of the choices available to performers and directors when tackling a Shakespeare production, Phyllida Lloyd addressed a series of questions including: why do so many actresses want to play Shakespearean roles, what are the traditional interpretations of the female role in Shakespeare, the crucial question of casting and the problem of casting women in men's roles and vice versa.

The existence of a large-scale session on women and Shakespeare at a Magdalena meeting clearly shows how the emphasis had changed in accordance with the needs expressed by former participants. From its beginnings as a place of encounter for women working primarily in experimental theatre, Magdalena was transforming itself into a forum for debate and practical exchanges amongst women working in many different kinds of theatre.

If the Magdalena organisers had taken to heart some of the misgivings articulated at the meeting in September 1987, they had also been affected by the impact of the second Holstebro Magdalena, that had taken place on 16–25 October of the same year. Organised by Julia Varley with the title 'Siren: A Woman's Voice in Theatre', the workshop was dedicated entirely to practical investigation of women's voices. Only five women took part in Siren: Brigitte Cirla, Jill Greenhalgh, Helen Chadwick and Julia Varley, who had all been present at the first Magdalena, and Francine Romain, from Guadaloupe, who had trained as an opera singer. Explaining the origins and aims of the workshop, Julia Varley claimed that after the July Magdalena there was a definite need for 'the different reality of a much smaller group', for something 'following different lines, smaller, more secret, deeper'.[6]

Despite the references in letters, reviews and other testimonies of the first Magdalena to the new experience of hearing so many women's voices, it was in fact the case that voice work had been consigned to a rather more marginal position in the final performance. Despite the huge success of Ida Kelarova's group singing and of the voice workshops and performances by women such as Helen Chadwick, Kozana Lucca, Lis Hughes Jones and Brigitte Cirla, the final performance consisted primarily of a string of visual images. The discussion of the last day had emphasised the word 'silence', and yet in retrospect what seems to have happened is that the group of women who came together to make a performance actually succeeded in silencing one another. Given all the possibilities that they had at their disposal, the fact that the female voice should have been heard too little in the final performance is a striking incongruity. Certainly Julia Varley, well known for her work on silence and stillness, felt that it was time for a group of women under the Magdalena umbrella to meet and engage directly with the issue of sound. In her introductory statement she notes the central importance

25. *Netta Plotsky in the final performance, Magdalena '86*

101

of voice and singing in previous Magdalena meetings, but significantly refers to voices in their non-theatrical context:

> The voices of women talking in the kitchen, in the changing rooms, round a table are impressed in me as something special and exciting. The secrets, the gossip, the cries, the songs at work have brought us together.
>
> In theatre it is still the area of mystery where all can be discovered, where experience counts, but rules are not written. The unknown, the curiosity to explore, the growing confidence, the attitude needed towards this research are the same found in the Magdalena Project's need to change and say something new in theatre.
>
> To find our voice: our own talking, singing voice and the voice which concretely expresses what is still hidden. The voice belonging to me and the voice belonging to a woman.[7]

Significantly, in September 1989, Magdalena plans to hold a Voice Festival.

By the end of 1987, with the Magdalena Project firmly established after a series of meetings in Wales and in Denmark, new lines of emphasis had also begun to emerge. The old charge of elitism amongst a closed group of alternative performers had been countered by the widening of Magdalena's aims and participants. Work on the creation of visual theatre was set alongside serious voice work and a new emphasis on text-based theatre, both with regard to newly written texts and traditional texts from the classic repertoire. Moreover, with the establishment of a permanent base for the Project in Cardiff, it became possible for the first time to discuss the setting up of an archive on women's theatre and the establishment of an international advisory committee for the furtherance of work by women in theatre.

In January 1988, Stacy Klein of Double Edge Theatre, Boston, organised a workshop conference called simply 'Electra', but advertised as an event pertaining to the Magdalena Project. Although the organisers of the previous Magdalena meetings were not part of the Boston organisational team, it is nevertheless an indication of the international status so suddenly and so rapidly acquired by the Project that Stacy Klein should have chosen to link her workshop specifically to Magdalena. Plans began to be discussed for future Magdalena

26. *Kozana Lucca's workshop, showing the Beasts in action*

meetings: in Argentina, proposed by Kozana Lucca and in Colombia for the anniversary celebrations of the discovery of the Americas in 1992 by Beatriz Camargo. More immediately, two further Magdalena conferences were proposed: a meeting in July 1988 on theatre and motherhood at Aradeo in the south of Italy organised by Silvia Ricciardelli of the Koreja Community Theatre Project and a meeting in July 1989 at Porsgrunn, Norway, on women as directors, organised by Geddy Aniksdal and Anne Erichsen of the Grenland Friteater.

Mothers and Directors

A great deal of controversy had been generated at the first Magdalena meeting over the question of the power relationship between performers and director. Jill Greenhalgh had specifically refused to take on the role of director for the final performance, despite being organiser of the whole enterprise, and the task of coordinating the various pieces of work had been taken on by Geddy Aniksdal and Gerd Christiansen. The relationship between the performers and the two volunteer directors was not altogether a happy one, and in subsequent workshop conferences the issue had again emerged, particularly when women used to working as directors were running workshops with participants whose experience of theatre was more limited.

In one sense, the problem of directorial power that kept surfacing at the Magdalena meetings was a direct off-shoot of the debates on the same topic that had characterised early feminist movements in the 1960s and 1970s.

At that time, one solution was proposed in the development of collaborative structures, co-operatives and communal decision-taking. Many women's journals set up editorial collectives, where all articles were read by all editors and assessed by the group. The idea of a 'leader', of one individual who took control and directed others, was unpalatable. Nevertheless, along with this ideological position went the process of rediscovering women's history, of establishing lists of names of 'great' women from the past, women whose successes in all kinds of fields had been forgotten. So, on the one hand, there was a feeling that the idea of collective rather than individual leadership was desirable, and on the other hand, there was the emergence of a growing list of names of key figures, women who began to serve as models and guru-figures for other women.

This kind of confusion, deriving from a desire to reject authoritarian structures, while at the same time looking towards the security of pioneering mother-figures from the past, has provided material for a long debate that is still far from resolved. In the theatre, that debate takes on special significance, especially in the West, where the role of the director has tended to increase in importance, and the boundary between director and performers is strongly marked. At the time of writing, the Porsgrunn Magdalena has yet to take place, but it seems highly likely that it will try to confront what has become one of the most problematic questions for women working in theatre.

The Porsgrunn Magdalena has been entitled A Room of One's Own and proposes to bring together 30 women from several countries. The preliminary statement, sent out to proposed participants contrasts the aims of the 1989 meeting with previous Magdalenas:

In earlier Magdalenas it was important to create an open structure in which all proposals could be tried out. As a result of these experiences we feel that the time is right for a more rigid structure in which we give skilled instructors and actresses the opportunity to enter more deeply into the material and work with definite aims towards a result.

The organisers also state very clearly that they intend this meeting to be principally for Scandinavian participants. In this respect, too, it differs from previous Magdalena meetings in its unabashed partisanship for what the organisers see as a marginalised group of nations.

The document contrasts what is termed 'an open structure' with the proposal for a new, 'more rigid structure' and suggests that only by passing through the experience of the former has it become clear that there is a need for the latter. It is tempting to look at the progression of Magdalenas from the first festival in 1986 and to suggest that as participants have acquired greater confidence through the continued exchange of ideas and practical skills, so they have moved away from what some felt was excessive idealism towards more specifically determined aims. In other words, and using the imagery of motherhood that has pervaded much of the discourse of Magdalena meetings, the childbirth was successful; the infant has gone through its first phase of discovery, exploration, conflict, tantrums and rejection of authority and is now looking for some more coherent structuring within which to locate herself.

The imagery of motherhood was felt by Silvia Ricciardelli in particular to be central to any discussion of women's role in theatre. When she came to organise her workshop in July 1988, she chose as the final title: Donne, Bambini e Teatro (Women, Children and Theatre). In the document sent out to participants, she notes that all the Magdalena meetings have been inspired in some respect by the personal priorities of the organisers and states her own primary concerns:

The Aradeo meeting derives from the question I have asked myself as to whether it is possible to reconcile 'mothers, children and theatre'. And I wanted to explore the possibilities of our relationship with childhood and our professional development. Motherhood is not just the topic for the workshop, but it is also the spirit in which I have tried to conceive and realise the workshop. I have left it to grow and gradually develop through the network of collaborations and difficulties encountered in the process.

The Aradeo workshop brought together a group of women from a variety of backgrounds: some from the professional theatre, some from education, some who were social workers specialising in children's problems and some from Italian feminist organisations. Silvia Ricciardelli explained the rationale behind her choice of participants: 'Magdalena '88 on Motherhood is not solely for those women who have children; it is for all those women for whom the choice either to reject motherhood or to become mothers has resulted in a specific change of direction in their work.'

Some of the participants did bring children with them, though others chose to leave their children behind, and as Silvia Ricciardelli had planned, some of the women came to discuss the dilemma of whether or not to choose to have children in the unstable milieu of small theatre companies.

The workshop was organised around practical sessions, workshop demonstrations and lectures. Two theatre historians from the University of Bologna, Eugenia Casini Ropa and Laura Mariani, discussed the question of female performers and motherhood in the nineteenth and early twentieth centuries, pointing out how the actress had traditionally occupied a special position of moral ambiguity in Western society. On the one hand, the actress enjoyed a freedom of movement denied to most other nineteenth-century women, and consequently often became both the object of envy for those denied their independence and the object of desire for those who equated the actress with the prostitute. On the other hand, a large number of actresses were forced into deeply ambiguous family relationships, often going to great lengths to conceal their pregnancies or to raise their children away from the theatre. The case of Eleonora Duse, the great Italian actress, is an excellent example of this kind of ambiguity. Herself the daughter of itinerant performers, Duse first appeared on stage at the age of four, and later in life her prime motivation as a mother seems to have been to prevent her daughter from following in her footsteps. Duse's drive to see her daughter raised as a respectable woman resulted in long periods of separation from her, as the child Enrichetta was sent away to convent schools, and Duse seems to have lived her maternity as an anguished conflict between a desire for bourgeois stability and her professional life. Prior to the birth of her daughter, there was the additional grief of a dead baby, born illegitimately when Duse was still very young, a fact that she tried hard to keep secret.

The Aradeo Magdalena thus moved the Magdalena project a stage further, by introducing from the outset an historical dimension. The lecture–demonstration by Susan Bassnett, entitled 'Anthropological Fragments' continued this line, and a furious debate followed the insertion into this lecture of a brief provocative sketch by Cora Herrendorf, depicting the boring daily routine of the Virgin Mary as she cycled home with the shopping, tried to calm a screaming Baby, prepared chicken for Joseph's dinner and reconciled all this with the Divine Will. Bassnett and Herrendorf raised the question of re-presentational taboos by introducing the image of the Supreme Mother, and opinion was divided as to whether such an extreme interpretation could be acceptable in theatre terms.

Debate also raged around the decision by Silvia Ricciardelli to work with a group of children, with a view to making a performance on the last evening of the workshop in the central square of Aradeo at a rally in support of the Mothers of the Plaza de Mayo, the Argentinian women's organisation founded as a result of the desperate endeavours of hundreds of women to trace their sons and daughters who were abducted and in many cases tortured to death by the military dictatorship of the mid-1970s. Silvia's group consisted of five local children, Silvia and Giuseppe Bonuso, Roberto Tarantino, Silvia Longo and Robert dell'Anna, and was extended on the first day to include Vanessa Bassnett and Tchoubin Pourhousseini, the 10-year-old daughter and son of two of the participants. The decision to make work with the children an integral part of the five-day work-shop was defended on the grounds that by working practically with children, participants would be forced to rethink their relationship to them. As an attempt to make this clear, in one session the children were chosen as directors and the women instructed to follow the children's guidance.

The counter-argument to Silvia Ricciardelli's view, expressed principally by Serena Sartori of the Milanese Teatro del Sole and one of Italy's most experienced women in the field of children's theatre, was that by introducing children the issue of theatre and motherhood was actually made more obscure. After the session with children as directors, Serena Sartori attacked simplistic notions of power relationships, arguing that all those involved in the work had known from the outset that the children had had no real authority and that the exercise had been grossly patronising. She also pointed out that the children had seemed bewildered and less than happy at being given

107

27. Nominatae
Filiae: *Gerd
Christiansen as
a daemonic
angel*

their supposed power and that children required the security of well-
defined power relationships with adults.

Reviewing the workshop in *Noi Donne*, the journalist Maria Antonietta Saracino declared that she had been moved both by the final
presentation of songs and music in the village square and by the sight
of women from so many different backgrounds struggling with the
'incessant, though diverse rhythms' of motherhood and work in the
theatre.[8] Her article discusses the dichotomy between the impulse to
create children and the impulse to create theatre, and she refers to
what Silvia Ricciardelli calls her own uneasiness with the compromise brought about by either a combination of the two or a rejection
of one of them.

The Aradeo Magdalena lasted five days only and was full of
tensions and contradictions, but in many respects it marked another
stage in the growth of the Magdalena Project. The theme of motherhood and theatre was from the start an impossible one, and it was
obvious that nothing definitive would be resolved. Nevertheless, the
workshop did bring into the open the whole question of the relation-

ship between the maternal drive and the drive for artistic improvement, a question that has been on the agenda of women's theatre collectives for the past twenty years and has been tackled in very many ways, from the extreme position of the Roy Hart Theatre in the 1960s that banned all female performers from ever becoming pregnant on pain of expulsion from the company, to the liberal collective position of Footsbarn, who travel the world with an ever-growing band of children and employ professional teachers to travel with them. The workshop also enabled women who have chosen not to have children to talk openly about their feelings of ambiguity and to compare experiences with women who have chosen to combine the two distinct needs of work and maternity.

Most importantly, the Aradeo Magdalena introduced an historical dimension to the workshop. Alongside the practical sessions, the voice work led by Nasdrin Pourhousseini, the demonstrations, discussions and performances, there were also talks putting the whole issue of theatre and motherhood into an historical context. Time and again, the debates could be located in an ongoing diachronic process, as women in the 1980s wrestled with the same, still unresolved problems confronting their predecessors in earlier theatres.

Nominatae Filiae

In January 1988, the hopes for a Magdalena production finally came to fruition, as Zofia Kalinska's *ad hoc* company of women met in Holstebro to start a three-month working period devising the performance known as *Nominatae Filiae*. The establishment of the company had been an arduous process, and right up to the last minute there were doubts about its viability.

The original Magic Circle group that had begun work with Zofia Kalinska at the first Magdalena consisted of Daria Anfelli, Brigitte Cirla, Maria Consagra, Anne Erichsen, Brigitte Kaquet and Michelle Kramers as performers and Susan Bassnett as writer. Through the whole of 1987, while Brigitte Kaquet in particular struggled to obtain funding, the original group began to alter, as one after another found herself unable to agree on the length of the working period. The fundamental division came from the different emphases placed upon the work itself. Some wanted to insist on a three-month period that would be followed by a public performance and an international tour, while others felt that it would be best to conceive of the three-month period as a form of research and that the pressures of creating a performance would simply reintroduce the tensions of the final days of the first Magdalena. It was argued that, although a three-month working period might seem like a long time in traditional theatre for the preparation of a show, in experimental theatre it was far too short, since during that time everything had to be first devised and then rehearsed. It was pointed out that many Third Theatre companies take up to a year to create a performance.

The decision to go ahead with a three-month working period followed by a tour was finally taken because of the need to comply with the conditions established by the funding bodies, which required public presentation of the work. This decision meant that several women were unable to take part, since although they had negotiated a period of absence of three months from their own companies, they felt that they could not enter into an open-ended commitment and consider a tour at a later date. Others left because they were uneasy with the idea of a tour and would have preferred to take part in a research project rather than a commercial venture. In the end, only one woman remained from the original group of performers. When the company came together in January 1988, its members were Zofia Kalinska (Poland) as director, Susan Bassnett (Britain) as writer, Gerd Christiansen (Denmark), Jill Greenhalgh (Britain), Maria Teresa Hincapie (Colombia), Brigitte Kaquet (Belgium), Adele Saleem (Britain/Afghanistan), Isabel Ubeda (Spain) and Celia West (New Zealand).

The one clear starting point for the company was Zofia Kalinska's stated intention about what she wanted to achieve. Her work at previous Magdalenas had focused on the notion of the 'daemonic woman', exploring the conflict and aggression inherent in a series of female archetypes such as Medea, Clytemnestra, Electra or Phaedra. In her notes on directing that were circulated among the company, she explained that:

> The object of the work is to explore feminine archetype. The circle of women represent different archetypal characters. I feel I see them returning to each after their deaths and repeating their lives, particularly those moments which they remember most strongly, the moments of great pain or greatest happiness. They will never be able to rid themselves of such memories, however many times they are born.

In the ritualised actions of daily life, I want to include what Susan Bassnett has described as the psychological interaction between the women as they move through space together. My working method is based on a long period of preparation, and it is impossible to give precise details of that preparatory work in advance because the rehearsal period is the time when the piece actually takes its shape. The best I can do is state that the purpose of the work is to develop and explore feminine archetypes and to show the beauty, weakness and daemonic power of all women as perceived by another woman, myself.

I believe this is an ideal time for new explorations by women in theatre and that women are uniquely placed to be able to try things out for themselves in a way that would not be possible for men.[9]

The company worked closely together with the director and writer in the early stages of preparation. A crucial first step was the need for each performer to find her own archetype. Through extensive reading, discussion and investigation of representational images of women, in particular a study of the work of women painters through the ages, figures began to emerge. Maria Teresa Hincapie centred her work on Medea, Adele Saleem focused on Salome, Brigitte Kaquet chose two figures, the eternal bride from Dicken's *Great Expectations*, Miss Havisham, and Faust's abandoned lover, Marguerite. The other three women experienced problems in finding an archetypal figure, and for the first weeks of intensive improvisations and study periods they worked with a set of images rather than with a character and a story. Celia West concentrated on female mystics, Gerd Christiansen on female suicides and Jill Greenhalgh on women artists.

The process of creating a piece of theatre from scratch is a highly complex one and virtually impossible to describe in any sensible way. Zofia Kalinska's directorial method consisted in lengthy practical sessions, during which certain rules were rigidly observed: all performers had to change into clothing in the three basic colours of the performance, red, white and black, and casual clothes were not allowed in the rehearsal room. By this means, Kalinska argued, the ritual aspect of the work would be reinforced. The second basic rule was the requirement of all performers to begin whatever actions they later developed by walking in a circle, moving progressively past six objects: a bed, a chair, a mirror, a window, a bowl of water and a

28. Nominatae
Filiae: *Two
moments of
interaction
between
archtypal figures*

broom, again to establish a sense of ritual in physical terms. What Kalinska most wanted to avoid was a form of theatre based on psychological realism, so the performers were required to approach their archetypes not through standard construction of character but instead through a series of situations into which the archetypal character was suddenly and unexpectedly thrown. For those performers who had never worked in this way before and who had always had the security of a script and a character, this proved extremely difficult.

The common language of the company was English, but since all the women came from different countries and since this had been a prime factor in the process of selecting them, care had to be taken to ensure that the performers worked in their own languages. Sometimes this produced striking results, as for example when one of Adele Saleem's pieces of text, taken from Oscar Wilde's *Salome*, was performed in Persian, the language of her childhood. Gerd Christiansen, who had been unable to find a single archetypal figure on which to work, began to mix languages and so found a metaphor for the sense of cultural displacement that characterised her suicidal figures. In later stages of rehearsal she began working with Danish archetypes and discovered the Little Mermaid, the woman who transformed herself into human shape out of love and who brought about her own death after a long period of suffering.

The pathways to the creation of archetypal figures were varied. In some cases the performers had clear ideas of what they wanted to do, in other cases archetypes were suggested by Bassnett and Kalinska. The decision to build the performance around the figure of a woman artist in search of material came as a result of Jill Greenhalgh's difficulties in finding any mythical female figure upon which to focus. The archetype of the Artist was finally agreed upon, and after that came the decision to structure the whole performance around the Artist.

Towards the end of January a crisis developed with the departure of Maria Teresa Hincapie, who felt unwilling to work with the theme of violence proposed by the director. The loss of Maria Teresa left the company without a Medea, and because she felt strongly that Medea was an essential character, Zofia Kalinska moved Celia West from her work with St Teresa into the role of Medea.

An early draft script explains the basic structure of the piece and the inter-relationship between the women:

Magdalena

An Artist's room somewhere in Europe at the close of the last
century, the age of the New Woman, when the process of
questioning the traditional roles of women has just begun. The
Artist is one of those troubled women who cannot accept the
place assigned to her in society, but whose dreams of an
alternative are unshaped and nebulous. She could be many such
women, Akne and Colette, Paula Modersohn Becker and
Elizabeth Siddall, Virginia Woolf, Isadora Duncan, Rosa
Luxemburg, Eleonora Duse. This Artist is a painter. Her room
is filled with unfinished canvases, clothes piled up, confusion and
chaos.

The room contains very little furniture, only the bare
essentials for survival. There is a bed, a table, a chair, a mirror.
There is a bowl of water and a broom. A dusty window gives a
little light from the outside world. These objects are spaced one
from another in such a way as to form a circle around the stage.
They are solid and real, but mounted on castors so that during
the performance they can be moved by the performers as the
room changes its appearance with new lives that come to
possess it.

The Artist was thus set apart from the other archetypes, just as Jill
Greenhalgh had remained apart from the other performers during the
first six weeks of work because of her failure to find a suitable role. In
this way, the working process undergone within the company found
its means of expression in the actual performance.

With the set established as the Artist's studio, the other women
became invaders of that space:

The five women are archetypal images from an imaginary past.
Summoned somehow, mysteriously, they have come despite
themselves into the Artist's room, not knowing what their task
might be. They have come from distant memory and now, in
time present, they are searching for a clue, for a place, an image,
a moment that will give them an identity again. The five women
are:

Medea, who destroyed what she loved best of all, her
children.

Salome, who ordered the death of John the Baptist and so
destroyed holiness and the man she desired together.

114

29. Nominatae
Filiae: *Celia
West as
Medea*

The Little Mermaid, whose desire for life on earth led to her
own self-destruction.

Miss Havisham, who spent a life in death, walled up in an
empty house, plotting revenge on all men because of her own
betrayal.

Cassandra, the Trojan prophetess who was cursed always to
speak the truth but never to be believed.

But because these five women are from the unformed world
of the imagination, they are not locked in a single self. Through
Medea runs the story of other queens whom life betrayed –
Phaedra and her lust for a forbidden man, her stepson;
Clytemnestra who killed her husband in a fatal act of revenge;
Hippolyta, the Amazon, brought back to Greece in chains to be

a bride. Through Salome runs the story of other child-women, caught in the act of reaching for the impossible, Alice in Wonderland falling down the rabbit hole, Iphigenia baring her throat to her father's knife, Antigone stamping her foot at Creon's law. Through the Mermaid runs the story of all those women whose search ended in darkness, the un-named women of asylums and convents, the anchorite walled up by her sisters, the rejected wife sealed up to go mad in the attic. Through Miss Havisham runs the story of the women who waited vainly, of Marguerite and her godless lover, Faust, of Mariana in the moated grange, of Tannhäuser's poor Elisabeth, of the Sleeping Beauty wrapped in cobwebs, waiting for a prince who never comes. And through the story of Cassandra runs the motif of silence and constraint that has been the lot of women in all cultures and for centuries. Unable to be heard, her words are lost as soon as she utters them.

As Medea, Salome, the Mermaid, Miss Havisham and Cassandra enter, they begin to circle, from mirror to chair, from bed to window, following the arrangement of the props and forming a circle. As they touch the objects, vague memories begin to shape themselves. At each place they pause, trying to remember, and so each point of focus in the room becomes a station on the Calvary that is each woman's remembered pain. Gradually the women find a place that is meaningful to each of them (the bed for Medea, the window for Miss Havisham, the mirror for Salome, the basin for Cassandra and for the Mermaid a space somewhere in the centre, but closest to the chair. As the performance progresses the women will work closely with each of these props, thereby establishing a clear relationship with and function of the prop in their individual stories.)

Nominatae Filiae opened at the Odin Teatret, Holstebro, on 18 April 1988 and then toured Denmark and West Germany before coming to Britain for a further six weeks. It was revived again in October 1988 and toured for a month in Poland. Reviews were generally excellent. The *Independent* described it as: 'a powerful, beautifully orchestrated work, welding together ideas that are quite disturbing – from folk-loric rituals to the classical Furies – to arrive at its own strange energy'.[10] The *Guardian* referred to its appeal to women in the audience:

Some of the visual imagery is spine-tinglingly powerful and the whole show – performed with immense style and some wit by an international company of actresses – is bound to strike a poignant chord with any woman who has tried to balance the demands of her own creative life against the trashy, limited images of womanhood handed down by our culture.[11]

Claire Armistead writing in the *Financial Times* discussed the piece in terms of the overall research project from which it had originated, that of trying to explore the possibility of a uniquely female form of theatre:

The rescue of women from the male imagination has become an almost obsessive preoccupation of the latterday women's movement. In this instance a Cardiff-based project, under Polish direction, sets about the task with the high seriousness of knights in pursuit of the Holy Grail. That they will fail to complete their mission is part of the tradition; the pursuit is all.

Nominatae Filiae is more specifically a collaboration between the theatre research arm of Belgium's Cirque Divers and the Magdalena Project, an international venture which grew out of a three-week women's festival in Wales two years ago. Its mission, broadly speaking, is to pool experience and creativity into the search for themes and variations that are uniquely female.

The first hurdle, which has yet to be successfully negotiated, is to find a language for the undertaking. Here is a piece rich with cultural resonance, which would seem in its own terms to be merely a preamble to the main cause. We are presented with a woman artist painting at the turn of the century, from whose pallette trip dying swans, murderesses and martyrs who speak in many tongues and idioms but who are historically closeted by male stereotypes and preconceptions – a state symbolised by a profusion of picture frames.

There is a Piaf figure in black lace who rasps out her role models (Medea, Roxane . . .) before submitting herself, in tremulous soprano, to a rendition of *La Vie en Rose*: there is a tousle-haired artist's model, who announces proudly that she specialises in suicide poses before dashing herself again and again to the floor. It is only at the very end of the reverie that the archetypes gather behind the largest of the picture frames and collectively claw their way out.

This single, barbaric concept gives a sudden, breathtaking coherence to a tapestry of images that is stitched together by director Zofia Kalinska in patterns that become increasingly wild.[12]

The success of *Nominatae Filiae* as a performance is indubitable, and the testimonies of those concerned show that the working experience was an enriching one for all the women involved. The enthusiastic reviews were an adequate reward for the weeks of frustration in the early stages of the work and the frenetic activity of the final month, when the designer Zofia de Inez Lewzuk arrived from Poland and began work on the costumes and set.

But the question of the uniqueness of the female experience and its articulation in terms of theatre remained a vexed one. During the three months of work, Zofia Kalinska complained at being constantly pushed back into what she termed a 'masculine' directorial position, where the performers demanded to be told what to do. She, for her part, kept insisting that they follow their own working pattern in exploring their relationships with the chosen archetypes, instead of having a series of demands placed on them by another person. These two very different perspectives often led to clashes, and in the moments of conflict the terminology used by both director and performers was that of the mother–daughter relationship.

The Aradeo workshop failed to discuss one aspect of women's theatre work that recurred in the *Nominatae Filiae* rehearsals, in much the same way as it had recurred in other Magdalena meetings – the impulse felt by many women to 'mother', to 'enable', to 'over-pro-tect' one another as a kind of compensation for what was perceived as the discrimination women endure in the world of men. Time and again discussion groups would take up the question of female soli-darity, the need for harmony amongst women, the need for a supportive environment. Both Zofia Kalinska and Susan Bassnett had wanted to challenge such assumptions in their work and investi-gate instead the violence and the destructive urges which are present in women just as they are in men. This, they felt, was a more honest position and one which could be exploded in view of the growth of women's self-confidence and public power during the decades of the women's movement. The equation of woman with caring and ma-

30. Nomínatae
Filiae: *Adele
Saleem as
Salome*

ternal instincts was one which they felt should be challenged, but despite the images of strength and power that the final performance managed to convey, the fundamental question was not tackled at all. The working method within the company consisting entirely of women was not notably different from that of any other company regardless of sex, except for the fact that the tensions between director and performers were articulated in other terms. Zofia Kalinska's desire to find a new way of collaborative working foundered on the need felt by the performers to work within the security of a structured directorial power system. In the event, she shaped some of the material brought by the performers, but for the most part the performance was the expression of the director's concepts and ideas, in the tradition of director's theatre. *Nominatae Filiae* did not in the end represent a breakthrough into new explicitly female ways of working.

Notes

1. See bibliography for full details.

2. Julia Varley, statement, 3 March 1987.

3. Quotation taken from the document sent to participants, *The Magdalena Project '87: A Woman's Language in Theatre?* II, 4, 5, 6 December.

4. Ibid.

5. Ibid.

6. Julia Varley, document entitled *The Magdalena Project: Siren: A Woman's Voice in Theatre*.

7. Ibid.

8. Maria Antonietta Saracino, 'E di scena Magdalena,' *Noi Donne* (October 1988).

9. Zofia Kalinska, Notes on Directing *Nominatae Filiae*, advance press statement prior to performances, March 1988.

10. Review by Sarah Hennings of productions at the 1988 Glasgow Mayfest, Festival of novel approaches, *The Independent*, 23 May 1988.

11. *The Guardian*, 23 May 1988.

12. *The Financial Times*, 25 May 1988.

IV
The Future for Women's Theatre

In her book, *Feminism and Poetry*, Jan Montefiore struggles with the question of whether there can be a genuinely female poetry written in a female language and concludes that, although there may be poetry of woman-centred sexuality, this does not constitute a new language because 'experience and language do not coincide, and there is nothing gendered about poetic form'.[1] She then adds that whenever women's poetry is looked at closely, it is still always engaged with the same masculine language and symbolism that it aspires to transcend:

> But this oppositional engagement, this struggle to transform inherited meanings, is where the real strength and specificity of women's poetry lies. Certainly, it is true that the notion of a specifically female language and identity is utopian, like that of any female tradition of poetry written without reference to any masculine discourse. But the value of utopias is that they enable us to imagine possibilities of difference for the brute, contingent world. . . .[2]

Jan Montefiore is writing about poetry, but the terms she uses can be equally applicable to theatre. Much of the work carried out at the Magdalena meetings has revolved around the question of 'a woman's language in theatre', and what is meant by that is whether there can be a form of theatre practice that is identifiably female. So far, the conclusions have tended towards the same view as Jan Montefiore – that the tradition of theatre is so strongly male-dominated that there is no clear way forward towards a women's theatre, other than one defined in terms of its content. Theatre forms, whether text-based or created in other ways, have not so far revealed anything that can be defined as specifically female, and it may be that such an aspiration is as utopian as the aspiration towards a specifically female form of poetic discourse. Nevertheless, the fact that such questions were not even being posed twenty years ago is a sign of how much progress there has been and how far the discussion and exploration has come, since the earliest manifestations of feminist theatre in the late 1960s.

In September 1986, shortly after the first Magdalena meeting, the International School of Theatre Anthropology (ISTA) held a meeting in Holstebro on the topic of 'The Female Role' as represented on the stage in various cultures. Present at that meeting were male and female performers from Europe, China, Japan, India and Bali and a large number of theatre practitioners, writers and anthropologists from all parts of the world. The basic premise of the meeting was to investigate the portrayal of gender roles by performers of both sexes; consequently there were female impersonators of extraordinary skill and Chinese women trained to play male roles, including the magnificent Pei Yan-Ling whose portrayal of a warrior was so exquisite that she received a standing ovation at the end of her workshop demonstration.

In an introductory statement that later appeared as an essay, Eugenio Barba argued that the notion of duality, though fundamental to most societies, does not necessarily contain positive and negative evaluations:

> At the origin, in the period of vulnerability, individual differentiation passes through the negation of the differentiation of the sexes. The field of complementarity dilates. This is seen in the Occident when, in training work on the pre-expressive level, no account is taken of what is masculine and what is feminine, or in the Orient, when an actor explores masculine and feminine roles indiscriminately. The double-edged nature of his particular energy becomes tangibly evident. The balance between the two poles, Animus and Anima, is preserved.
>
> In this context, the Balinese speak of a continual interweaving of Manis and Kras. The Indians speak of Lasya and Tandava. These terms do not refer to women and men or to masculine or feminine qualities, but to Softness and Vigour as flavours of energy. The warrior god, Rama, for example, is often represented in the 'soft' manner: Lasya. In our culture, Anima

31. Nominatae
Filiae:
*Archtypes
passing through
the frame*

and Animus refer to the two sides of a pair of scales, a *concordia discors*, an interaction between opposites, which brings to mind the poles of a magnetic field or the tension between body and shadow. It would be arbitrary to particularise them sexually.[3]

Except, of course, that societies do particularise the 'soft' and the 'vigorous', and the values that come to be attributed to these qualities tend to be associated with gender roles. This was the problem that came to the fore during the three days of the Holstebro meeting and mirrored the kinds of issues that had been discussed so intensely at Magdalena '86 and have remained on the agenda ever since. Eugenio Barba and the ISTA meeting appeared to be starting from the utopian position of an asexual idea of energy, whereas many of the women present, particularly theatre practitioners, argued that it was impossible to ignore an actor's sex and that any theoretical position on performing must take into account sexual differences.

123

A basic premise of ISTA work since the early 1980s has been the notion of pre-expressivity. By this is meant what the actor communicates by presence and dynamic energy and consists of what Barba calls 'a heritage of knowledge that is substantially similar in the theatres of all cultures'.[4] This pre-expressive level is also known as the 'biological' level of theatre, and is defined as follows:

> This 'biological' level of the theatre permits us to make an intercultural examination of the various theatrical traditions, not as historically determined systems, but as extra-daily techniques based on a particular use of the actor's energy and manifested in particular styles and forms.
> The principles underlying extra-daily technique and use of energy are:
> (1) an alteration of balance, resulting in new posture and gait.
> (2) a dilation of muscular tensions according to the dynamics of opposites in relationship
> (3) a consistent inconsistency with respect to the 'arbitrary' rules the actor decides to follow.
> The use of these principles result in a new architecture of muscular tones and corporal rhythms which are the basis of the actor's pre-expressivity.[5]

The actor's training, according to this model, is therefore somehow desexualised, and regardless of the sex of the individual and the ways in which the roles of male and female may be perceived in society at large, the biological level of theatre remains a constant meeting point where sexual differentiation can be either ignored or overcome.

But many of the women present at the ISTA meeting did not agree with this view of the actor's training and the actor's role. They argued strongly that focus on the actor's technique of body and voice work should not obscure the wider issues of the social position of both the actor as individual and the roles he or she plays. In many parts of the world women have been forbidden to perform in public; in some cases women have been excluded from the stage after having played on it for centuries; while in other cases they have never been allowed to begin, and consequently female roles have been portrayed by male performers. These historical facts, it was argued, remain on the table despite the idealistic discussions of asexual technique. And, perhaps inevitably, the refusal in Holstebro to acknowledge that social dimension resulted in accusations of discrimination against women, the suggestion that the theory of pre-expressivity as asexual was male-determined.

It is difficult not to feel some sympathy with this point of view. On the one hand, it would be grossly over-simplistic to assume that Eugenio Barba's notion of pre-expressivity is sexist, but on the other, it does fail to take into account the fact that despite training from a very early age, male and female bodies undergo a series of biological changes that cannot but have an impact on the physical results. Puberty for men and for women is a time of enormous change, but the great difference between the sexes is that after puberty women menstruate, and consequently their biological time-clock is altered in ways that men cannot imagine. A performer may rise above her monthly period pains and produce marvellous work regardless, but she will still be aware of those physical changes, controlled by hormonal alterations, and will therefore have to make a conscious effort to try to blot them out of her awareness if that is how she chooses to work. In planning the Magdalena meeting on motherhood at Aradeo, Silvia Ricciardelli chose to deal with precisely one such issue: the way in which the possibility of child-bearing weighs on the life and training of the female performer.

Eugenio Barba's seminal work on acting and the research of the ISTA group has been deemed to be of great value throughout the world by large numbers of actors in and out of traditional theatres. But it was not until 1986, the year of the first Magdalena, that women began to ask questions, and the challenge mounted to his theory of pre-expressivity by women with an alternative viewpoint is an important stage in the development of work in women's theatre. It may still not be possible to say precisely what a women's theatre language might be, but it does seem to be possible to say what it is not and to identify flaws in the theories of even the most experienced and sympathetic men in the theatre world.

Discussing the tradition of the *onnagata*, the Japanese male actor portraying female roles, Jan Kott makes an extraordinary statement about representations of femininity on stage:

If one asks an actress to portray a woman, to walk like a woman, to drink tea like a woman, she will be astonished and will ask: 'But which woman?'. In fact, femininity only exists in the eyes of men, just as blackness only exists for whites. The

onnagata portrays femininity to a much greater degree than if the
actor was a woman. His femininity is the result of study by
generations of actors, and perhaps even more importantly,
generations of painters. It is at one and the same time magical
and a joke, adoration and humiliation, idealization and desire. It
is a femininity doubly ambiguous, seen through the eyes of a
man and played by a man. An actress who undresses on stage
plays a woman who is undressing. When the strip-tease is over,
she has nothing on. First she was almost nude, but now she is
only nude and can only exhibit herself.

It is as Obrasov said: 'With a box of matches one can show
everything which is not a box of matches. But the box itself can
only be exhibited'.[6]

In proposing the theory that woman is the Other, that she comes
into existence only when perceived by men, Jan Kott follows the old
Existentialist view of the dichotomy between the sexes. But by
suggesting that woman cannot perform except as herself and that
femininity on stage can only be ideally represented by a man, Kott
ends up making a statement remarkable for its discrimination. The
logical counter-argument would surely be that if femininity can only
be represented by a male performer, masculinity could only be
represented by a female performer, and yet there is nothing in the
history of representation, whether pictorial, sculptural or theatrical,
that would confirm this hypothesis. Nor have women performers
ever sought to do such a thing on any scale (there are certain
traditions of female cross-dressing in some forms of theatre, but
always as a minority interest). Jan Kott's suggestion reveals the
magnitude of the problem facing women who are endeavouring to
create their own form of theatre. For in his view, that is *a priori* an
impossibility. Woman, like Obrasov's emblematic box of matches,
can only represent herself, can only be exhibited.

If a leading theatre critic can make such statements, there is clearly
still a great deal of groundwork to be done. Those women who are
endeavouring to create a women's theatre have to take on board the
views of the Jan Kotts of the world. However much such opinions
may be disliked, they cannot be ignored because of their grounding in
tradition and in audience expectations. The strength of women, the
struggle for a voice and a language, the complex processes of
women's artistic production, all the issues that preoccupy women

theatre practitioners today are completely absent from Jan Kott's vision of women's theatrical presence, in which femininity is an external set of signs perceivable only by men and not an intrinsic value system belonging primarily to women.

The work of the Magdalena Project so far has been that of widening areas of debate and bringing out into the open problems that are both practical and theoretical. The questions posed in the first Magdalena, which tended to be more abstract, have gradually shifted as the context has altered, and the range of people involved has widened. No longer only concerned with experimental theatre, the Magdalena Project now has links with many kinds of theatre and links also with educational establishments. The Inroads project, for example, was designed to introduce some of the ideas of Magdalena into schools. This project has not materialised, but instead the Write On project, designed particularly for younger women interested in writing and performing, took place during the last week of February 1989. The programme of workshops is constantly being enlarged. In short, the scope of the Magdalena Project is now considerably larger than was ever dreamed of when plans were first laid down for a meeting of women interested in theatre.

What is also apparent is that the Magdalena meetings have offered such women a unique opportunity to meet and share their experiences. Sometimes those meetings have functioned as a support group, as a consciousness-raising group or as a forum where conflicting opinions can be voiced among women, but always as a focal point for women sharing a common interest. Time and again comments from participants have stressed the rarity of such encounters and the value of having them.

What the Magdalena Project has done so far is to open doors that many women had previously either never seen or had felt were closed to them. As the Project increases in size and in complexity, it will no doubt encompass even more. Principal on the agenda, now that women in theatre can feel assured that they do have their own organisation and consequently a platform from which to speak more loudly, is the need to rediscover their own history. As Joan Kelly, the late feminist historian puts it, the dual goal of women's history is to 'restore women to history and to restore our history to women'.[7] In the theatre, the history of women has been ignored or minimalised for so long that it is hardly surprising that many women working in theatre today have a sense of uneasiness because they are unaware of their own past. Now perhaps, as women come together to share techniques and traditions and to exchange ideas and histories, they will begin also to turn to their own heritage. The 1992 Magdalena meeting that is being planned in Colombia will focus on exactly this question. It seems, finally, that as the twentieth century draws to a close, the future of women's theatre, revitalised by a rediscovery of its own history, has never looked brighter.

32. Zofia Kalinska directing Nominatae Filiae

Notes

1. Jan Montefiore, *Feminism and Poetry, Language, Experience, Identity in Women's Writing* (London, Pandora, 1987), p. 178.

2. Ibid., p. 179.

3. Eugenio Barba, 'The Actor's Energy: Male–Female versus Animus–Anima,' *New Theatre Quarterly*, Vol. III, No. 11 (August 1987), pp. 237–41.

4. Eugenio Barba, document for The Female Role, ISTA Congress, 17–22 September 1986.

5. Ibid.

6. Jan Kott, document for The Female Role, ISTA Congress, 17–22 September 1986.

7. Joan Kelly, *Women, History and Theory* (Chicago, University of Chicago Press, 1984), p. 1.

Select Bibliography

Aston, Elaine, 'Feminism in the French Theatre: A Turn of the Century Perspective,' *New Theatre Quarterly*, Vol. II, No. 7 (Aug. 1986)

——, 'Male Impersonation in the Music Hall: The Case of Vesta Tilley,' *New Theatre Quarterly*, Vol. IV, No. 15 (Aug. 1988)

Auster, Albert, *Actresses and Suffragists: Women in American Theatre 1890–1920*, New York, Praeger, 1984

Barba, Eugenio, 'The Actor's Energy: Male–Female versus Animus–Anima,' *New Theatre Quarterly*, Vol. III, No. 11 (Aug. 1987)

Bassnett, Susan, 'Notes on the Work of Monstruous Regiment,' in *British Drama and Theatre from the Mid Fifties to the Mid Seventies* (Proceedings of Conference, April 1978), Rostock, Wilhelm-Pieck-Universität, 1979

——, 'Towards a Theory of Women's Theatre,' in *Semiotics of Drama and Theatre*, Herta Schmid and Aloysius Van Kesteren, eds, Amsterdam and Philadelphia, John Benjamin, 1984

——, 'Women Experiment with Theatre: Magdalena '86' and 'Perceptions of the Female Role: The ISTA Congress,' *New Theatre Quarterly*, Vol. III, No. 11 (Aug. 1987)

——, 'The Magdalena Experiment: New Directions in Women's Theatre,' *The Drama Review*, Vol. 31, No. 4 (T116) (Winter, 1987)

——, with John Stokes and Michael Booth, *The Actress in her Time: Bernhardt, Terry, Duse*, Cambridge, Cambridge University Press, 1988.

Batchelor, Eleanor, ed., *Plays by Women*, New York, Womanbooks, 1977

Brown, Janet, *Feminist Drama: Definition and Critical Analysis*, Metuchen, NJ, Scarecrow Press, 1979

Brunner, Cornelia, 'Roberta Sklar: Toward Creating a Women's Theatre,' *The Drama Review*, Vol. 24, No. 2 (T86)(June, 1980)

Case, Sue-Ellen, *Feminism and Theatre*, London, Macmillan, 1988

Chinoy, Helen Krich, 'Art versus Business: The Role of Women in American Theatre,' *The Drama Review*, Vol. 24, No. 2 (T86)(June, 1980)

——, and Linda Walsh Jenkins, *Women in American Theatre*, New York, Crown, 1981

Churchill, Carol, 'The Common Imagination and the Individual Voice, Interview with Geraldine Cousin,' *New Theatre Quarterly*, Vol. IV, No. 13 (Feb. 1988)

Cohn, Ruby, 'Joan Holden and the San Francisco Mime Troupe,' *The Drama Review*, Vol. 24, No. 2 (T86)(June, 1980)

Cotton, Nancy, *Women Playwrights in England, 1363–1750*, London, Associated University Presses, 1980

Craig, Sandy, ed., *Dreams and Deconstructions: Alternative Theatre in Britain*, London, Amber Lane Press, 1979

Davis, Tracy, 'Questions for a Feminist Methodology in Theatre History' in T. Postlethwait and B. McConachie, eds, *Interpreting the Theatrical Past: New Directions in the Historiography of Performance,* Iowa City, University of Iowa Press, 1989

——, 'Sex and the Victorian Actress' in *Victorian Scandals: Decorum and its Enemies*, Kris Gariga, ed., forthcoming

De Lauretis, Teresa, *Alice Doesn't: Feminism, Semiotics and Cinema*, Bloomington, Indiana University Press, 1984

France, Rachel, ed., *A Century of Plays by American Women*, New York, Richards Rosen, 1979

Gardner, Viv, *Sketches from the Actresses Franchise League*, Nottingham, Nottingham University Drama Texts, 1985

Gilder, Rosamond, *Enter the Actress: The First Women in the Theatre*, London, Harrap, 1931 (repr. New York, Theatre Arts Books, 1960)

Gordon, Mel, 'Laurie Anderson: Performance Artist,' *The Drama Review*, Vol. 24, No. 2 (T86)(June, 1980)

Hanna, Gillian, *Feminism and Theatre (Theatre Papers,* 2nd series, No. 8), Dartington, Devon, Dartington College, 1978

Hirschfield, Claire, 'The Actresses' Franchise League and the Campaign for Women's Suffrage, 1908–1914,' *Theatre Research International*, Vol. 20, No. 2 (Summer, 1985)

Holledge, Julie, *Innocent Flowers: Women in Edwardian Theatre*, London, Virago, 1981

Itzin, Catherine, *Stages in the Revolution: Political Theatre in Britain since 1968*, London, Methuen, 1980

Jardine, Lisa, *Still Harping on Daughters: Women and Drama in the Age of Shakespeare*, Brighton, Harvester Press, 1983

Johnson, Claudia, D., *American Actresses: Perspective on the Nineteeth Century*, Chicago, Nelson-Hall, 1984

Keyssar, Helene, *Feminist Theatre*, London, Macmillan, 1984

Leavitt, Dinah Louise, *Feminist Theatre Groups*, Washington, DC, McFarland, 1980

Malpede, Karen, *Women in Theatre: Compassion and Hope*, New York, Drama Book Specialists, 1983

McLusky, Kathleen, 'The Act, the Role and the Actor: Boy Actresses on the Elizabethan Stage,' *New Theatre Quarterly*, Vol. III, No. 10 (May 1987)

Miles, Julia, ed., *The Women's Project*, New York, Performing Arts Journal Publications and American Place Theatre, 1980

——, ed., *The Women's Project II*, New York, Performing Arts Journal Publications and American Place Theatre, 1984

Moore, Honor, ed., *The New Women's Theatre: Ten Plays by Contemporary Women*, New York, Vintage Books, 1977

Morgan, Fidelis, *The Female Wits: Women Playwrights of the Restoration*, London, Virago, 1981

Natalle, Elie, *Feminist Theatre*, Metuchen, NJ, and London, Scarecrow Press, 1985

O'Quinn, Jim, 'Linda Mussman's Time and Space Limited Theatre,' *The Drama Review*, Vol. 24, No. 2 (T86)(June, 1980)

Pasquier, Marie-Claire, 'Women in the Theatre of Men: What Price Freedom?,' in Judith Friedlander et al., eds, *Women in Culture and Politics: A Century of Change*, Bloomington, Indiana University Press, 1986

Reinhardt, Nancy S., 'New Directions for Feminist Criticism in Theatre and the Related Arts,' in Elizabeth Langland and Walter Gore, eds, *A Feminist Perspective in the Academy: The Difference It Makes*, Chicago, University of Chicago Press, 1981

Roth, Moira, ed., *The Amazing Decade: Women and Performance Art in America, 1970–1980*, Los Angeles, Astro Artz, 1983

Rutter, Carol, *Clamorous Voices*, London, The Women's Press, 1988

Sargent-Wooster, Ann, 'Yvonne Rainier's *Journeys from Berlin/1971*,' *The Drama Review*, Vol. 24, No. 2 (T86)(June, 1980)

Speakman, Diane, 'The Next Stage: Devaluation, Revaluation and After,' *Themes in Drama*, No. 11 (*Women in Theatre*), Cambridge, Cambridge University Press, 1989

Spender, Dale and Carole Hayman, *How the Vote was Won and Other Suffragette Plays*, London, Methuen, 1985

Stewart, Ellen, 'Ellen Stewart and La Mama,' *The Drama Review*, Vol. 24, No. 2 (T86)(June, 1980)

Sullivan, Victoria and James Hatch, eds, *Plays by and about Women*, New York, Vintage Books, 1973

Todd, Susan, *Women in Theatre: Calling the Shots*, London, Faber and Faber, 1984

Venables, Clare, 'The Woman Director in the Theatre,' *Theatre Quarterly*, Vol. X, No. 38 (Summer, 1980)

Wandor, Michelene, *Understudies: Theatre and Sexual Politics*, London, Methuen, 1981

——, *Carry On, Understudies*, 2nd edn, London, Routledge, 1986

——, *Orlando's Children: Gender, Sexuality and the Family in Post-War British Plays*, London, Methuen, 1986

——, *Strike While the Iron is Hot: Three Plays on Sexual Politics*, London, Journeyman Press, 1980

——, ed., *Plays by Women*, Vol. I, London, Methuen, 1982; Vol. II, 1983; Vol. III, 1984; Vol. IV, 1985; Vol. V, 1987

——, *Look Back in Gender: Sexuality and the Family in Post-War British Drama*, London, Methuen, 1987

Wilson, Katharina, M., ed. & transl., *The Dramas of Hrostvitha of Gandersheim*, Saskatoon, Sask., Matrologia Latina, Peregrina Publishing Co., 1985

The American Journal *Women and Performance*, published twice yearly, is the only periodical devoted entirely to women and theatre.

Index

INFORMIX-SQL

A tutorial

and reference

INFORMIX-SQL®

A tutorial

and reference

Tony Lacy-Thompson

Prentice Hall

New York · London · Toronto · Sydney · Tokyo · Singapore

First published 1991 by
Prentice Hall International (UK) Ltd
66 Wood Lane End, Hemel Hempstead
Hertfordshire HP2 4RG

A division of
Simon & Schuster International Group

NOTICE
The author and the publisher have used their best efforts to prepare
the book, including the computer examples contained in it. The
computer examples have been tested. The authors and the publisher
make no warranty, implicit or explicit, about the documentation.
The authors and the publisher will not be liable under any
circumstances for any direct or indirect damages arising from any
use, direct or indirect of the documentation or the computer
examples contained in this book.

INFORMIX is a registered trademark of INFORMIX Software Inc.

UNIX is a registered trademark of AT&T in the USA and other countries.

Computer hardware and software brand names and company
names mentioned in this book are protected by their respective
trademarks and are acknowledged.

Printed and bound in Great Britain by
Dotesios Ltd, Trowbridge, Wiltshire

Library of Congress Cataloging-in-Publication Data

Lacy-Thompson, Tony.
  INFORMIX-SQL: tutorial and reference / by Tony
  Lacy-Thompson.
    p.   cm.
  Includes bibliographical references.
  ISBN 0-13-465121-9
  1. Relational data bases.   2. INFORMIX-SQL (Computer
  program)
  3. UNIX (Computer operating system)   I. Title.
  QA76.9.D3L33   1990   90-35382
  005.75'8–dc20   CIP

British Library Cataloguing in Publication Data

Lacy-Thompson, Tony
  INFORMIX-SQL: tutorial and reference.
  1. Relational databases
  I. Title
  005.756

  ISBN 0-13-465121-9

2 3 4 5   95 94 93 92 91

Contents

Foreword

When I first pulled my chair up to a computer terminal at UC Berkeley in 1976, I was amazed at how hard it was to deal with the machine (which I couldn't even see). Logging in was difficult, the instructions were poor, and the BASIC programming language was hard to get going in. However, the alternative was worse. I had a huge amount of biology laboratory data, and if I could analyse it all 30 to 100 different ways, I could determine if we had found a white blood cell that killed cancer tumour cells, the way we wanted them killed. So, I was motivated.

To do it the old fashioned way was a horrifying thought. I would have to plug the numbers into a hand held calculator, 30 to 100 times (this was actually considered the new way by most). But instead, I figured that computers, since they have disk drives to hold data, could be persuaded to keep the numbers around after I punched them in once, and I would be able to run my different formulae on the numbers as many times as I could change the program.

This worked well, although I had trouble structuring what the data should look like on the disk. It took a little thinking. Then I began using the word processor instead of the typewriter, so I could do revisions of my lab write-ups more easily. I discovered that the data model for how those characters got stored on the disk drive was very different to the way my lab numbers got stored.

So, it dawned on me that computers actually didn't do too much for you. Yes, they remembered the data on the disks, and let you run programs on the data, make changes and get another printout and such, but you were on your own to figure out how to get them to do these things. You didn't just walk up to the machine and speak sentences at it and expect it to understand, like in the movies. You had to deal with the fact that computers dealt in bytes, not sentences or words or even complete numbers, it only knew about bytes and the eight bits that were in them.

What was missing? What could be added to the interaction between humans and things they know and machines and the things they know that could make the communication easier? Modelling.

What is modelling? What is a model? A model is a set of atomic elements and operations that work on those elements. Fancy talk, I know, but let's take a look at this concept. Temperature is something that humans and most organisms can sense quantitatively, but we had to develop a model to *talk* about it quantitatively. The boiling point and melting point of water were chosen to be 100 and 0, and the units and the word degree are used to give context to these units. The operations on these elements are mostly arithmetic, like 80 degrees is hotter that 70 degrees. Experiments can be done to determine how much oil must be burned to raise the temperature of a building from 60 degrees to 70 degrees. It's a good model for quantitatively dealing with temperature.

So what modelling should we employ for humans and computers to use together to make information easier to store, retrieve and analyse? What should the elements be? What should be the operations on those elements?

Well, what has happened in the past few decades is this. 'Word processing' sorts of information and 'database' sorts of information are still stored very differently, and thus have different models. A spreadsheet or a drawing of a house, these have their own formats. But in the modelling of database type data, a great deal of progress has been made. Database type data is uniquely identifiable as 'things that repeat'. A list of customers, or a list of car parts, or a list of ships in the Navy all have the property that the same information is recorded for each entity − the structure of what is being stored repeats. Information about each customer is stored in a record for each customer. The records are different, but the structure is the same.

What operations should there be on this type of database data elements, these records? What other elements should there be? What other operations on these other elements? What will these operations do for me?

Well, you should be able to add records, delete them, update them, print them out, print out only some of them, print out only parts of some of them, and print out only parts of some of them only if they are related in a certain way. That is the *relational* data model. There have been other data models, but they were a little more complicated and limiting than they had to be − the networked data model and the hierarchical data model. The relational model is better almost every time, trust me. Only computers of the '80s and '90s can run the relational model well, so it is new in its widespread use.

Actually, the relational model can be, and is, implemented differently in different products. The basic principles are the same, and most products incorporate a language called SQL to form the base of the implementation of the relational model. Tony's book will take you through what is and what you can do with one such implementation of SQL and the relational data model. I am sure by understanding the model and using it, you will fair far better than I did as a student in your interactions with computers for data management.

Good luck.

Roger J. Sippl
Chairman
Informix Software Inc.

Preface

When I first learned **INFORMIX-SQL** on a course at Sphinx in 1986, little did I know that I would be writing a book about it four years later. But having subsequently taught courses on it (as well as UNIX and Q-OFFICE) at the Olivetti International Training Centre in Haslemere, it struck me that there was a need for a readable reference book; one that included all the tips and traps that I had found from experience, and *all* the information about a particular part of the product under a *single* heading. This book is based on **INFORMIX-SQL** Version 2.10.03, but includes all the additional features present in Version 4.0. It can be used as a manual for formal training courses, as a self-teach book, or as a reference for the more experienced user.

Chapter 1 covers the loading of the product under both UNIX and MS-DOS, the Help menus and an overview of the changes in Version 4.0. There is also a section on setting up the 'environment'. This will normally have been done already for a new user in an existing site, but the information is important to all users. Chapter 2 is the obligatory Database Design Principles chapter, that you will find in any good book on a database product. It really is essential to have a working knowledge of the relational model and normalisation before creating a relational database; actually creating a database is covered in Chapter 3, as are the subjects of transactions, indexes and null values.

SQL is quite a large subject which can easily confuse the novice user, particularly when all that is required by most users is a basic knowledge of the SELECT statement for ad hoc queries. So I have split SQL into two chapters: an Introduction to SQL, covering basic SELECT, INSERT, UPDATE and DELETE statements, and Further SQL, which includes all the material from the introductory chapter but goes much, much further (there are thirty pages on the SELECT statement alone!).

Chapters 6 and 7 cover the forms design package **PERFORM**, for both the end-user and the application developer, and Chapter 8 covers the **ACE** report generator. User menus are covered in Chapter 9 and Chapter 10 summarises how all the **INFORMIX-SQL** tools would be used together to develop a real application. The Appendices cover the **property** example database (on which all the exercises are based), answers to selected exercises, and a guide to Informix database products, including notes on upgrading from **INFORMIX 3.3** to **INFORMIX-SQL**.

This book was written on an AT&T 3B2/300 using Quadratron's Q-ONE wordprocessor. It was typeset by the author using LASER-Q, a typesetting package for Q-ONE (written by William Strudwick of Olivetti with contributions from the author), and printed on a Hewlett Packard LaserJet II with soft fonts.

I would like to thank the many people who helped me to complete this book: Roger Sippl and John Bruzas from Informix Menlo Park, Anna Hipkiss, Charles Anderson and Kim Robinson from Informix UK, Graham Twaddle of Beta Computers, Ivor Murray and Jeremy Russell of SkillAdvance, David Goodall of the OpenSoft Consultancy, William Strudwick of Olivetti Haslemere and, lastly, Mike Cash of Prentice Hall UK, for his help and patience. But of course my most special thanks are reserved for my family: Laura, Claire and Robert, who had to put up with a lot to see this book finished. I hope it was worth it.

Tony Lacy-Thompson
September 1990

Chapter 1

Introducing INFORMIX-SQL

1.1 What is INFORMIX-SQL?

INFORMIX-SQL is a Database Management System based on the *relational* model. It is thus a Relational Database Management System or RDBMS (for definitions of these terms, see Chapter 2, Database Design Principles). **INFORMIX-SQL** consists of a number of modules which may be executed from the command line, or through a menu system. The modules comprising **INFORMIX-SQL** are:

isql   A menu-driven database management system which glues together all the other modules into a complete system.

PERFORM   A screen form design and transaction processing module.

ACE   A powerful report writer.

SQL Editor   A menu-driven interface to SQL – the industry standard Structured Query Language which originated at IBM. SQL is a powerful, free-form query language which also includes statements for inserting, updating and deleting data. Informix has added a number of useful extensions to ANSI standard SQL.

User-menu   Allows the creation and execution of a user-defined menu system. These may include options for executing screen forms, writing reports or indeed any function (including operating system functions) that may be executed from the command line.

Schema Editor An interactive screen-based utility for the creation and modification of database tables. One of the most powerful features of **INFORMIX-SQL**, the Schema Editor allows the database administrator to create, verify and alter database table schemas without using SQL.

All of the above functions may be run either from the menu system or individually, directly from the command line.

1.1.1 Version 4.0 unbundling

Prior to Version 4.0, **INFORMIX-SQL** was a product consisting of a C-ISAM based database engine (now known as the Standard Engine) and a set of tools – **PERFORM** forms designer, **ACE** report writer, etc. From Version 4.0, **INFORMIX-SQL** has been 'unbundled' and consists only of this set of tools, which may be coupled with either the Standard Engine (**INFORMIX-SE**) or the OnLine engine (**INFORMIX-OnLine**). OnLine is Informix' second generation OLTP (on-line transaction processing) engine, the first being **INFORMIX-TURBO**, and offers high performance and availability, as well as support for multimedia and distributed databases.

1.2 Loading INFORMIX-SQL

On all systems, both UNIX and DOS, **INFORMIX-SQL** may be accessed by typing, from the command line

```
isql
```

However, this assumes that the environment on your terminal or PC has been set up correctly. This section lays out the basic ground rules for this environment.

1.2.1 On UNIX systems

To load **INFORMIX-SQL** from your terminal (assuming it has been successfully installed on your system) you must first have set up some *environment variables* (covered in detail in Section 1.4). These are variables that belong to your current UNIX shell, the contents of which may be read by programs which are run in that shell. There are a number of environment variables which may be read and acted upon by **INFORMIX-SQL** but the two minimum and most important ones are **INFORMIXDIR** and **PATH**. **INFORMIXDIR** must be set to the base directory of the **INFORMIX-SQL** package, which is usually /usr/informix, and **PATH** must include the **INFORMIX-SQL bin** directory, which is usually /usr/informix/bin. These may be set by adding the following lines to your **.profile** file (for Bourne shell users):

```
INFORMIXDIR=/usr/informix
PATH=$PATH:/usr/informix/bin
export INFORMIXDIR PATH
```

or add the following to your **.login** file, for C shell users:

```
setenv INFORMIXDIR /usr/informix
setenv PATH $PATH:/usr/informix/bin
```

You must now logout and log back in again (or you may re-execute your startup file by typing **. .profile** or **. .login**). To enter **INFORMIX-SQL**, you just type

```
isql
```

at the command line prompt.

Notes

(i)   If you encounter the message

Unknown message number 32766.

you have either mistyped the variable **INFORMIXDIR** or you have not exported it.

(ii) If you encounter the message

The type of your terminal is unknown to the system

then your terminal type (contained in the **TERM** variable) is not listed in the `/etc/termcap` file which **INFORMIX-SQL** uses by default. It may be listed in the `/usr/informix/etc/termcap` file however, in which case you must set the **TERMCAP** variable by adding the following lines to your **.profile** file, after which you must log out and log back in again:

```
TERMCAP=/usr/informix/etc/termcap
export TERMCAP
```

If you are a C shell user, this line should be added to your **.login** file:

```
setenv TERMCAP /usr/informix/etc/termcap
```

See also the **INFORMIXTERM** environment variable, Section 1.4.

(iii) If you need to access a database in a directory other than your current directory, you will need to set the **DBPATH** variable; see Section 1.4.

1.2.2 On DOS systems

On DOS systems you should set the **FILES** and **BUFFERS** parameters in your **config.sys** file to these values:

```
FILES=40
BUFFERS=8
```

You should also put these settings into your **autoexec.bat** file:

```
SET INFORMIXDIR=c:\informix
SET PATH=c:\informix\bin[;dirname]
```

where *dirname* is any directory or directories required by other programs on
your machine. Note that these changes are implemented automatically when
you first install **INFORMIX-SQL** on your machine. Also, the **DBCOLOR** variable
is set to blue (see Section 1.4). You should now reset your machine.

Real- and protected-mode
The DOS version of **INFORMIX-SQL** comes in two halves: the database engine
and the front-end tools. If your PC is 8086- or 8088-based (compatible with an
IBM PC/XT), then you may only use the real-mode versions of the engine and
front-end tools (i.e. both must run in 640K of memory). If, however, you have
an 80286- or 80386-based PC (compatible with an IBM PC/AT) and at least
1MB of extended memory, you have the choice of running either the engine or
front-end tools in extended memory.

In general, you will get faster performance by running the engine in real-mode
and the front-end tools in protected-mode.

Two commands are required to load **INFORMIX-SQL**: one to load the engine,
and one to load the front-end tools. There are two versions of each command,
as follows.

`startsql`	(loads the engine in real-mode)
`pstartsql`	(load the engine in protected-mode)
`isql`	(loads the front-end tools in real-mode)
`pisql`	(loads the front-end tools in protected-mode)

The required combination can be entered on one line, as in

```
startsql pisql
```

If the engine is loaded separately, as in

```
startsql
pisql
```

then on exit from **INFORMIX-SQL**, the engine will remain in memory until you
type in the `exit` command.

Note that individual users may be given passwords by use of the **IPASSWD**
utility, described in detail in an Appendix of the **INFORMIX-SQL** manual.

1.3 The INFORMIX-SQL Menu System

INFORMIX-SQL is based on a series of *ring menus*. A ring menu is one in

which all the options are displayed on a single line and an option is selected
by one of two methods:

(a) Type the first letter of the option, or

(b) Use the **SPACE** and **BACKSPACE** keys to move the highlight to the
required option and press **RETURN**. If you carry on pressing **SPACE**,
you eventually return to the first option, hence the name *ring* menu.

The first line of a menu always displays the available options, and the second
line always displays information about the highlighted option. If there are
more options than may be displayed on one line this will be indicated by an
ellipsis (. . .), as in Figure 1.1 below. More information on the highlighted
option may be obtained by pressing the **HELP** key which is *Ctrl-W* (or
alternatively **F1** on DOS machines).

PERFORM : Query Next Previous Add Update Remove Table Screen . . .
Searches the active database table.

Figure 1.1 The ellipsis . . . indicates more options.

The **INFORMIX-SQL** master menu is shown below in Figure 1.2.
INFORMIX-SQL consists of a hierarchy of menus the majority of which contain
an **Exit** option. This option will always take you back to the previous menu or,
from the master menu, back to the operating system. If there is no **Exit** option,
you may use the **INTERRUPT** key (marked **DEL, DELETE, RUBOUT** or *Ctrl-C* on
DOS machines). Note that this key may be changed to another key on UNIX
terminals by typing

```
stty intr Ctrl-key
```

at the command line prompt.

INFORMIX-SQL: Form Report Query-Language User-menu Database Table Exit
Run, Modify, Create, or Drop a form

--- Press CTRL-W for Help --------

Figure 1.2 The INFORMIX-SQL master menu.

Here is a brief summary of the options available from the master menu:

Form   Calls the FORM menu which allows the user to run, modify, generate and compile a **PERFORM** screen form.

Report   Calls the REPORT menu which allows the user to run, modify, generate and compile an **ACE** report.

Query-   Calls the SQL menu, allowing the user to enter, edit and execute
Language   SQL statements and command files. Ad hoc queries (and inserts, updates and deletes) may be made from this menu.

User-menu   Enables the operator to design or call user-written menus.

Database   Allows the creation, selection and dropping of databases.

Table   Calls the interactive schema editor for database table management, including the creation, modification and display of information about database tables.

Exit   Returns to the operating system.

1.3.1 Help menus

Every option on a menu screen in **INFORMIX-SQL** has a HELP screen associated with it which may be accessed by pressing the **HELP** key (*Ctrl-W*, or **F1** on DOS systems). Figure 1.3 below is an example of a HELP screen.

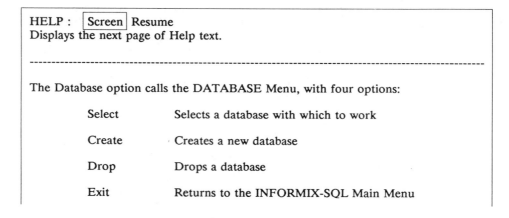

HELP : | Screen | Resume
Displays the next page of Help text.

The Database option calls the DATABASE Menu, with four options:

    Select   Selects a database with which to work

    Create   · Creates a new database

    Drop   Drops a database

    Exit   Returns to the INFORMIX-SQL Main Menu

Figure 1.3 An INFORMIX-SQL HELP screen.

If the help extends to more than one screen then further screens may be displayed by selecting the **Screen** option (i.e. by pressing **RETURN**).

1.4 Environment Variables

By setting and changing certain *environment variables,* an Informix user can change some of the default settings that **INFORMIX-SQL** normally uses for things such as date and money formats and the location of its executable files. On UNIX systems environment variables may be set by editing the user's **.profile** or **.login** files and adding lines such as:

```
INFORMIXDIR=/usr/informix
export INFORMIXDIR
```

for Bourne shell users, or, for C shell users:

```
setenv INFORMIXDIR /usr/informix
```

On DOS systems lines must be added to the **autoexec.bat** file, of the form:

```
SET INFORMIXDIR=\informix
```

There follows a complete list and explanation of all the environment variables used by **INFORMIX-SQL**.

PATH
The user's **PATH** variable must include the **bin** directory of the **INFORMIX-SQL** base directory. For UNIX systems this will usually be:

```
/usr/informix/bin
```

and for DOS systems:

```
\informix\bin
```

INFORMIXDIR
This variable specifies the base directory of the **INFORMIX-SQL** directory structure. For UNIX systems this will normally be:

```
/usr/informix
```

and for DOS systems:

```
\informix
```

DBPATH
Gives **INFORMIX-SQL** a list of directories to search for databases, form and report files, in addition to the current directory. The current directory is always searched first, and is the only directory searched if **DBPATH** is not set. For example:

```
DBPATH=/usr/tony/dbdir:/db/testdir
```

DBMONEY   In **INFORMIX-SQL** this variable specifies both the currency symbol and the decimal separator, where the defaults are the dollar sign and a decimal point. The format of the variable is:

[front][.|,][back]

Thus   DBMONEY=,Bf

gives   1.234,56Bf

whereas DBMONEY=£

gives   £1,234.56

DBDATE   The date format, for both data input and display, may be specified with this variable. For instance December 28, 1989 would be displayed differently according to the value of **DBDATE**:

DBDATE	Result
MDY2	12/28/89
DMY4 -	28-12-1989
Y4MD.	1989.12.28
DMY2	28/12/89

New for Version 4.0

You may now also specify a zero as a separator, to indicate no separator:

DBDATE	Result
MDY40	12281989

DBCOLOR   Available for DOS only. Specifies the colours for foreground (text) and background (screen). The syntax is

SET DBCOLOR = *background/foreground*

where the default is blue/white. Allowable colours are white, yellow, magenta, red, cyan, green, blue and black.

DBDELIMITER   Specifies the field separator to be used for LOAD and UNLOAD statements. The vertical bar (|) is the default. This may be set to null (i.e. no separator) by setting the variable as follows:

DBDELIMITER=

DBEDIT   Allows the user to specify an editor other than **vi** (or **edlin** on DOS) for creating forms and reports. This may be any editor or word processor that produces ASCII output.

DBPRINT   Specifies the print command. The default is **lp** on UNIX or **lpt1** for DOS.

DBTEMP   The directory for temporary files created by **INFORMIX-SQL**. The default is **/tmp** for UNIX and the current directory for DOS.

New for Version 4.0

INFORMIXTERM   Specifies whether **INFORMIX-SQL** should use **termcap** or **terminfo** for terminal capability information. For example:

```
INFORMIXTERM=terminfo
export INFORMIXTERM
```

or

```
INFORMIXTERM=termcap
export INFORMIXTERM
```

Exercise

1.   Using an editor, examine the **.profile** (or **.login**, or **autoexec.bat**) in your home directory and check that the **PATH** and **INFORMIXDIR** variables are set correctly.

2.   Invoke **INFORMIX-SQL** and, using the **HELP** key (*Ctrl-W*), familiarise yourself with the options on the main menu.

1.5 New Features in INFORMIX-SQL Version 4.0

Version 4.0 of INFORMIX-SQL contains a number of enhancements, some of which relate to INFORMIX-SQL as a front-end tool, and some of which are relevant to the particular database engine you are using, be it INFORMIX-SE or INFORMIX-OnLine.

1.5.1 General and engine-related changes

ANSI SQL compliance
INFORMIX-SQL Version 4.0 is now fully compliant with ANSI level I SQL and partially compliant with level II (with two exceptions).

Data type synonyms   The following data type synonyms are supported:

> REAL for SMALLFLOAT
> DOUBLE PRECISION for FLOAT
> CHARACTER for CHAR
> NUMERIC for DEC and DECIMAL
> INT for INTEGER

UNIQUE and   These keywords are now synonyms (DISTINCT is ANSI
DISTINCT   SQL).

NULL values   Previously, each NULL value was treated as a separate group when evaluated within a GROUP BY clause. Now all NULL values are considered identical.

Comments   You may now use a double dash (--) to indicate a comment line in either an SQL command file, a form specification or a report specification.

MODE ANSI databases
In a MODE ANSI database, each and every SQL statement is automatically a transaction, and there are no BEGIN WORK or COMMIT WORK statements. Also, the name of an object (for instance a table), must be qualified by the owner of the object (where *owner* is the login name of the user that created the object) wherever that object name is used.

ANSI compatibility checking
There are a number of Informix extensions to ANSI standard syntax. You may define the **DBANSIWARN** environment variable to check for these. **DBANSIWARN** does not require a value, you may set it equal to null using either

```
DBANSIWARN=
export DBANSIWARN
```

or

```
setenv DBANSIWARN
```

New data types and keywords
The following are available in both **INFORMIX-SE** and **INFORMIX-OnLine**:

DATETIME allows an exact moment in time to be stored in the database. You may set the precision from years down to fractions of a second.

INTERVAL allows a time span to be stored, with a similar precision range to that of DATETIME.

The keywords UNIQUE CONSTRAINT may now be used in the CREATE TABLE statement to automatically generate a unique index on a column or composite column.

These are available in **INFORMIX-OnLine** only:

VARCHAR allows a variable length character field to be stored, the number of characters actually stored being either the true length or the *minimum* size (user-definable for this column), whichever is the greater.

Binary Large OBjects or BLOBs
TEXT allows the storage of up to 2 Gigabytes of textual data, including tabs, returns and form feeds. Possible uses include memos, reports, program source code. In Version 4.0 there is no free text retrieval on this type of column.

BYTE columns allow the storage of up to 2 Gigabytes of binary data. This can be anything that can be digitised, from scanned images, photographs and signatures to sound, video, spreadsheets and program object code.

All of these are of course accommodated in the Interactive Schema Editor, as is the *owner.object* naming convention for MODE ANSI databases.

New Query Optimiser
Version 4.0 database engines (both the Standard Engine and OnLine) include a new cost-based optimiser which determines the time-cost of a number of different ways of executing a query. It then chooses the most efficient, which is sometimes not the most obvious. You may examine the query path chosen by means of the new SQL statement SET EXPLAIN ON/OFF.

The TRANSACTION menu
Whenever a user fails to terminate a transaction, and then attempts to open a new database, run a form or user-menu, or leave **INFORMIX-SQL**, the TRANSACTION menu (see Figure 1.4) is displayed, forcing the user to either commit or rollback the changes in the transaction.

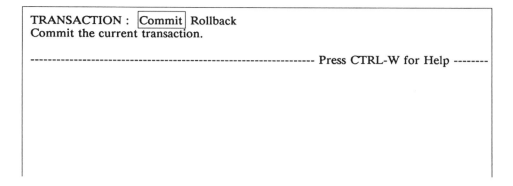

Figure 1.4 The TRANSACTION menu.

Support for terminfo
Support is now given for terminfo as well as termcap.

1.5.2 Changes to PERFORM

Screen sizes and attributes
Forms may now be larger than 24 x 80 and may include colour and graphics. For long CHAR fields (and the new TEXT and VARCHAR data types in OnLine) a wordwrap feature and multiline editor are provided.

Output
A new **Output** option allows you to write out one or all rows from the current list in UNLOAD format.

Version 2.10 forms
Forms compiled by Version 2.10 may be run by Version 4.0, but not vice versa.

BLOBs in PERFORM
The new **View** option in **PERFORM** allows you to display, though not update, TEXT or BYTE type BLOBs. BYTE type BLOBs may have a program associated with them which may be optionally executed by entering an exclamation mark (!).

1.5.3 Changes to ACE

READ statement
The new READ statement may optionally replace the SELECT statement to retrieve data from an ASCII file instead of from the database.

1.5.4 New utilities

The utilities **dbimport** and **dbexport** are now provided which allow you to import and export a complete database, including both schemas and data.

Chapter 2

Database Design Principles

2.1 What is a Database?

- A database is any organised collection of interrelated data stored together to serve one or more applications in an optimal fashion.

- The data is stored so that it is independent of programs using it and the database is designed so that it may be used by different programmers.

- A common and controlled approach is used in adding new data and modifying and retrieving existing data within the database.

In earlier data processing one or more files of records were kept for each application. The object of a database is to allow the same collection of data to serve as many applications as possible.

2.1.1 What is a database management system or DBMS?

Whatever form a database may take, there are certain basic operations that need to be performed:

- Creating a structure in which the data is to be stored

- Entering data into that structure

- Modifying data when it changes

- Removing obsolete data

- Extracting data in various forms and combinations

- Ensuring consistency, security and integrity of the data

A database management system or DBMS is a collection of programs which, using the facilities of the operating system, enables the users to manipulate the database in the ways mentioned above.

One of the intentions of a database is to make data independent of the programs that use it. The data can be easily reorganised or its contents added to; data structures, layouts and their physical storage devices can change without the old application programs being rewritten. Data independence is one of the most important features of a DBMS.

In most file systems, a massive amount of duplication exists in the data stored. Many data items are stored redundantly in files for different purposes. Not only does this waste space, but it can lead to inconsistencies, since it may happen that not all occurrences of the same data item are updated at the same time. A DBMS should remove most if not all of this redundancy.

2.2 Database Models

In the early days of data processing, all files were flat files. In a flat file each record contains the same types of data items. One (or possibly more than one) data item is designated the key and is used for sequencing the file and for locating records. These files may well duplicate data, leading to inconsistencies when the data is updated and inefficiency due to the extra amount of storage space required.

In the database world however a number of file structures are used which are not flat. They are variously described as *hierarchical, network* (or *Codasyl*) and the *relational* model.

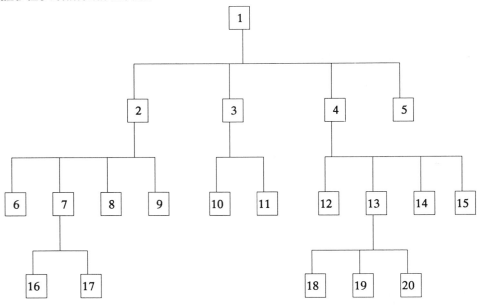

Figure 2.1 A hierarchical database can be likened
to an upside-down tree.

2.2.1 Hierarchical databases

A hierarchical database can be likened to an upside-down tree (see Figure 2.1 opposite), the element at the top of the tree being known as the *root*. With the exception of the root, every element or node has one node related to it at a higher level and no element can have more than one parent. Each element can have one or more elements related to it at a lower level, known as children.

If Figure 2.1 were a customer accounts system, then elements 2, 3, 4, and 5 might represent different regions. Elements 6-15 would represent customer records, and elements 16-20, transactions. To retrieve all the transactions for customer 7, it is a simple matter to traverse the tree, finding all the elements in the path 1/2/7. However to summarise the information from all the transactions in the database involves traversing all the paths 1/2/6, 1/2/7, etc., and checking if there are any children for each of those parent nodes. We can summarise the pros and cons of the hierarchical model thus:

Pro: Fast access for retrieving individual transactions, also for adding new records (transactions or customers).

Con: Slow and difficult for retrieving summary information, for changing the structure of the database and for more complex relationships. Consider the effect of inserting a new level of nodes, say for *area*, or if a customer has more than one address (e.g. personal and business) each of which is in a different region.

2.2.2 Network databases

If a child in a data relationship has more than one parent, the relationship cannot be described as a tree or hierarchical structure. Instead it is described as a network or plex structure, giving rise to a network database.

Any item in a network database can be linked to any other item and thus a child can have more than one parent, as in Figure 2.2 overleaf. Although network databases are more flexible than hierarchical databases, since they allow the addition of new relationships and entry points for data access at any node, this can lead to immense complexity, resulting in problems for both maintenance and application programmers.

2.2.3 The relational model

Hierarchical and network databases have a tendency to get more and more complex as data is added and new relationships are set up between the data items. But in the 1970s, Dr Ted Codd working at IBM started to apply a branch of mathematics called relational theory to the storage of data in a computer. In effect he invented the relational database.

Any data representation, tree or network structure, can be reduced to a combination of one or more two-dimensional tabular forms called *relations*.

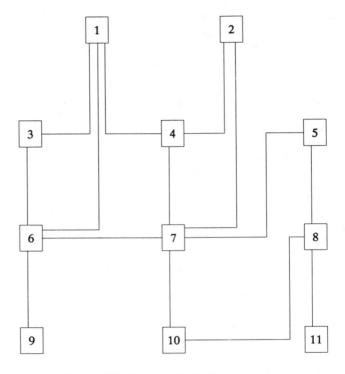

Figure 2.2   A network database structure.

Relationships between data items can be replaced with relationships in two-dimensional tabular form by a step-by-step process known as *normalisation* (see Section 2.4). The tables must be set up in such a way that no information about the relationships between data elements is lost.

The tables are rectangular arrays with rows and columns, as in Figure 2.3 opposite, which can be described mathematically and have the following properties:

1.   Each entry in a table represents one data item.

2.   In any column, all data items are of the same kind.

3.   Each column is assigned a distinct name.

4.   All rows are distinct; duplicate rows are not allowed.

5.   The ordering of the rows is not significant; the rows can be interchanged without affecting the information content of the table.

6. The ordering of the columns is not significant; this is true because of point 3.

The table is referred to mathematically as a relation and a database constructed using relations is known as a *relational database*.

table   **stock**

Part No.	Description	Quantity
P2	nut 10mm	4500
P1	bolt 8mm	8350
P3	washer 10mm	7000
P4	nut 12mm	2520

Row (label at left of P1 row)

Column

Figure 2.3   A table is composed of rows and columns.

The table in Figure 2.3 is named **stock**. It consists of three *columns* (sometimes referred to as domains) each of which is headed by the name of an attribute type, or column name, and four *rows* (also known as tuples – rhymes with couples). At the intersection of each row and column is an attribute occurrence or attribute value. For example, **bolt 8mm** is an attribute value of the attribute type Description.

Projections, joins and views
One of the great advantages of the relational model is the ease with which relations can be cut and pasted to form new relations. The operation of splitting a relation into subrelations is known technically as *projection* and is illustrated in Figure 2.4 overleaf. In practice projection is achieved by means of the SQL SELECT statement, covered in detail in Chapter 5.

The converse of projection is connecting different relations together to form a new relation. This operation is known as a *join*. Since it is not necessary to use all the attribute types of the relations, the resulting relation may be smaller than the sum of the joining relations.

Since projections and joins form new tables from data that is current at the time the projection or join is executed, any change to the data in the originating tables will not be reflected, unless the projection or join is re-executed. Views, however, are dynamic windows on to the database, giving the user a different logical view of the data. Although they are actually made up of projections and joins, they appear to the user as actual tables. Views are covered in detail in Chapter 5.

EMPLOYEE

Emp_no	Employee_name	Dept_no	Salary	Location
53702	Anderson C	721	1200	London
53703	Hipkiss A	721	2300	London
53791	Haney J	007	5000	Lenexa
53800	Bork J	402	1100	Menlo Park
53805	Nash B	721	1900	London

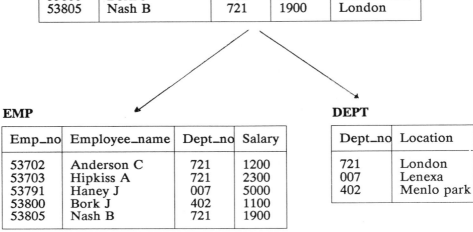

EMP

Emp_no	Employee_name	Dept_no	Salary
53702	Anderson C	721	1200
53703	Hipkiss A	721	2300
53791	Haney J	007	5000
53800	Bork J	402	1100
53805	Nash B	721	1900

DEPT

Dept_no	Location
721	London
007	Lenexa
402	Menlo park

Figure 2.4 Projection splits a relation into subrelations.

HOUSE

HOUSE-AGENT

ref_no	owner	h_adrs1
23	Smith	151 Malden Way
35	Jones	62 Sheephouse Way
37	Adams	43 Manor Drive

ref_no	agent
23	Allen & Co
23	Mitchells
35	Mitchells

NEW-HOUSE

ref_no	owner	h_adrs1	agent
23	Smith	151 Malden Way	Allen & Co
23	Smith	151 Malden Way	Mitchells
35	Jones	62 Sheephouse Way	Mitchells
37	Adams	43 Manor Drive	Grabit

Figure 2.5 A join connects two relations together.

Pros and cons of the relational model
The main advantages of a relational database are:

1. The two-dimensional tables are a very simple and understandable way of representing data.

2. Operations such as projections and joins allow cutting and pasting of relations giving the users different local views of the global structure.

3. The relational model is the epitome of data independence. Rows can be very simply added, deleted or updated, columns can be changed, extended and added, all without disrupting current application programs or existing data.

The major disadvantage of the relational model is that its great flexibility impinges on its performance. Early implementations suffered greatly from this and they often lost out to hierarchical databases. However as the need to retrieve more information from the same data increased and the price/performance ratio of computers decreased, these speed limitations fell away and the relational model's simplicity and flexibility has seen it win the day, at least for the foreseeable future.

2.3 Models, Entities and Attributes

Let us suppose that we have decided to build a database containing information about the houses for sale in a particular area. Since our database is likely to have certain restrictions and assumptions about the real-world data, it would be wise to first build a *model* on paper, in the same way as an aircraft designer would build a wind-tunnel model to test the design of a new aircraft. Our model will be made up of a number of *entities*, each of which will represent a real-world object such as a house or an estate agent. Each entity will have a number of *attributes*, such as an address or a number of bedrooms, and there will be *relationships* between the entities.

Let us begin with one very simple entity, HOUSE. In the first version of our model, the HOUSE entity has attributes of owner, address, number of bedrooms, a price and some information about the agent with whom the house is registered. As we must have a way of uniquely identifying each house record, we must decide which one or more of the attributes we can designate as the identifier or *primary key* of the entity. Since a house may be registered with more than one agent, a suitable candidate could be the attributes **h_adrs** and **agent** (the prefix **h_** refers to a house attribute, the prefix **a_** to an agent attribute). The entity may then be written like this, with the key underlined:

HOUSE(owner, h_adrs, no_bedrooms, price, agent, a_adrs, a_phone)

2.4 Normalisation and Normal Forms

The first stage in the analysis of data is to list the obvious entity types. As the analysis proceeds, it may be that these original entities are broken down to form new entities, and relationships formed between them. These new entities may more closely model the real-world situation and may make operations on the eventual database such as insertion and updating simpler and less prone to error. Normalisation is a step-by-step process for analysing data into its constituent entities and attributes.

2.4.1 First Normal Form – atomic values/repeating groups

In the above HOUSE entity, the two attributes **h_adrs** and **a_adrs** are not single attribute values, but *composites*. For example the address

> 151 Malden Way, New Malden, Surrey

is made up of a number of pieces of information. A simple design principle that leads us to the First Normal Form, or 1NF, is that the smallest pieces of information that may be required by users should be allocated to separate attributes. As it stands, it would be difficult to search for all the houses in a particular town or county (or all the agents). Thus it would be much more useful to have the following attributes:

> HOUSE (owner, h_adrs1, h_adrs2, h_town, h_county, no_bedrooms, price, agent, a_adrs1, a_adrs2, a_town, a_county, a_phone)

However, the question now arises as to which attributes to use for the key. Since **h_adrs** has now been split into four it would be much more convenient to have a single new attribute for the key. We shall call it **ref_no**:

> HOUSE (ref_no, owner, h_adrs1, h_adrs2, h_town, h_county, no_bedrooms, price, agent, a_adrs1, a_adrs2, a_town, a_county, a_phone)

Let us now consider some additions to our HOUSE entity. It would be useful to have some information about the bedrooms in the house, such as size and the presence of an *ensuite* bath. Since the number of bedrooms will vary, we have what is known as a *repeating group*. Here is a possible solution:

> HOUSE (ref_no, owner, h_adrs1, h_adrs2, h_town, h_county, no_bedrooms, bed_size1, ensuite1, bed_size2, ensuite2, bed_size3, ensuite3, bed_size4, ensuite4, price, agent, a_adrs1, a_adrs2, a_town, a_county, a_phone)

We have allocated enough space for up to four bedrooms, but this solution is unsatisfactory on two counts. Firstly, if a house has less than four bedrooms we are wasting space, and secondly, if a house has more than four bedrooms we cannot accommodate it. We must separate the repeating group from HOUSE and make it into a new entity, which we shall call BEDROOM. Our new entities are now:

HOUSE-1   (ref_no,   owner,   h_adrs1,   h_adrs2,   h_town,   h_county,
           no_bedrooms,   price,   agent,   a_adrs1,   a_adrs2,   a_town,
           a_county, a_phone)

BEDROOM-1   (ref_no, bedroom_no, bedroom_size, ensuite)

The suffix 1 on the entity names denotes that these entities are in First Normal
Form, or 1NF. Notice that BEDROOM-1 has a key made up of two attributes:
ref_no relates a bedroom to a particular house, and **bedroom_no** identifies a
particular bedroom in that house. This is known as a *composite key*.

To summarise:

The first stage of normalisation is accomplished by ensuring that all attributes
contain only *atomic* values, i.e. values which cannot or will not need to be
broken down any further, and by the removal of repeating groups, rewriting
them as new entities with the appropriate identifier or identifiers.

2.4.2 Second Normal Form – functional dependencies

Our model allows the assumption that an agent may have more than one
house on his books. This gives rise to occurrences of the HOUSE entity of the
form shown in Figure 2.6 below:

HOUSE-1

ref_no	owner	h_adrs1	---	agent	a_adrs1	---
23	Smith	151 Malden Way	---	Allen & Co	32 High St	---
35	Jones	62 Sheephouse Way	---	Mitchells	21 New Road	---
37	Adams	43 Manor Drive	---	Allen & Co	32 High St	---
40	Sewell	11 Thetford Road	---	Allen & Co	32 High St	---

Figure 2.6 Occurrences of the HOUSE entity in 1NF.

This suffers from three disadvantages:

1. If all the houses registered with a particular agent are sold and the rows
    deleted, the agent's name and address are lost from the database.

2. It would not be possible to insert a new agent who has no houses
    registered in this area.

3. If an agent changes his address or phone number and more than one
    house is registered with him, then the address or phone number has to be
    changed in *every* record involving that agent – a time-consuming process,
    and one prone to error.

These disadvantages are due to the *functional dependencies* within the HOUSE entity. We know that a valid key of the HOUSE entity is made up of the attributes **h_adrs1** and **agent**. All the house attributes are dependent on the **h_adrs1** part of the key, and the agent's address is dependent on the agent's name. The solution is to separate the attributes which are dependent on only part of the key into a new entity, giving this result (the suffix 2 denotes that the entities are in Second Normal Form):

HOUSE-2   (ref_no, owner, adrs1, adrs2, town, county, no_bedrooms, price, agent)

AGENT-2   (agent, adrs1, adrs2, town, county, phone)

Having separate entities allows us to dispense with the prefixes **h_** and **a_**. Notice that the **agent** attribute in the HOUSE-2 entity is also the key identifier of the AGENT-2 entity. The **agent** attribute in the HOUSE-2 entity is therefore known as a *foreign key*.

The same occurrences now appear as shown in Figure 2.7 below.

HOUSE-2

ref_no	owner	adrs1	---	agent
23	Smith	151 Malden Way	---	Allen & Co
35	Jones	62 Sheephouse Way	---	Mitchells
37	Adams	43 Manor Drive	---	Allen & Co
40	Sewell	11 Thetford Road	---	Allen & Co

AGENT-2

agent	adrs1	---
Allen & Co	32 High St	---
Mitchells	21 New Road	---

Figure 2.7   Occurrences of HOUSE and AGENT in 2NF.

From these new entities it can be seen that the agents' details are separate from those of the houses, allowing us to:

1.   Delete all the house rows registered with a particular agent without losing that agent's details (they are in AGENT-2).

2.   Insert a new agent without any houses (this follows from point 1).

3.   Update an agent's details by changing just one row, the particular

occurrence of the AGENT-2 entity. This change is then reflected for any house registered with that agent.

To summarise:

Entities are said to be in Second Normal Form, or 2NF, when all non-key attributes are functionally dependent only on the primary key, and the *whole* of the primary key. Notice that BEDROOM is already in 2NF because the details of a particular bedroom are dependent on both **ref_no** and **bedroom_no** (i.e. the whole of the primary key). If you are in any doubt about whether an entity is in 2NF, consider what will happen in various insertion, updating and deletion situations as discussed above.

2.4.3 Third Normal Form – transitive functional dependencies

Let us consider an extension to the AGENT entity. Most agents nowadays have a tie-up with a financial institution and we should like to record this together with the maximum amount of money the lender will lend (this is usually a percentage of the asking price). Our AGENT entity is now

AGENT-2   (agent, adrs1, adrs2, town, county, phone, lender, max_loan)

The attribute **lender** is dependent on **agent**, the key of AGENT. However **max_loan** is dependent on **lender**, and is only *transitively* dependent on **agent** because **lender** is. If **max_loan** needs to be changed for a particular lender, it will have to be changed in all the rows where that lender occurs. In Third Normal Form, or 3NF, we remove any transitive dependencies by creating a new entity, LENDER. Our full entity model in 3NF now looks like this

HOUSE-3   (ref_no, owner, adrs1, adrs2, town, county, no_bedrooms, price, agent)

BEDROOM-3   (ref_no, bedroom_no, bedroom_size, ensuite)

AGENT-3   (agent, adrs1, adrs2, town, county, phone, lender)

LENDER-3 (lender, max_loan)

2.4.4 Summary of normalisation

The three steps of normalisation may be summarised thus:

1NF   Remove all repeating groups.

2NF   Ensure that all non-key attributes for an entity are dependent on the *whole* of the key, and not just a part of it.

3NF   Ensure that all non-key attributes are mutually independent (i.e. they are only dependent on the key).

It may seem to you that normalisation has increased the amount of data to be held in the database, since the technique involves increasing the number of entities and duplicating some attributes. However, databases grow; new entities and attributes are added, and the data is used in new ways. New relationships arise and old ones disappear. Data models structured in 3NF offer data integrity for the present, and the promise of minimum disruption through restructuring in the future.

2.5 Entity Relationships

In our current model, there are a number of relationships between entities. An agent has many houses, and a house has many bedrooms. These are known as **one-to-many** relationships and are often drawn using a single arrowhead to represent the 'one' side and a double arrowhead to represent the 'many' side. We can illustrate this by means of an **entity-relationship** or **E-R diagram**, as in Figure 2.8 below.

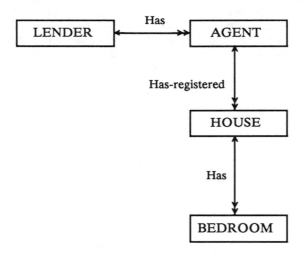

Figure 2.8   The entity-relationship diagram.

In this model, each house is only registered with one agent, but it is quite likely that some houses will be registered with more than one agent. We then have a **many-to-many** relationship, as in Figure 2.9 opposite.

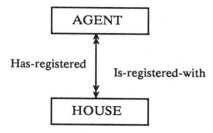

Figure 2.9   A many-to-many relationship.

This would lead to occurrences of the HOUSE entity of the following form:

HOUSE

ref_no	owner	h_adrs1	---	agent
23	Smith	151 Malden Way	---	Allen & Co
35	Jones	62 Sheephouse Way	---	Mitchells
23	Smith	151 Malden Way	---	Mitchells
40	Sewell	11 Thetford Road	---	Allen & Co

Figure 2.10   House 23 is registered with both Allen & Co
and Mitchells.

We are once again back to our old problem of updating. If the price of a houses changes, all the rows with that house but a different agent must be updated. The solution to this problem is to add a third entity in between, with two one-to-many relationships to it, as in Figure 2.11 below.

Figure 2.11   The solution to the many-to-many problem.

The attributes of HOUSE-AGENT are **ref_no** and **agent**, and possible occurrences are as in Figure 2.12 overleaf. Note that the HOUSE entity no longer needs an **agent** attribute.

HOUSE-AGENT

ref_no	agent
23	Allen & Co
35	Mitchells
23	Mitchells
40	Allen & Co

HOUSE

ref_no	owner	h_adrs1	---
23	Smith	151 Malden Way	---
35	Jones	62 Sheephouse Way	---
37	Adams	43 Manor Drive	---
40	Sewell	11 Thetford Road	---

Figure 2.12   House 23 is registered with both
Allen & Co and Mitchells.

We can now change the price of a house just by updating one row in the HOUSE table, and we can register the house with an additional agent by adding a row to HOUSE-AGENT, associating the house's **ref_no** with the agent's name.

2.6 Summary

We have seen that a database based on the relational model, such as **INFORMIX-SQL**, has certain advantages over one based on the hierarchical or network models. Not least of these is simplicity and flexibility, and the ability to produce new relations through the use of projections and joins. Entity modelling is a way of building a model on paper of real-world data and normalisation is a step-by-step process which ensures that the entities we are using model the real world as closely as possible, making operations such as deletion and updating simpler and less prone to error.

The relationships between the entities can be modelled using an entity-relationship diagram. We have built up a model for a local property database, and throughout the rest of the book we shall implement a simplified form of this model as a database in **INFORMIX-SQL**, with associated forms and reports. Our implementation will not contain either the LENDER or HOUSE-AGENT entities, and so a house may be registered with only one agent. Should the reader wish to implement the full model, I think he will find everything he needs in the following pages.

Chapter 3

Creating a Database

3.1 Transactions

A transaction is one or a number of database operations which together are considered to be a unit of work. A transaction is assumed to be indivisible in that, if any part of the transaction fails, the whole transaction has failed. For example if updates are to be performed on two tables whose records are closely related, and only those on one table are successful, the database would be left 'out of sync'. By packaging the updates on the two tables together as a transaction, the successful updates may be 'rolled back', leaving the database in the same state as before the transaction started.

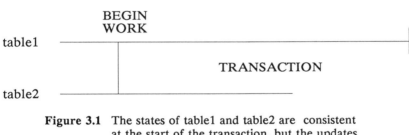

Figure 3.1 The states of table1 and table2 are consistent at the start of the transaction, but the updates on table2 do not complete.

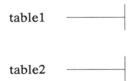

Figure 3.2 After ROLLBACK WORK, the two tables are consistent again, in the same state as at the start of the transaction.

The concept of transactions is implemented in **INFORMIX-SQL** by the use of some special SQL statements, and a *transaction log file*, where all modifications to the database are recorded. The special statements are:

BEGIN WORK   Denotes the start of a transaction.

COMMIT WORK   Denotes that all successful operations since the start of the transaction are to be written to disk.

ROLLBACK WORK   Undoes all modifications to the database since the last BEGIN WORK statement. Data definition statements however (those affecting the structure of the database as opposed to its data) may not be rolled back; they are automatically committed even if they are part of a transaction.

Since all modifications to the database are recorded in the transaction log file, the database may be recovered from a crash by reinstating a backup copy of the database and replaying the current log file. This is achieved through the ROLLFORWARD DATABASE statement (see Chapter 5, Section 5.8.2). It is a good idea to create the log file on a different disk to that containing your database since this shares the access time and reduces the risk of losing both database and log file.

Although a transaction log file does add an extra write to every database operation, this overhead is more than compensated for by the safety features it provides. When you create a database, you have the choice of creating it with or without transactions, as the next section will show.

Notes

(i)   A single statement is also treated as a transaction so that if a hundred updates are to be performed on a table using a single UPDATE statement but for some reason only fifty are successful, then **INFORMIX-SQL** will automatically discard the modifications, leaving the database in a consistent state.

(ii)   All the rows in the database affected by a transaction are locked in *share* mode (other users have read access only) until the transaction is either committed or rolled back.

(iii)   The location of the current database's log file may be found by using the following SQL statement:

```
select dirpath from systables
where tabtype = "L"
```

(iv)   If you cannot open the database because you have lost the transaction log file, its location (or where it should be) can be found by searching the **systables.dat** file for the **syslog** entry. In UNIX this may be achieved by executing the following command line:

```
grep syslog dbname.dbs/systables.dat
```

(v)   The log file can be moved to a new location with the START DATABASE statement. For example:

```
start database property
with log in "/usr2/newlog"
```

(vi) The transaction logging facility may be disabled altogether by executing the following statement:

```
delete from systables
where tabtype = "L"
```

3.2 Creating a Database

To create an **INFORMIX-SQL** database, follow these steps:

1.   Make sure you are in the directory in which you wish to create the database, since the **DBPATH** variable is not checked at this stage.

2.   Select **Database** from the main menu.

3.   Select the **Create** option.

4.   Give your database a name, bearing in mind the following:

      You may use up to ten characters for UNIX or eight for MSDOS.

      There is no distinction between upper and lower case.

      The name must start with a letter, and you may use any combination of letters or numbers plus the underscore character.

      There are a number of reserved words that may not be used. They are listed in an Appendix of the **INFORMIX-SQL** Reference Manual.

5.   If your version of **INFORMIX-SQL** is 2.0 or greater, skip to Step 6. In versions prior to 2.0, you will be asked if you want to *have transactions with the database.* This option allows you to create a database with a transaction log (discussed in the previous section). Enter the full pathname of your transaction log file (you must have write permission in the new log file's directory). You may skip Step 6.

6.   In Versions 2.0 and greater, the database will always be created *without* transactions; to start a transaction log you must either use the SQL statement START DATABASE (see Chapter 5, Section 5.8.2), which is not available with **INFORMIX-OnLine**, or instead use the complete CREATE DATABASE statement (Chapter 5, Section 5.6.1). For the first of these choices, follow these steps:

6.1 Select **Query-Language** from the main menu.

6.2 Select **New** from the SQL menu and type the following:

```
start database dbname
with log in "pathname"
```

Example

```
start database property
with log in "/usr/tony/dblog"
```

6.3 Press **ESC** and select the **Run** option from the SQL menu. This will create the transaction log file with the pathname specified.

6.4 Select **Exit** to return to the main menu.

You have now created your database, which consists of your transaction log file (probably) and a directory with the name *dbname***.dbs**, where *dbname* is your chosen database name. This directory contains eighteen files (twenty two in Version 4.0), called **system catalogues** which together make up the database dictionary for your database. Each catalogue is itself a table and has a **.dat** and a **.idx** file, so there are in fact nine (or eleven) system catalogues. You have also made this the current database.

3.3 System Catalogues

The system catalogues contain a wealth of information about the database. A full listing of all the catalogues and their column names (for they are in themselves database tables) may be found in the respective Appendix of the **INFORMIX-SQL** manual. They are described briefly here.

systables	contains information on the database tables, such as name, owner, location, size and creation date.
syscolumns	contains information on all the columns in the database.
sysindexes	describes the database's indexes, including the index name, owner, table, index type (clustered, unique or duplicate) and indexed columns.

systabauth	describes table-level privilege information such as permission grantor and grantee and type of permission for each table.
syscolauth	describes column-level privilege information.
sysdepend	describes which tables or views other views depend on.
syssynonyms	contains information on table synonyms, such as owner name, synonym name and date created.
sysusers	contains information about users and their database-level privileges – DBA, RESOURCE, CONNECT.
sysviews	describes the SELECT statements that make up the views present in the database.

New for Version 4.0

sysconstraints	records constraints placed on database tables.
syssyntable	used for the mapping of synonyms, particularly for extended (distributed) tables in **INFORMIX-OnLine** and **INFORMIX-STAR**, the Informix product which provides distributed database capabilities.

Exercise

1.   Create a database called **property** in your current directory.

2.   Create a transaction log file for your database, in your home directory. Remember to give the *full* pathname of your log file.

3.   Using a shell escape (`!sh` for UNIX, or `!command.com` for DOS), list the system catalogues in your **property.dbs** directory.

3.4 Data Types

The data type of a column determines the kind of data which can and cannot be stored in that column, and how it may be manipulated and presented. The data types available in **INFORMIX-SQL** are as follows. In Version 4.0, certain synonyms (such as INT for INTEGER) are also allowed, to provide ANSI compatibility.

Type	Description
Character CHAR[(*n*)]	Or CHARACTER[(*n*)]. Any combination of *n* letters, numbers or symbols, where *n* is less than 32,512. *n* defaults to 1.
Numeric SMALLINT	Whole numbers in the range -32,767 to +32,767.
INTEGER	Or INT. Whole numbers in the range approximately -2 billion to +2 billion.
DECIMAL[(*m*[,*n*])]	Or NUMERIC, or DEC. Decimal floating-point numbers with *m* significant digits (up to 32) of which *n* are decimal digits.
SMALLFLOAT	Or REAL. Floating-point numbers with up to 8 significant digits.
FLOAT[*n*]	Or DOUBLE PRECISION. Floating point numbers with up to 16 significant digits.
Serial SERIAL[(*n*)]	Contains integers, allocated automatically when a row is added and guaranteed to be unique. The starting number may be set to *n*, but defaults to 1.
Date DATE	Date values, formatted on display and verified on entry according to the environment variable **DBDATE** (see Chapter 1).
Money MONEY[(*m*[,*n*])]	Money values, with *m* significant digits (up to 32) of which *n* are decimal digits, formatted on display according to the environment variable **DBMONEY** (see Chapter 1). Note that MONEY(*m*) is interpreted as DECIMAL(*m*,2) and that the default MONEY = DECIMAL(16,2).

New for Version 4.0

The following data types are all new with Version 4.0. The first two are available with both the Standard Engine and OnLine, whereas the variable length and BLOB data types are available only with OnLine.

Type	Description
Time	
DATETIME *first* TO *last*	Holds a value representing a precise moment in time, with a precision (which you determine) of years down to fractions of a second. Covered excellently in an Appendix to the **INFORMIX-SQL** manual.
INTERVAL	Used to store values representing a period of time. Has a similar precision range to datetime. Also covered in an Appendix to the **INFORMIX-SQL** manual.
Variable length (OnLine only)	
VARCHAR	Allows you to store up to 255 characters in a variable-length column.
BLOBs – Binary Large OBjects (OnLine only)	
TEXT	Up to 2 Gigabytes of textual data (including tabs, returns and form feeds) may be stored in this column.
BYTE	Up to 2 Gigabytes of binary data may be stored in this type of column. The data may be anything from spreadsheets and programs to digitised images and sound.

3.5 Indexes

A book is a collection of words and phrases arranged in an arbitrary manner (leaving aside dictionaries, encyclopaedias and phone books), and as far as any alphabetical ordering is concerned, the words are in random order. How then does one find a particular word, subject or phrase? Without an index one must search through all the words in the book in the order in which they appear – a *sequential* (and rather tedious) search through a random file.

So what is an index and how does it help? An index is a separate section containing a selection of words and phrases from the book ordered alphabetically. Associated with each word or phrase is the location in the book (page number) where that word or phrase may be found. The task of finding a word or phrase is now much simpler. We must first make a sequential search through an *ordered* file – the index (although this search is not entirely sequential since we are able to go very quickly to section M or section A etc.). Having found the word or phrase we then also have the location (page number) where we must make a further sequential search.

Figure 3.3 An index is a separate section containing a selection of words and phrases from the book ordered alphabetically.

Although there is a certain amount of 'flitting about' with searches in different sections of the book, the process is faster by many orders of magnitude than a sequential search through the whole book. From this discussion, we can postulate a general theory:

Indexes speed up data retrieval.

But is this always true? Let us consider a small book, a very small book, of say three pages. The average number of pages that need to be searched to find a word or phrase without using an index is $(1 + 3) / 2 = 2$ (since the least number of pages is 1 and the most is 3). Let us suppose that the index to our book takes up one page and that the index has a header page. Since these are easy pages to search, we can say that they take half the time a normal page takes to search. We must also search the page indicated by the index.

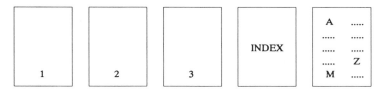

Figure 3.4 A small book of three pages, with an index.

This then gives us $1/2 + 1/2 + 1 = 2$ page searches, which is the same as the average time taken to search the book without an index! I have used rough estimates based on a rough model, but the principle remains valid since any index will always impose an overhead. This leads us to Rule 1, which we can apply to a relational database as follows:

Rule 1:   An index will not speed up *and may actually slow down* data retrieval from a table with a small number of rows.

The break-even point for both the Standard Engine and OnLine is about 200 rows, since both use B-Tree+ indexing.

Consider an index entry for the first word of every sentence. There would be a relatively small number of entries, each having a large number of occurrences (such as 'the', 'if', 'in', 'there'). Because of the large number of occurrences, probably at least one per page, the index will not speed up your search at all, and will just waste space. In an actual database, columns falling into this category would be those with a small range of values such as Y or N, sex or marital status.

Rule 2:   Do not create an index on a column with a small number of possible values. It wastes space and will not speed up retrieval at all. (Moreover, it will *considerably* decrease the speed of inserts and deletions, but see Section 3.5.3, Multi-column indexes.)

In general then, with certain exceptions, indexes speed up data retrieval. Since the entries in an index are already ordered, its presence will also speed up the sorting of data. What about insertion, deletion and updating? When a row is added to a table it is added at the end of the data file holding the table. But if there is an index associated with the table, then a new entry must be inserted here as well. But an index is an *ordered* set of entries, so the new entry must be inserted at the correct place. When the number of entries reaches certain pre-defined limits, the insertion of one more entry causes a large number of disk blocks to be rewritten. This is not usually a problem when rows are being added interactively and the speed of insertion is not too important, but if a large number of rows are being added using **dbload** or some other batch insertion program, the presence of an index will slow the insertion down considerably. This also applies to a batch update where indexed columns are being changed. Luckily, **INFORMIX-SQL** is flexible enough to allow us to create indexes when they are needed (for sorting and retrieval) and drop them when they are not (for batch insertion and updating).

Rule 3:   Indexes slow down insertion and updating, particularly by batch programs like **dbload** or an UPDATE statement which affects a large number of rows. A dynamic approach should be adopted, creating and dropping indexes as required.

3.5.1 Creating indexes

Indexes may be created and dropped either through the Interactive Schema Editor (see Sections 3.7 and 3.8), or through the following SQL statements:

CREATE INDEX *index-name* ON *table-name* (*column-name*)

DROP INDEX *index-name*

Note that *index-name* is a name that you associate with a particular index. It is only used by the creator of the index (or the DBA – database administrator) in definition statements such as CREATE INDEX, DROP INDEX and ALTER INDEX. It should be as meaningful as possible, with some clue as to the column name or names from which it is made up. For example:

```
create index i_hprice on houses(price);
```

Notes

(i)   You have no influence over the *index-name* created by the Interactive Schema Editor, though you may display the index names for a particular table through the **Info** choice on the TABLE menu.

(ii)   The total length of an index may not exceed 8 columns and 120 bytes (16 columns and 256 bytes in **INFORMIX-OnLine**). Multi-column indexes are discussed in Section 3.5.3.

(iii) You may not create an index on a *view* (see Chapter 5, Section 5.6.3).

3.5.2 Duplicate and unique indexes

Where queries are required on a surname or town it would be reasonable to put an index on these columns. However, it would also be reasonable to expect that there will be more than one row with the same value, e.g. Smith, or London. But where a column may only have a single occurrence of a particular value, such as a part number, or a bank account number, there is a simple way of enforcing this, and that is by creating a *unique* index on that column. While this unique index exists, the user will be prevented from entering a duplicate value in this column.

Unique indexes may be specified in the Interactive Schema Editor or may be created using a variant of the CREATE INDEX statement:

CREATE UNIQUE INDEX *index-name* ON *table-name* (*col-name*)

Note

(i)   You may not create a unique index (or change a duplicate index to unique) on a column that already contains duplicate values. In particular a column which allows NULL values (see Section 3.6) will almost certainly contain more than one NULL.

New for Version 4.0

(ii)   A unique index is automatically created by the use of the UNIQUE CONSTRAINT keywords in the CREATE TABLE statement (see Chapter 5, Section 5.6.2).

3.5.3 Composite or multi-column indexes

There are sometimes instances where rows cannot be uniquely identified by a single column, but only by a combination of columns, particularly in a join or sorting operation. You may, for instance, want to sort names in first name within last name order, giving an output such as:

Smith Andy
Smith David
Smith Harry
West   Bert
West   Fred

This retrieval would be speeded up by creating a multi-column or *composite* index on the last name and first name columns. Composite indexes may not be created through the Interactive Schema Editor, but by using the following CREATE INDEX statement:

CREATE INDEX *index-name* ON *table-name* (*col1, col2* [,...])

Notes

(i)   You may create a composite index on up to eight columns whose total length may not exceed 120 bytes. This may seem a lot, but bear in mind that it could be used up by only *four* columns of data type CHAR(30). (In **INFORMIX-OnLine** this limit is increased to sixteen columns and up to 256 bytes.)

(ii)   Creating an index on a column with a large number of duplicates can slow down inserts and deletions considerably. The situation can be improved, however, by creating a multi-column index consisting of the highly duplicate column and another column which is either unique, or has a small number of duplicate values. For instance, the **county** column in the **houses** table has a large number of duplicates. A composite index could be created with the **ref_no** column, which is unique. This would allow an index to be placed on the **county** column without imposing a large overhead on insert and delete operations:

```
create index i_comp on houses(ref_no, county);
```

3.5.4 Ascending or descending?

Normally, when you create an index, it will be created in ascending order, i.e. from low to high values of letters (A to Z), numbers (1 to 9) and dates (1900 to 1989). But you may reverse this order for a particular index by creating a descending index. For example, a report may require data from our **houses** table to be sorted on the **price** column, with the highest price first. The direction of the index may be specified in the Interactive Schema Editor or by using another variant of the CREATE INDEX statement:

CREATE INDEX *index-name* ON *table-name* (*column-name* DESC)

Note

A composite index may comprise a mixture of column names *and* directions. For instance the following is perfectly valid (note that ASCending is the default and has been specified here for clarity only):

```
create index i_comp2
   on houses(ref_no asc, price desc);
```

3.5.5 Clustered indexes

Consider the set of London telephone directories. Each of the directories holds names in one of four ranges of letters: A-D, E-M, N-R, S-Z, and these ranges are displayed on the spine of the respective book. They in fact represent an index to the data, since they help us to locate a particular name and phone number. But when we open say the A-D book, we find that not only does it contain all the names whose first letter is between A and D, but that the names are sorted, in order of name. This makes it very much easier to find a particular name, or even better, a group of names such as all the Blacks or Baileys. We say that the index is a *clustered* index, in this case with respect to the name field. As you can see from this example, a clustered index actually refers to a property of the *data*, whereby its physical ordering is the same as that of the index.

Since both UNIX and MSDOS read data from the disk in blocks, clustering will greatly increase the speed of an indexed retrieval or sorting operation.

A clustered index may not be created through the Interactive Schema Editor but by using the CREATE INDEX statement like this:

CREATE CLUSTER INDEX *index-name*
    ON *tablename* (*col-name* [,...])

or you may cluster the data according to an existing index by executing the statement:

ALTER INDEX *index-name* TO CLUSTER

Notes

(i)   The data may of course only be ordered in one way, so you may only have one clustered index at a time on a table. You may move the cluster attribute to another index by first removing it:

ALTER INDEX *index-name1* TO NOT CLUSTER

and then placing it on the other index:

ALTER INDEX *index-name2* TO CLUSTER

or

CREATE CLUSTER INDEX
index-name2 ON *table-name* (*col-name* [,...])

(ii)   As new rows are added or existing rows updated, the clustering will gradually disappear and may have to be re-applied using the statement:

ALTER INDEX *index-name* TO CLUSTER

(iii)   Since no ordering is possible in a **PERFORM** form, a clustered index is the only way to impose an order when a number of rows are retrieved. But remember that it can take a long time to create a clustered index, since the data file must be rewritten in its entirety.

(iv)   As with all indexes, a clustered index may not be created on a view.

3.6 NULLs

A NULL value for a column is a value which is unknown or meaningless. In our **property** database, if the price of a house has not yet been decided, its value is clearly not zero, but just unknown. In some older DBMSs (including **INFORMIX** prior to Version 2.0 of **INFORMIX-SQL**), NULL values were represented by zeros in numeric fields and spaces in character fields, which can be misleading. Although there is obviously a place for NULL values, their presence can cause problems. For instance, what is the value of the following expression if the value of **price** is NULL?

```
price + 1000
```

Since the value of **price** is unknown (NULL), then the result of unknown + 1000 must also be unknown. NULL values are like black holes – no matter what you put into them, you never get anything out, except another NULL. So whatever operation they take part in, be it addition, subtraction, multiplication or whatever, the result is always a NULL.

But it does not stop there. If the value of **book_date** in a particular row is NULL (i.e. unknown), then that row can never be selected from a WHERE clause of the form:

```
where book_date < (today - 90)
```

The purpose of this WHERE clause (WHERE clauses are covered in Chapter 5, Section 5.4.2) is to select those houses that have been on the books for more than 90 days. But if a house's **book_date** is unknown, then there is no way of comparing it with (**today** - **90**), or any other value for that matter! You will see in Section 5.4.2 (and in the notes for this section) that there are ways of testing specifically for NULL values.

According to one of Ted Codd's twelve rules, a database must handle NULL values to call itself relational. Using zero instead of NULL, for instance, could make a calculation such as an average completely erroneous. But there are times when you may want to consider disallowing NULLs in columns that are likely to be used in expressions or comparisons. You may do this when you create a table (see the next section), though *not* when altering one (see note (iv) below).

Notes

(i)   Although NULL values are normally taken to be unknown, for the purposes of sorting they are treated as being less than non-NULL values, coming first in an ascending sort.

(ii)   To use the latest version of **INFORMIX-SQL** on databases created with **INFORMIX-SQL** 1.10 or earlier, in which NULL values were represented by zeros and spaces, you must execute the **dbupdate** utility which is described in an Appendix of the **INFORMIX-SQL** manual.

(iii)   You may test specifically for a NULL value by using the test condition

WHERE *column* IS [NOT] NULL

but note that the word IS is mandatory and may not be replaced with an =. For example:

```
select * from houses
where book_date < (today - 90)
or book_date is null;
```

(iv)   When a table is first created, it contains no rows, and so it is easy to impose the condition that no future values of a column may be NULL. However, once data has been entered into a table, two things must be borne in mind: (i) a column may not be altered to NO NULLs if it already contains some NULL values, and (ii) a new column specifying NO NULLs may not be added, since by default the initial values in this new column *must* be NULL.

3.7 Creating Tables

Tables may be created in the current database either by using the SQL statement CREATE TABLE or, which is much simpler, by using the CREATE TABLE menu of the Interactive Schema Editor. The steps to create a table using the schema editor are as follows:

1. Make sure that the current database (whose name is displayed in the middle of the line of dashes under the menu options) is the one in which you wish to create your table. If not, select the right one by choosing the **Database** option from the main menu.

    If the required database is not listed in the SELECT DATABASE menu, either you are in the wrong directory, or your **DBPATH** environment variable is not set correctly (see Chapter 1).

2. Select **Table** from the main menu.

3. Select **Create** from the TABLE menu.

4. Give your table a name.

    You may use up to eighteen characters (UNIX or DOS).

    There is no distinction between upper and lower case.

    The name must start with a letter, and you may use any combination of letters or numbers plus the underscore character.

    There are certain reserved words (such as *table, public, average*) that must not be used for table or column names. A full list may be found in an Appendix of the **INFORMIX-SQL** manual. Sometimes these words will only cause errors in an **INFORMIX-4GL** program.

5. You are now in the CREATE TABLE menu of the schema editor. Select **Add** to add a new column to the table.

```
CREATE TABLE houses :   | Add | Modify  Drop  Screen  Exit
Adds columns to the table above the line with the highlight.

----- Page 1 of 1 ----------- property --------------------- Press CTRL-W for Help ------

Column Name                     Type        Length   Index   Nulls

 _____
```

Figure 3.5   The CREATE TABLE menu of the schema editor.

Because the schema editor is interactive, the screen display behaves slightly differently from the normal menu screens. It is now in two parts: the top part consists of the menu options as usual, except that the cursor keys may not be used to select a menu option, only **SPACE**, **BACKSPACE** or the appropriate first letter of an option. The second part of the screen is where you edit the *schema* of a table and this is where the cursor keys do have an effect.

If you make a mistake in the database column you are editing (remember that a database *column* is displayed *across* the screen in the schema editor) you may go left and right to correct the error. If you spot an error in another part of the schema, you must return to the main CREATE TABLE menu by pressing the **INTERRUPT** key (this may be marked **DEL**, **DELETE**, or *Ctrl-C*). You may then use the cursor keys to move to the part that needs correcting and select **Modify**.

6. Specify the name of the column

    Column names follow the same rules as for tables (see Step 4).

    Use names that are meaningful, but not too long, since you will need to type them in again when retrieving data.

7. You must now define the data type of your column (data types are covered in Section 3.4). You are presented with the ADD TYPE menu:

ADD TYPE adrs1 :   [Char] Number Serial Date Money date-Time Interval
Permits any combination of letters, numbers, and punctuation.

----- Page 1 of 1 ----------- property --------------------- Press CTRL-W for Help ------

Column Name	Type	Length	Index	Nulls
adrs1	[ ]			

Figure 3.6   The ADD TYPE menu of the schema editor.

7.1   **Char.** If you choose **Char** you will be asked to specify the maximum length expected for this character column (the default length is 20).

7.2   **Numeric.** Choosing **Numeric** will cause the ADD NUMERIC menu to be displayed, from which you must choose one of the numeric data types.

ADD NUMERIC houses :   Integer Smallint Decimal Float
Permits whole numbers in the approximate range -2 billion to 2 billion.

----- Page 1 of 1 ----------- property --------------------- Press CTRL-W for Help ------

Column Name   Type   Length   Index   Nulls

no_bedrooms

Figure 3.7 The ADD NUMERIC menu of the schema editor.

7.2.1   **Integer.** Choosing this option will take you on to Step 8.

7.2.2   **Smallint.** Choosing this option will take you on to Step 8.

7.2.3   **Decimal.** If you choose **Decimal** you will be asked to specify first the length of the number, which is the *total* number of significant digits, and the scale, which is the number of *decimal* digits.

7.2.4   **Float.** Choosing the **Float** option will bring up the ADD PRECISION menu for floating point numbers, which asks you to choose between **Smallfloat** and **Float** (see Section 3.4 for the difference).

7.3   **Serial.** If you select the **Serial** data type you will be asked to specify a starting number (the value of the column when the first row is added to this table), which will default to 1 if you press **RETURN**. The starting number will be displayed under the Length heading.

7.4   **Date.** The display of **Date** values is controlled by the **DBDATE** environment variable; there are no other questions to be asked for this type, so go to Step 8.

7.5   **Money.** The **Money** data type is a special form of **Decimal** which is formatted on display according to the **DBMONEY** environment variable. You will be asked for the length, which is the *total* number of significant digits to be allowed for, and the scale, which is the number of *decimal* digits.

New for Version 4.0

7.6 **date-Time.** The **Datetime** data type allows you to hold a value which represents a precise moment in time. It can hold any value from a year down to a fraction of a second, and you determine the precision through the ADD DATETIME QUALIFIER menu, which is displayed next.

   7.6.1 From the ADD DATETIME QUALIFIER menu you must select a **First** and **Last** field for the precision, from the available choices. A standard DATE data type, for instance, would have a precision of YEAR TO DAY, whereas a daily timestamp would have a precision of HOUR TO SECOND. If you wanted to store just the year, you could specify YEAR TO YEAR. This data type, together with INTERVAL, is covered in detail in an Appendix to the **INFORMIX-SQL** User Guide manual.

7.7 **Interval.** The **Interval** data type allows you to hold a value which represents a precise span of time. It can hold any value from a year down to a fraction of a second, and you determine the precision through the ADD INTERVAL QUALIFIER menu, which is displayed next.

   7.7.1 From the ADD INTERVAL QUALIFIER menu you must select a **First** and **Last** field for the precision, from the available choices. There are two exclusive lists to choose from, either YEAR and MONTH, or DAY down to FRACTION. Each field represents a number of that particular field, as in a number of years or a number of days and hours. A work period might have a precision of HOUR TO MINUTE. If you wanted to store just a number of years, you could specify YEAR TO YEAR. This data type, together with DATETIME, is covered in detail in an Appendix to the manual.

7.8 **Variable-length.** With **INFORMIX-OnLine** as your database engine you may select the **Variable-length** option, which then displays the VARIABLE-LENGTH menu, as in Figure 3.8.

   7.8.1 **Varchar.** Specify a maximum size that this column will accept, up to 255 characters, and a minimum space which will always be reserved, from 0 to *maxsize*. Use VARCHAR with caution, as updates which exceed the minimum space will impinge on performance. See the OnLine Programmer's Manual for more details.

VARIABLE-LENGTH :   Varchar   Text Byte
Variable-length data containing a maximum of 255 characters.

----- Page 1 of 1 ----------- property --------------------- Press CTRL-W for Help ------

Column Name   Type   Length   Index   Nulls

adrs2

Figure 3.8 The VARIABLE-LENGTH menu of the schema editor.

7.8.2   **Text.** The ADD BLOBSPACE menu is displayed and you are asked whether you want to store the column data in the same dbspace as the rest of the database (the **Table** option), or in a separate BLOBspace (the **BLOBSpace-name** option).

7.8.3   **Byte.** The ADD BLOBSPACE menu is displayed and you are asked whether you want to store the column data in the same dbspace as the rest of the database (the **Table** option), or in a separate BLOBspace (the **BLOBSpace-name** option).

8. Decide whether or not this column will have an index (indexes are discussed in Section 3.5) and whether or not duplicate values are to be allowed in this column.

    Note

    Remember that you can press *Ctrl-W* at any time to get help for whichever part of the schema editor you are currently on.

9. Decide whether NULL values (discussed in Section 3.6) will be allowed in this column.

10. Repeat Steps 6-9 for all the required columns.

11. Press **RETURN** again after you have entered the information for the last column. **INFORMIX-SQL** exits the ADD NAME screen and displays the CREATE TABLE menu.

12. Select **Exit** followed by the **Build-new-table** option of the EXIT menu.

```
EXIT houses :   | Build-new-table | Discard-new-table
Builds a new table and returns to the Table Menu.

----- Page 1 of 1 ---------- property --------------------- Press CTRL-W for Help ------

Column Name                  Type        Length   Index    Nulls

ref_no                       Serial      1        Unique   No
adrs1                        Char        20                Yes
adrs2                        Char        20                Yes
town                         Char        20       Dups     No
```

Figure 3.9 The EXIT menu of the schema editor.

Exercise

1. Create the following tables in your **property** database:

Table: houses

Column Name	Type	Length	Index	Nulls
ref_no	Serial	1	Unique	No
owner	Char	20		No
adrs1	Char	20		No
adrs2	Char	20		Yes
town	Char	20		No
county	Char	20		No
no_bedrooms	Integer			No
no_baths	Integer			No
lounge_size	Char	11		Yes
dining_size	Char	11		Yes
thru_lounge_size	Char	11		Yes
notes	Char	30		Yes
price	Money	11,0		No
agent	Char	20		No
book_date	Date			No

Table: bedrooms

Column Name	Type	Length	Index	Nulls
ref_no	Integer		Dups	No
bedroom_no	Smallint			No
bedroom_size	Char	11		No
ensuite_bath	Char	1		No

Table: agents

Column Name	Type	Length	Index	Nulls
company	Char	20	Unique	No
adrs1	Char	20		No
adrs2	Char	20		Yes
town	Char	20		No
phone	Char	12		No

3.8 Modifying tables

To change a table schema, select **Table** from the main menu and from the TABLE menu select **Alter**. Select the required table from the list presented to you (just move the highlight up or down and press **RETURN**). You are now in the schema editor again. You can make changes to your table by moving the cursor to the appropriate line in the schema and selecting one of the following options from the ALTER TABLE menu.

```
ALTER TABLE houses :     | Add | Modify  Drop  Screen  Exit
Adds columns to the table above the line with the highlight.

----- Page 1 of 1 ----------- property --------------------- Press CTRL-W for Help ------

Column Name                    Type        Length   Index    Nulls

| ref_no                  |    Serial      1        Unique   No
 adrs1                          Char        20                Yes
 adrs2                          Char        20                Yes
 town                           Char        20       Dups     No
```

Figure 3.10 The ALTER TABLE menu of the schema editor.

Add   Adds a new column to the table, above the highlighted column (but see note (i) below). Pressing **RETURN** at the ADD NAME screen closes the column addition.

Modify   Using the cursor keys, move the highlight to the part of the schema you want to change, *then* select **Modify** to change the highlighted column definition (but see note (ii) below).

Drop   Removes the highlighted column. You are given a last chance to confirm or deny this choice.

Screen   If your schema goes over the page, this option allows you to move to the next page.

Exit   Brings up the EXIT menu. Selecting **Discard-new-table** discards the *changes* you have made, leaving the table schema as it was previously. The **Build-new-table** option implements the changes you have made. If any inconsistencies are found then the changes are not made, an appropriate error message is displayed and you are left in the ALTER TABLE menu (but see note (iii) below).

Notes

(i)   One of the beauties of a relational database is that you can add columns anywhere in a table schema, of any size (within **INFORMIX-SQL** limits) without disrupting any data currently in the table. There are certain restrictions however:

(a) A new column will by default contain a NULL value for every row already present in the table, therefore you cannot specify a new column as NO NULLs.

(b) It follows that if a column contains more than one NULL value, you may not specify a unique index for it. You must first insert unique data into every row of the table.

(c) You may not add a column of type SERIAL to a table that already contains data. You must first unload the data to a temporary file, rebuild the schema to include the SERIAL column, and reload the data.

(ii) If there is data in the table, there are certain restrictions that apply when you select the **Modify** option:

(a) You may not change a data type to SERIAL (but see note (i) above).

(b) You can always *increase* the size of a data type, such as SMALLINT to INTEGER or a CHAR of length 20 to one of length 30, but you cannot always *decrease* the size. If the column already contains numbers larger than the limit of SMALLINT then you may not change the data type to SMALLINT. You can decrease the size of a CHAR column, but you may lose data through truncation if any rows contain data that exceeds the new length.

(c) You may get rounding errors if you change the type of a column from FLOAT to DECIMAL.

(d) You can always change from NUMERIC to CHAR, but only from CHAR to NUMERIC if there are no non-numeric characters present.

(iii) Early versions of **INFORMIX-SQL** had non-specific and rather terse error messages. Check notes (i) and (ii) above to see what you have done wrong (or upgrade to the latest version!).

(iv) The **dbschema** utility exists to recreate the SQL command file used to create a table or tables in an existing database. Its syntax is:

dbschema [-t *tabname*] **-d** *database* [*filename*]

where *filename* contains the **dbschema** output. In Version 4.0, the *owner.object* naming convention is used, so you may need to edit the file. To run the command file from the SQL menu, it will need a **.sql** extension. The utility is covered in depth in the **INFORMIX-SQL** manual.

Exercise

1. Modify the **houses** table, changing the data types of **no_bedrooms** and **no_baths** from Integer to Smallint.

2. Modify the **houses** table, putting an index allowing duplicates on the **agent** field.

3. Modify the **agents** table, changing the column name **company** to **agent**.

4. Modify the **agents** table, adding a new column called **county**, of type Char and Length 20, between **town** and **phone**. Do not allow any NULLs.

Your table schemas should now look like this:

Table: houses

Column Name	Type	Length	Index	Nulls
ref_no	Serial	1	Unique	No
owner	Char	20		No
adrs1	Char	20		No
adrs2	Char	20		Yes
town	Char	20		No
county	Char	20		No
no_bedrooms	Smallint			No
no_baths	Smallint			No
lounge_size	Char	11		Yes
dining_size	Char	11		Yes
thru_lounge_size	Char	11		Yes
notes	Char	30		Yes
price	Money	11,0		No
agent	Char	20	Dups	No
book_date	Date			No

Table: bedrooms

Column Name	Type	Length	Index	Nulls
ref_no	Integer		Dups	No
bedroom_no	Smallint			No
bedroom_size	Char	11		No
ensuite_bath	Char	1		No

Table: agents

Column Name	Type	Length	Index	Nulls
agent	Char	20	Unique	No
adrs1	Char	20		No
adrs2	Char	20		Yes
town	Char	20		No
county	Char	20		No
phone	Char	12		No

Chapter 4

Introduction to SQL

4.1 Introduction

Structured Query Language (SQL) was developed by IBM for creating and querying databases. The Informix SQL language (previously known as RDSQL, from Informix Software's old name – Relational Database Systems Inc.) is fully compliant with ANSI level I SQL, and partially compliant with level II. Informix additions to the language permit the user to load and unload database tables into system files, to modify table schemas and to rename tables and columns.

SQL is the interactive query language for **INFORMIX-SQL**. It is powerful and flexible and is essential for the following operations:

- Batch (i.e. multiple row) updates and deletes

- Database administration

- Displaying multiple rows on the screen at a time

- Complex queries and subqueries

However, it is not screen-orientated; for this type of application you would use **PERFORM** (see Chapters 6 and 7). It also has no output formatting facilities – these are provided by the **ACE** report generator (see Chapter 8), which uses the SQL SELECT statement to extract data from the database.

4.2 The SQL Menu

To use the **INFORMIX-SQL** Structured Query Language you must select the **Query-Language** option from the main menu. The SQL menu (or RDSQL in older versions) has ten options which allow you to create, modify, save and retrieve SQL command files, as well as running and deleting them. There are also options to output the results to the printer or a system file and to obtain information on tables in the current database. The SQL menu is shown in Figure 4.1 and the functions provided by the various options are as follows:

New   The **New** option is used to enter and edit SQL statements on the screen, using the SQL editor. Selecting this option also clears the current statements, *without warning*, so be sure to save them first with the **Save** option if you think you may need them again.

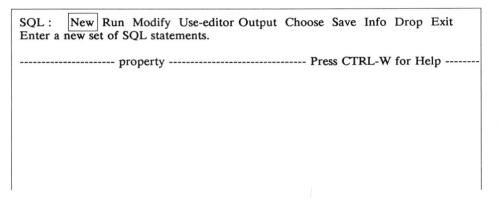

SQL :   New Run Modify Use-editor Output Choose Save Info Drop Exit
Enter a new set of SQL statements.

---------------------- property ----------------------------- Press CTRL-W for Help --------

Figure 4.1 The SQL menu.

Run   Runs the current set of SQL statements. If errors are detected the **Modify** option is highlighted although the **Use-editor** option may be used instead. In either case the first error detected will be indicated.

Modify   Is used to change the current statements using the SQL editor. If an error is detected while running the current statements, the cursor points to the position of the error.

Use-editor   Is used to enter and edit SQL statements on the screen using a system editor. Any editor producing ASCII output and accepting a filename from the command line (in other words without using a menu system) may be used. Normally the system editor (**vi** on UNIX machines, **edlin** on DOS machines) is used but the default may be changed by setting the environment variable **DBEDIT** (see Chapter 1).

Output   This option sends the results of running the current statements to the printer, a system file, or another program.

Save   Is used to save the current set of SQL statements in a command file for later retrieval using the **Choose** option. The extension **.sql** is added automatically.

Choose   Having saved a number of command files, you may select the contents of one of them to be the current statements (allowing you to either **Run** or **Modify** them) by selecting the **Choose** option. You may omit the **.sql** extension.

Info   The **Info** option gives a wealth of information about the current database tables and indexes.

Drop   Allows the user to delete a command file from the list of command files.

Exit   Returns you to the **INFORMIX-SQL** main menu.

4.3 Entering SQL Statements

SQL statements may be entered singly or as SQL scripts by selecting **Query-Language** from the main menu. While you are working with the SQL menu, **INFORMIX-SQL** remembers the last sequence of statements, if any, with which you were working. These statements are called the **current statements**.

SQL statements are written free-form and may include all 'white space' characters (spaces, tabs, returns). Statements are separated by semicolons. Note that the semicolon is a *separator,* not a terminator, so the last or only statement does not need one (although in this Module and the following one it is used, as a reminder).

Since you may use either the SQL editor or another such as **vi** or even a word processor such as **Q-ONE** (as long as the editor takes a filename from the command line in the form *editor filename*) you have a choice of two routes:

If you prefer to choose your favourite editor, you must first make sure that the environment variable **DBEDIT** is set correctly (see Chapter 1, Section 1.4), although the default is **vi** for UNIX or **edlin** for DOS. You may then follow these steps:

1. Select **Use-editor** from the menu.

2. Enter your SQL statements and save the file. At this stage, your statements are saved in a temporary file, these being the current statements.

3. To save your statements permanently in a command file that can be reused, select the **Save** option from the menu. (**INFORMIX-SQL** adds the **.sql** extension to the filename you select.)

4. Select **Run** to run the current SQL statements.

5. You may modify the current statements using your system editor by again selecting the **Use-editor** option.

If you prefer to use the SQL editor, follow these steps:

1. First select **New** from the menu and enter a new set of current statements. **N.B.** The current statements will be lost if you have not saved them with the **Save** option.

2. Exit from the SQL editor by pressing **ESC** and, if required, save the file using the **Save** option.

3. You may now run the current statements using the **Run** option.

4. To modify the current statements using the SQL editor you must select the **Modify** option.

```
NEW: ESC     = Done editing    CTRL-A = Typeover/Insert  CTRL-R = Redraw
     CTRL-X = Delete character CTRL-D = Delete rest of line

-------------------- property ---------------------------- Press CTRL-W for Help --------




```

Figure 4.2 The SQL editor.

4.4 SQL Statement Summary

There are five different kinds of statement in SQL: Data Manipulation Language (or DML) statements, Data Definition Language (or DDL) statements, Data Access Control statements, Data Integrity statements and Auxiliary statements. In the following table the statements are presented in their appropriate classifications.

DML	SELECT, INSERT, UPDATE, DELETE
DDL	CREATE, ALTER, DROP, RENAME
Access	GRANT, REVOKE, LOCK, UNLOCK, SET LOCK MODE
Integrity	BEGIN WORK, COMMIT WORK, ROLLBACK WORK, ROLLFORWARD DATABASE, START DATABASE, CLOSE DATABASE, DATABASE, CHECK TABLE, RECOVER TABLE, REPAIR TABLE, CREATE AUDIT, DROP AUDIT
Auxiliary	INFO, LOAD, UNLOAD, OUTPUT TO, UPDATE STATISTICS

Figure 4.3 The Informix SQL statement set.

In this chapter we will be taking an introductory look at the DML statements only, and concentrating on the SELECT statement in particular. These, together with all the other SQL statements, are covered in detail in the next chapter.

4.5 The SELECT Statement

SQL stands for Structured Query Language. Is it not strange then that in Informix SQL, in common with other implementations of SQL, out of forty SQL statements, only one statement allows you to query a database! That statement is the SELECT statement and will be used, in one form or another in nine out of ten of your SQL statements. For this reason we shall cover it first.

Let us first consider the simplest form of the SELECT statement:

SELECT *select-list* FROM *table-list*

where:

select-list   is a list of column names, expressions or aggregates. To select all the columns from a table use an asterisk (*).

table-list   is a list of one or more table names.

For example:

```
select * from houses;
```

This statement will retrieve all the columns from the **houses** table and display their values for each row in the **houses** table. In the figure below, the shaded area represents what has been selected.

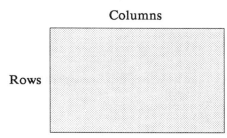

Figure 4.4   An * selects all the columns from a table.

When displaying the output on the screen, **INFORMIX-SQL** attempts to display the rows across the screen if it can fit all the columns in. For instance:

```
select owner, adrs1, town
    from houses;
```

will be displayed as in Figure 4.5:

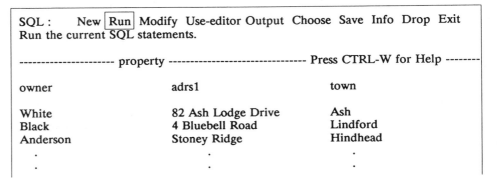

Figure 4.5 Selected rows displayed across the screen.

whereas the output from the following query:

```
select * from houses;
```

will be displayed as in Figure 4.6, with a single row displayed on each screen.

```
RUN :    Next  Restart  Exit
Display the next page of query results.

--------------------- property ----------------------------- Press CTRL-W for Help --------

ref_no               1
owner                White
adrs1                82 Ash Lodge Drive
adrs2                Ashley Park
town                 Ash
county               Surrey
no_bedrooms          4
no_baths             2
lounge_size
dining_size
thru_lounge_size     21'6 x 13'3
notes                Double garage, private gardens
price                £108900
agent                Thompson & Bayles
book_date            26/06/90
```

Figure 4.6 Selected rows displayed one per page.

The next case to consider is when we want to select only certain columns from every row in the table:

```
select owner, adrs1, town
   from houses;
```

The shaded area in Figure 4.7 illustrates what has been selected:

Columns

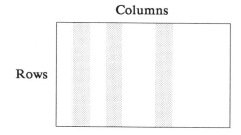

Rows

Figure 4.7   Specific columns may be selected.

4.5.1 The ORDER BY clause

The output from your SELECT statement may be sorted by using the ORDER BY clause. You may sort in either ascending order of a particular column, which is the default, or in descending order of a column, by specifying the keyword DESC.

For example:

```
select owner, adrs1, town
    from houses
    order by owner;
```

This will sort the output of the query according to the **owner** column. The following query will sort the output in **town** order within **county**:

```
select adrs1, town, county
    from houses
    order by county, town;
```

producing the following output:

```
SQL :      New Run Modify Use-editor Output Choose Save Info Drop Exit
Run the current SQL statements.

--------------------- property ------------------------------- Press CTRL-W for Help --------

adrs1                      town                  county

82 Ash Lodge Drive         Ash                   Hampshire
4 Bluebell Road            Lindford              Hampshire
Cliffe Cottage             Guildford             Surrey
        .                       .                      .
        .                       .                      .
```

Figure 4.8 The result of an ORDER BY clause.

Exercise

1. Access the SQL menu by selecting **Query-Language** from the main menu. You will have to select a database, so make sure that **property** is in your **DBPATH** or current directory.

2. Peruse the single-line explanations of the various options and obtain help on some of them by typing *Ctrl-W.*

3. Select **New** to access the SQL editor and note the editing options at the top of the screen. These are the only editing functions available (so you may sometimes prefer to use another editor through the **Use-editor** option). However, a useful feature of the editor is the availability of help, which gives the syntax of all the SQL statements. Type *Ctrl-W* on the editor screen to access this help.

4. Enter your first SQL statement:

    ```
    select * from houses;
    ```

    and press **ESC** to exit the editor.

5. Select **Run** to run the statement and examine successive screens of the output by selecting the **Next** option, and eventually **Exit.**

6. **Save** your statement under the name **allhouses.**

7. Select **Modify** (or you may care to try **Use-editor** if you prefer **vi**).

8. Change your query to:

    ```
    select owner, adrs1, town
    from houses
    order by town desc;
    ```

    and run it.

9. Now **Save** your new query and select **Choose** from the menu. You should see your two queries listed. Moving the cursor to one of them and pressing **RETURN** will make the statements in that query the current statements.

4.5.2 The WHERE clause

The most important optional clause of the SELECT statement is the WHERE clause. This clause allows you to set conditions defining which rows are retrieved from the database. For example:

```
select * from houses
    where town = "Woking";
```

This will retrieve all the information in the database on houses in Woking. The action of the WHERE clause can be expressed diagrammatically as:

Columns

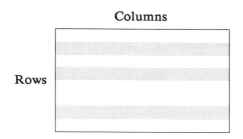

Rows

Figure 4.9   The WHERE clause defines which rows are retrieved.

The syntax of the WHERE clause is very simple:

WHERE *condition*

However, *condition* can be very complex, being a collection of one or more *search conditions* which may be connected by AND or OR. The operator NOT may also be used to negate any particular condition. The following query will select those 4-bedroomed houses which are not in Woking:

```
select owner, adrs1, price
    from houses
    where no_bedrooms = 4
    and not town = "Woking";
```

A search condition can be either a comparison, a join condition, or a subquery. In this chapter we will examine some simple comparison and join conditions only, and leave the rest for discussion in Chapter 5, Further SQL.

4.5.3 Comparisons and expressions

The simplest form of the comparison condition is:

expr rel-op expr

where:

expr   is an *expression*. An expression is a column name or a constant (including the system constant TODAY) or any combination of these (with certain restrictions) connected by one of the arithmetic operators:

+   addition
–   subtraction
*   multiplication
/   division

The following are all valid expressions:

```
town
"Woking"
price * 1.15
150000
price / no_bedrooms
2 * ((price + 1000) / no_bedrooms)
today - 9
```

These are invalid, because they attempt to mix different data types:

```
town + 10
price / county
"Woking" / no_bedrooms
```

rel-op   is short for *relational operator*. This has nothing to do with relational database theory, but is just one of the following:

=   equal
!= or < >   not equal
>   greater than
> =   greater than or equal
<   less than
< =   less than or equal

Examples

Let us now consider some examples of simple search conditions:

```
select ref_no, adrs1
    from houses
    where town = "Guildford";
```

This will retrieve the **ref_no** and **adrs1** columns from the **houses** table for houses in Guildford.

```
select owner, adrs1, price
    from houses
    where price > 120000
    order by price desc;
```

This will retrieve the **owner, adrs1** and **price** columns from the **houses** table for houses valued at more than £120,000 and display them in descending order of price.

```
select owner, adrs1, town
    from houses
    where no_bedrooms > 3
    and price < 130000;
```

This query will retrieve information on houses with more than three bedrooms but costing less than £130,000.

```
select ref_no, adrs1, town, price
    from houses
    where town = "Woking"
    or not (no_bedrooms > 3 and price < 130000);
```

This query will retrieve information on houses which are either in Woking or which have not more than three bedrooms *and* which cost more than £130,000.

```
select adrs1, town
    from houses
    where book_date > (today - 90)
    order by town;
```

Finally, this query will retrieve address information on houses which have been on the books for less than ninety days, ordered by town.

4.5.4 Simple join conditions

The theory of joins was covered in Chapter 2, but here we put the theory into practice. Consider the two tables **houses** and **bedrooms**. For each row in the **houses** table there are a number of rows in the **bedrooms** table, one row for each bedroom. What we would like to do is display the corresponding rows in the **bedrooms** table for a particular house. You may recall that both tables have a **ref_no** field and this field is used to join the tables together. Since the column name is the same in both tables we must state which table we are referring to using the construct *table.column-name*. Our query will then look like this:

```
select adrs1, town, bedroom_size, bedroom_no
    from houses, bedrooms
    where houses.ref_no = bedrooms.ref_no;
```

resulting in output of the form in Figure 4.10 below.

At this point it would be useful to introduce the idea of a *table alias*. A table alias gives us a shorthand name for a table which we can use in other parts of the query. The query above could be written using table aliases like so:

```
select adrs1, town, bedroom_size, bedroom_no
    from houses h, bedrooms b
    where h.ref_no = b.ref_no;
```

```
SQL :    New Run Modify Use-editor Output Choose Save Info Drop Exit
Run the current SQL statements.

---------------------- property ------------------------------ Press CTRL-W for Help --------

    adrs1                        town            bedroom_size    bedroom_no

    82 Ash Lodge Drive           Ash             13' x 12' 6"           1
    82 Ash Lodge Drive           Ash             12' 9" x 12'           2
    82 Ash Lodge Drive           Ash             10' x 10' 6"           3
    82 Ash Lodge Drive           Ash             10' x 10' 3"           4
    Mon Choise                   Woking          14' x 11'             1
    Mon Choise                   Woking          11' 6" x 10'          2
    Mon Choise                   Woking          8' 9" x 9'            3
            .                        .               .                  .
            .                        .               .                  .
```

Figure 4.10   The output from a join of the **houses** and **bedrooms** tables.

Table aliases are essential for *self-joins* which are covered in Chapter 5, Further SQL. The simple two-table join can be easily extended to give a multi-table join. We would like now to display an agent's name, the addresses of houses on his books, and the bedroom details of those houses:

```
select a.agent, h.adrs1, bedroom_size, bedroom_no
    from agents a, houses h, bedrooms b
    where a.agent = h.agent
    and h.ref_no = b.ref_no;
```

We can of course combine other search conditions with the join conditions:

```
select a.agent, h.adrs1, bedroom_size
    from agents a, houses h, bedrooms b
    where a.agent = h.agent
    and h.ref_no = b.ref_no
    and h.price between 100000 and 120000;
```

A report generator is required here to format the output properly. **ACE** is covered in Chapter 8.

4.6 INSERT, UPDATE and DELETE Statements

Together with the SELECT statement, these complete the DML (Data Manipulation Language) statements and are as follows:

INSERT

> Adds one or more rows to a table:

> > INSERT INTO *table-name* [(*col-list*)]
> >   {VALUES (*value-list*) | *SELECT-statement*}

> There are two main forms of the INSERT statement. The first is where you specify the VALUES keyword and a list of values to be inserted into a row, for example:

```
insert into houses (ref_no, owner, adrs1, adrs2,
                    town, county, no_bedrooms)
     values (0, "Thompson", "9, The Street", null,
          "Bagshot", "Surrey", 4);
```

> The second is where the values are to be taken from rows from another table in the database according to the SELECT statement specified, for example:

```
insert into temph
    select * from houses
       where town = "Woking";
```

> In either case you may either specify a list of column names to contain the values, the rest being set to NULL, or the list may be omitted in which case a value must be specified for every column in the row (the keyword NULL may be used as a value).

Notes

(i) The keyword NULL may be used to insert a NULL value in a particular column.

(ii) If a serial column is being inserted, a zero must be used as the value. This will be replaced with the next appropriate serial value when the row is added.

UPDATE

Modifies data in one or more rows of a table:

UPDATE *table-name* SET *col-name* = *expr* [,...]
    [WHERE *condition*]

UPDATE *table-name* {(*column-list*) | *} = (*expr-list*)
    [WHERE condition]

See Section 4.5.2 for details of the WHERE clause.

Examples

This example increases the prices of all the houses in the **houses** table by 10%. Because no WHERE clause is specified and therefore all the rows are affected, **INFORMIX-SQL** gives a warning and a second chance (unless it is executed from within a command file):

```
update houses set price = price * 1.10;
```

This example changes all the **county** columns to Surrey, if the **town** column is Guildford, and sets the **notes** column to Modified:

```
update houses (county, notes) =
                ("Surrey", "Modified")
    where town = "Guildford";
```

DELETE

Deletes one or more rows from a table:

DELETE FROM *table-name* [WHERE *condition*]

See Section 4.5.2 for details of the WHERE clause.

Examples

In this example all houses costing less than £100,000 are deleted from the **houses** table:

```
delete from houses where price < 100000;
```

In the next example all houses which have been on the books for more than three months (ninety days) are archived to an operating system file using the UNLOAD statement (covered in Section 5.9) and then deleted from the database:

```
unload to "/usr/dbarchive"
     select * from houses
        where book_date < (today - 90);
delete from houses
     where book_date < (today - 90);
```

Exercise

1. Display the **owner** and **adrs1** columns for all the houses in Woking.

2. Display the **adrs1, town** and **price** columns for all the houses with 3 bedrooms. Order the output by price.

3. Modify the previous query to order the output by price within town.

4. Display the **ref_no, adrs1, town** and **price** columns for houses with more than 3 bedrooms, but costing less than £130,000 (look back at the examples). See what happens without the brackets.

5. Display the **owner, adrs1** and **price** columns from the **houses** table, together with the **agent** and **adrs1** columns from the **agents** table for each house in Guildford. Use table aliases and sort the output in descending order of price.

6. Insert a new row into the **houses** table being the details of your own house (or the Queen's or the President's).

7. Now increase the price of this house by 10%.

8. Delete the house from the **houses** table (it's been sold!).

Chapter 5

Further SQL

5.1 Introduction

In the previous chapter, the Data Manipulation Language statements (SELECT, INSERT, UPDATE and DELETE) were covered, though not in depth. For the majority of users this is all the SQL needed, and on a first pass through the book, you can safely skip this chapter, Further SQL, which deals with these statements, and all the other SQL statements, in some depth.

Everything in Chapter 4, Introduction to SQL is included in this chapter, so this chapter alone may be used later for reference.

5.2 SQL Syntax

A word about the syntax of SQL statements. In this book, as in the **INFORMIX-SQL** manuals, when describing the syntax of statements, there are certain conventions and symbols which have particular meanings:

UPPER CASE LETTERS	these denote keywords, which must be entered as shown, though you may use lower case.
italics	denote variables, for which you must substitute identifiers or expressions (e.g. *column-name*).
|	you may choose one of the options either side of the | symbol (e.g. DISTINCT | UNIQUE).
[ ]	the clause, sub-clause or word enclosed in the square brackets is optional (e.g. *column-name* IS [NOT] NULL).
{ }	you *must* choose one of the options between the curly brackets (e.g. LOCK TABLE *table-name* IN {SHARE | EXCLUSIVE} MODE).

( )   parentheses where present are entered as part of the command, as in AVG(*column-name*).

. . .   the ellipsis denotes optional repetition of the previous clause, as in *column-name* [ASC | DESC][, . . .].

For instance:

INSERT INTO *table-name* [(*column-list*)]
{VALUES (*value-list*) | *SELECT-statement*}

The first part of the statement may be broken down as follows:

INSERT INTO   are keywords.

table-name   is the name of a table which you must supply.

[(*column-list*)]   is an optional (note the square brackets) list of column names which you may supply. The items in a *list* are separated by commas. In this case, if present the list must be enclosed in parentheses ( ).

You must then supply either:

VALUES (*value-list*)   the keyword VALUES plus a list of values

or:

SELECT-statement   a SELECT statement.

The following is a valid INSERT statement:

```
insert into houses (ref_no, lname, adrs1, price)
      values (0, "Smith", "12, The Street", 115000);
```

5.3 SQL Statement Summary

There are five different kinds of statement in SQL: Data Manipulation Language (or DML) statements, Data Definition Language (or DDL) statements, Data Access Control statements, Data Integrity statements and Auxiliary statements. In Figure 5.1 the statements are presented in their appropriate classifications.

5.3.1 Comments

Comments may be inserted anywhere within an SQL statement either by preceding the comment with a hash (#), (or in Version 4.0 with a double dash (−−)), or by enclosing the comment in curly brackets { }.

DML	SELECT, INSERT, UPDATE, DELETE
DDL	CREATE, ALTER, DROP, RENAME
Access	GRANT, REVOKE, LOCK, UNLOCK, SET LOCK MODE
Integrity	BEGIN WORK, COMMIT WORK, ROLLBACK WORK, ROLLFORWARD DATABASE, START DATABASE, CLOSE DATABASE, DATABASE, CHECK TABLE, RECOVER TABLE, REPAIR TABLE, CREATE AUDIT, DROP AUDIT
Auxiliary	INFO, LOAD, UNLOAD, OUTPUT TO, UPDATE STATISTICS

Figure 5.1 The Informix SQL statement set.

5.4 The SELECT Statement

SQL stands for Structured Query Language. Is it not strange then that in Informix SQL, in common with other implementations of SQL, out of forty SQL statements, only one statement allows you to query a database! That statement is the SELECT statement and will be used, in one form or another in nine out of ten of your SQL statements. I intend to cover it in detail before mentioning any other statement.

Let us begin by setting out the full syntax of the SELECT statement, with all its options:

```
SELECT [DISTINCT | UNIQUE] select-list
    FROM {table-name [table-alias]
        | OUTER table-name [table-alias]} [,...]
    [WHERE condition]
    [GROUP BY column-list] [HAVING condition]
    [ORDER BY column-list [ASC | DESC]] [,...]
    [INTO TEMP table-name]
```

We can continue by considering the simplest form of the SELECT statement:

SELECT *select-list* FROM *table-list*

where:

select-list   is a list of column names, expressions or aggregates (expressions and aggregates will be covered in the following sections). To select all the columns from a table use an asterisk (*).

table-list   is a list of one or more table names.

For example:

```
select * from houses;
```

This statement will retrieve all the columns from the **houses** table and display their values for each row in the **houses** table. In the figure below, the shaded area represents what has been selected.

Columns

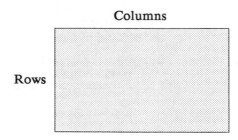

Rows

Figure 5.2   An * selects all the columns from a table.

The next case is when we want to select only certain columns from every row in the table:

```
select owner, adrs1, town
    from houses;
```

The shaded area in Figure 5.3 illustrates what has been selected:

Columns

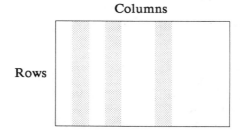

Rows

Figure 5.3   Specific columns may be selected.

The DISTINCT keyword

Consider this statement:

```
select town, county
    from houses;
```

We would like to display all the different towns and their counties in the database, but this is what we get:

```
town         county

Guildford    Surrey
Guildford    Surrey
Guildford    Surrey
Woking       Surrey
Haslemere    Surrey
Woking       Surrey
   .            .
   .            .
   .            .
```

Because town and county do not uniquely specify a row in the **houses** table, duplicates are returned. Note that the output from a SELECT statement should be a table itself; but a relational table cannot contain duplicate rows. This represents a flaw in the SQL language but it can be rectified by use of the DISTINCT or UNIQUE keyword (the choice is yours):

```
select distinct town, county
    from houses;
```

This produces the required output, without duplicates:

```
town         county

Guildford    Surrey
Woking       Surrey
Haslemere    Surrey
   .            .
   .            .
   .            .
```

Note

Unfortunately, the query processor is not quite intelligent enough to know when you want duplicates and when you do not. For instance when using the aggregate function AVG to get the average value of a column you would clearly get different results from these two queries:

```
select avg(price)
    from houses;
```

and

```
select avg(distinct price)
    from houses;
```

5.4.1 The ORDER BY clause

The output from your SELECT statement may be sorted by using the ORDER BY clause. You may sort on up to eight columns, but the total length of all the ORDER BY columns added together may not   exceed 120 bytes (sixteen columns and 255 bytes if you are using **INFORMIX-OnLine** instead of the Standard Engine). You may also reverse the order of the sort by specifying the keyword DESC, for descending (the default being ASC for ascending). The syntax of the ORDER BY clause is as follows:

ORDER BY *column-name* [ASC | DESC][,...]

For example:

```
select owner, adrs1, town
    from houses
    order by owner;
```

This will sort the output of the query according to the **owner** column. The following query will sort the output in **town** order within **county**:

```
select adrs1, town, county
    from houses
    order by county, town;
```

producing the following output:

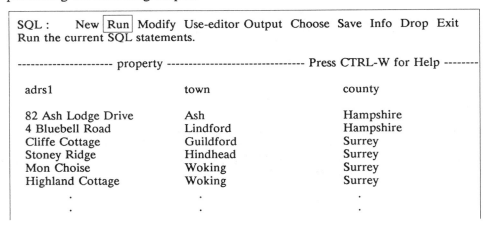

SQL :   New Run Modify Use-editor Output Choose Save Info Drop Exit
Run the current SQL statements.

--------------------- property ----------------------------- Press CTRL-W for Help --------

adrs1	town	county
82 Ash Lodge Drive	Ash	Hampshire
4 Bluebell Road	Lindford	Hampshire
Cliffe Cottage	Guildford	Surrey
Stoney Ridge	Hindhead	Surrey
Mon Choise	Woking	Surrey
Highland Cottage	Woking	Surrey
.	.	.
.	.	.

Figure 5.4 The result of an ORDER BY clause.

Notes

(i)   You may only ORDER BY columns which are named in the *select-list*. Note that using the asterisk (*) as the *select-list* implicitly names *all* the columns, so you can ORDER BY any of them.

(ii)   The ORDER BY clause must be the last clause in a SELECT statement (unless there is an INTO TEMP clause, in which case you may not use an ORDER BY clause).

(iii)   If you have an *expression* (see Section 5.4.2, The WHERE clause) in your *select-list* you may ORDER BY the expression by using an integer to refer to the position of the expression in the *select-list*. For example:

```
select adrs1, price * 1.15, town
    from houses
    order by 2;
```

5.4.2 The WHERE clause

The most important optional clause of the SELECT statement is the WHERE clause. This clause allows you to set conditions defining which rows are retrieved from the database. For example:

```
select * from houses
    where town = "Woking";
```

This will retrieve all the information in the database on houses in Woking. The action of the WHERE clause can be expressed diagrammatically as:

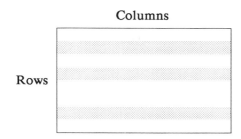

Figure 5.5   The WHERE clause defines which rows are retrieved.

The syntax of the WHERE clause is very simple:

WHERE *condition*

However, *condition* can be very complex, being a collection of one or more *search conditions* which may be connected by AND or OR. The operator NOT may also be used to negate any particular condition. The following query will select those 4-bedroomed houses which are not in Woking:

```
select owner, adrs1, price
   from houses
   where no_bedrooms = 4
   and not town = "Woking";
```

A search condition can be either a comparison, a join condition, or a subquery. We will examine each of these in turn.

5.4.3 Comparisons and expressions

The simplest form of the comparison condition is:

expr rel-op expr

where:

expr   is an *expression*. An expression is a column name or a constant (including the system constants TODAY and USER) or any combination of these (with certain restrictions) connected by one of the arithmetic operators:

> +   addition
> −   subtraction
> *   multiplication
> /   division

An expression may also include an aggregate or group function (though not in combination with a column name) or a date function.

The following are all valid expressions:

```
town
"Woking"
price * 1.15
150000
price / no_bedrooms
2 * ((price + 1000) / no_bedrooms)
town[1,3]
today - 9
max(price)
avg(price) / 2
weekday(book_date)
```

These are invalid, because they attempt to mix different data types:

```
town + 10
price / county
"Woking" / no_bedrooms
avg(price) / no_bedrooms    {aggregate/column!!}
```

rel-op   is short for *relational operator*. This has nothing to do with relational database theory, but is just one of the following:

=	equal
!= or <>	not equal
>	greater than
>=	greater than or equal
<	less than
<=	less than or equal

Examples

Let us now consider some examples of simple search conditions:

```
select ref_no, adrs1
    from houses
    where town = "Guildford";
```

This will retrieve the **ref_no** and **adrs1** columns from the **houses** table for houses in Guildford.

```
select owner, adrs1, price
    from houses
    where price > 120000
    order by price desc;
```

This will retrieve the **owner, adrs1** and **price** columns from the **houses** table for houses valued at more than £120,000 and display them in descending order of price.

```
select owner, adrs1, town
    from houses
    where no_bedrooms > 3
    and price < 130000;
```

This query will retrieve information on houses with more than three bedrooms but costing less than £130,000.

```
select ref_no, adrs1, town, price
    from houses
    where town = "Woking"
    or not (no_bedrooms > 3 and price < 130000);
```

This query will retrieve information on houses which are either in Woking or which have not more than three bedrooms *and* which cost more than £130,000.

```
select adrs1, town
   from houses
   where book_date > (today - 90)
   order by town;
```

Finally, this query will retrieve address information on houses which have been on the books for less than ninety days, ordered by town.

Notes

(i)   Subscripts may be used with CHAR columns to extract a portion of the column, in the form *column-name*[*m,n*], to extract the *m* th through to the *n* th character of the column (*m* and *n* may be equal). For example:

```
select adrs1[1,10]
   from houses;
```

will display the first ten characters of the **adrs1** column.

(ii)   The system constant USER returns your login name on UNIX systems and your login or machine name on DOS systems.

(iii)   The system constant TODAY returns the current system date.

New for Version 4.0

(iv)   The short version of the CURRENT function (i.e. without any qualifiers) returns your system's current date *and time* in the same form as the DATETIME data type, i.e.

       yyyy-mm-dd hh:mm:ss.ffff

(v)   A new function in Version 4.0, LENGTH(*string*) returns the number of bytes (after clipping trailing blanks) in *string* which can be a character constant, a CHAR column, or in OnLine, a VARCHAR, TEXT or BYTE column. For example:

```
select length(adrs1) + length("Address") adr_len
   from houses;
```

Date and datetime functions
The following date functions (and in Version 4.0, datetime functions) may be used in expressions (in either a *select-list* or a WHERE clause condition), allowing you to convert from a DATE (or DATETIME) data type to various other types, and back again. The start of time for **INFORMIX-SQL** is 31st December, 1899 and all dates are stored as a number of days relative to this

date. If necessary this can be a negative number. Dates are formatted on output and validated on input according to the **DBDATE** environment variable (see Chapter 1, Section 1.4).

New for Version 4.0

CURRENT [*first* TO *last*]

The CURRENT function returns a DATETIME value with the system's current date and time. The qualifiers *first* and *last* determine the precision of the returned value and are taken from the following list (*first* obviously being greater then *last*): YEAR, MONTH, DAY, HOUR, MINUTE, SECOND and FRACTION. For example:

```
current hour to minute
```

would return the current time, in hours and minutes, whereas

```
current year to day - 1 units year
```

would return today's date (year, month and day) for the previous year (the UNITS keyword is covered shortly).

Note

The CURRENT function may be executed at any time during the execution of the statement. You should not, therefore, use it to mark the start, end or any particular time crucial point in the statement.

DATE(*expr*)

This function converts the given expression into a DATE type value. The expression may be a string or a number. For example:

```
date(32585)
```

returns "19/03/89", being the 32,585th day after 31/12/1899. On the other hand,

```
date("26/8/89")
```

returns "26/08/89" which you could have typed without using the date function!

```
date(-1000)
```

returns the date of 1000 days before 31/12/1899. The following query uses the **sysusers** table, to which everyone has access, as a 'dummy' table:

```
select distinct (today - date(0)) day_num
    from sysusers;
```

It displays the number of days since 31/12/1899 using the display label day_num (display labels are covered shortly).

New for Version 4.0

DATETIME(*datetime-expr*) *first* TO *last*

DATETIME, as well as being a data type, may also be used as a function to convert a string into a DATETIME value, either for inserting, or to participate in a DATETIME expression. For instance:

```
current - (datetime(55-5-19) year to day)
```

would return how old I am today, as an INTERVAL value, where my birthday is May 19, 1955. The *first* and *last* qualifiers are covered under the CURRENT function, but see the manual Appendix for more details.

DAY(*date-expr*)

This function returns the day of the month from the given expression, which must be of type DATE (or DATETIME). For example:

```
select adrs1, town
    from houses
    where day(book_date) < 16;
```

This query retrieves houses which were placed on the books in the first half of the month.

```
day(today)
```

returns today's day of the month.

New for Version 4.0

EXTEND(*value*[,*first* TO *last*])

This function adjusts the precision of a DATETIME value. (The *first* and *last* qualifiers are covered under the CURRENT function, but see the manual Appendix for more details.) Any fields not specified and more significant than *value* are filled with values from the CURRENT function. Less significant fields are filled with a 1, for a MONTH or DAY field, and a 0 for the fields HOUR to FRACTION. For example:

```
insert into mytable(name, tax_start)
   values ("mybusiness",
             extend(datetime(4-5)month to day,
                 year to minute));
```

This example inserts a DATETIME value into **mytable** consisting of April 5, extended to include the current year (taken from the CURRENT function) and hour and minute (set to 0s).

New for Version 4.0

INTERVAL(*datetime-expr*) *first* TO *last*

INTERVAL, as well as being a data type, may also be used as a function to convert a string into an INTERVAL value, either for inserting, or to participate in a DATETIME expression. (The *first* and *last* qualifiers are covered under the CURRENT function, but see the manual Appendix for more details.) For instance:

```
update time_record set work_week =
   (interval("37:30") hour to minute);
```

This example sets the **work_week** column to thirty seven and a half hours.

MDY(*expr1,expr2,expr3*)

The MDY function returns a DATE type value when called with three expressions which evaluate to integers representing the month, day and year. It is commonly used to convert back values which have been stored using the DAY, MONTH and YEAR functions. For example:

```
select tab1.* from tab1, tab2
   where tab1.date_col
          = mdy(tab2.mcol, tab2.dcol, 1990);
```

MONTH(*date-expr*)

The MONTH function returns the number of the month from the given expression, which must be of type DATE (or DATETIME). For example:

```
select adrs1, town, month(book_date) _month
   from houses;
```

displays the address of each house in the database and the month it was placed on the books, using the display label _month. Display labels are covered in more detail shortly (note the use of the underline in the display label, since **month** is a reserved word).

New for Version 4.0

UNITS

This keyword gives you a shorthand way of specifying single-field INTERVAL values for use in datetime arithmetic. Its syntax is:

number UNITS *field-name*

For example:

```
datetime(1955-5-19) year to day + 65 units year
```

gives my retirement date!

WEEKDAY(*date-expr*)

The WEEKDAY function returns an integer in the range 0-6 representing the day of the week of the given DATE (or DATETIME) type expression, where 0 represents Sunday, 1 represents Monday, etc. For example:

```
select adrs1, town, price
    from houses
    where weekday(book_date) = 0;
```

displays information on houses placed on the books on a Sunday.

YEAR(*date-expr*)

The YEAR function returns an integer corresponding to the year of the given DATE (or DATETIME) type expression. For example:

```
select owner, adrs1, town, book_date
    from houses
    where year(book_date) in (1989, 1990);
```

retrieves houses placed on the books in 1989 or 1990.

Display labels
Expressions may also be used in the SELECT clause itself, for instance:

```
select adrs1, price * 1.15, book_date
    from houses;
```

would give us a list of houses and their prices plus 15%. However the display would read as in Figure 5.6 below, with the column heading (expression).

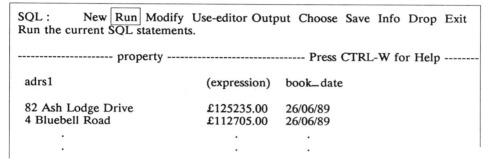

Figure 5.6   An expression in a SELECT statement.

We can improve the display by using a *display label*:

```
select adrs1, price * 1.15 price_plus_15, book_date
    from houses;
```

which displays as:

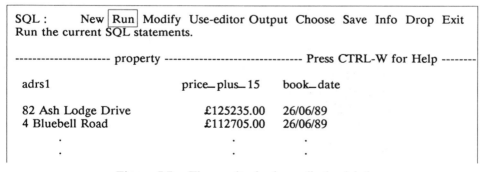

Figure 5.7   The result of using a display label.

Display labels are also useful when displaying two columns of the same name from different tables (note that this query uses a *join* which is covered in the next section):

```
select houses.adrs1 h_adrs1, agents.adrs1 a_adrs1
   from houses, agents
   where houses.agent = agents.company;
```

Ranges, value lists, nulls

The comparison condition can be extended to include a range search:

    expr [NOT] BETWEEN *expr* AND *expr*

a value list search:

    expr [NOT] IN (*value-list*)

and a specific search for a NULL value:

    column-name IS [NOT] NULL

This last comparison is the only way to specifically search for a NULL (note the mandatory keyword IS). In all these conditions the NOT keyword is optional.

Consider some examples of the above:

```
select adrs1, town, county, price
   from houses
   where price * 1.15 between 100000 and 150000;
```

This query will retrieve information on houses whose price plus 15% is between £100,000 and £150,000.

```
select owner, adrs1, town
   from houses
   where book_date
            not between "1/1/90" and "30/6/90";
```

This query will retrieve information on houses whose **book_date** column is outside the range January-June 1990.

```
select price, adrs1, town, no_bedrooms
   from houses
   where town in ("Guildford", "Woking")
   order by town, price;
```

This query selects information on houses in both Guildford and Woking, ordering the display by price within town.

```
select adrs1, agent, book_date
   from houses
   where price is null;
```

This last query retrieves houses where the **price** column is NULL. NULLs are covered in detail in Chapter 3, Section 3.6.

String matching
No set of comparison conditions would be complete without some form of string matching comparison, and **INFORMIX-SQL** boasts two!

 column-name [NOT] LIKE "*string*"

 column-name [NOT] MATCHES "*string*"

Why two? Well LIKE is part of the SQL standard whereas MATCHES comes from the pre-SQL version of **INFORMIX**. With LIKE, you may use the following wildcard characters as part of your search string:

 % matches zero or more characters

 _ matches any one character.

For example:

```
select owner, adrs1, town, price
    from houses
    where owner like "A%";
```

will select all those rows whose **owner** column begins with A.

MATCHES, on the other hand, has a number of wildcard characters:

 * matches zero or more characters (as % in LIKE)

 ? matches any one character (as _ in LIKE)

 [...] matches any one of the enclosed characters. For instance "[abc]def" matches either **a, b** or **c** followed by **def** (note that the square brackets are mandatory).

 [a-z] matches any character in the range specified (in this case lower case characters). Note that the square brackets are mandatory.

 [^...] matches any character *not* in the brackets. For instance [^abc] matches any character other than **a, b** or **c** (note that the square brackets are mandatory).

 \ nullifies any special significance of the next character, as in:

```
where expression matches "(x+y)\*2z"
```

New for Version 4.0

column-name [NOT] LIKE "*string*" [ESCAPE "*escape-character*"]

column-name [NOT] MATCHES "*string*"
                    [ESCAPE "*escape-character*"]

In Version 4.0 you may specify an escape character to nullify the significance of a special character, such as % or *. For instance:

```
select student_id, score from scores
    where mark like "8_\%" escape "\";
```

Here the backslash character has been used to escape the significance of the % character, returning the student id's of students with exam marks between 80% and 89%.

The range of comparisons using MATCHES is much richer than that of LIKE due to its UNIX heritage. Let us look at some examples:

```
select owner, adrs1, town
    from houses
    where owner matches "A*";
```

retrieves all rows with an **owner** column starting with A.

```
select owner, adrs1, town
    from houses
    where owner matches "[A-M]*";
```

retrieves all rows whose **owner** column starts with any letter in the range A-M.

```
select owner, adrs1, town
    from houses
    where owner matches "[XYZ]*";
```

retrieves all rows whose **owner** column starts with either X, Y or Z.

Lastly, you can combine any of the above search conditions using the logical operators AND, OR and NOT. For example:

```
select adrs1, town, county, price
    from houses
    where price between 100000 and 130000
    and town = "Woking";
```

retrieves houses in Woking whose price is between £100,000 and £130,000. When combining more than two search conditions, it may be necessary to use parentheses to ensure that the query does exactly what you want it to. For instance:

```
select adrs1, town, agent
   from houses
   where no_bedrooms = 4
   and not (town = "Woking" or town = "Guildford");
```

will retrieve all houses with 4 bedrooms which are not in either Woking or Guildford. However this statement:

```
select adrs1, town, agent
   from houses
   where no_bedrooms = 4
   and not town = "Woking"
   or town = "Guildford";
```

would retrieve all houses with 4 bedrooms and not in Woking, *plus* all houses in Guildford, regardless of the number of bedrooms. The only difference between the two is the use of parentheses.

Exercise

1. Retrieve the **owner, adrs1, town** and **price** columns for all the houses having three bedrooms and costing less than £120,000, ordered by price within town.

2. Display the addresses and agents' names of houses placed on the books on a Sunday.

3. Display the addresses, towns and prices less 10% of houses costing less than £115,000 after the reduction is applied (i.e. use the expression in the WHERE clause as well). Use a display label for the new price column.

4. Display all the towns having 4-bedroomed houses. Be sure to remove duplicates.

5. Display information on houses in Guildford and Woking placed on the books in the first four months of the year.

6. Display the addresses and booking dates of houses whose price is null.

7. Retrieve the **owner, adrs1, town** and **price** columns of houses whose owner's name starts with a letter in the range A-M and the houses are in Woking or Guildford, or the price is between £100,000 and £140,000.

5.4.4 Join conditions

The theory of joins was covered in Chapter 2, but here we put the theory into practice. Consider the two tables **houses** and **bedrooms**. For each row in the **houses** table there are a number of rows in the **bedrooms** table, one row for each bedroom. What we would like to do is display the corresponding rows in the **bedrooms** table for a particular house. You may recall that both tables have a **ref_no** field and this field is used to join the tables together. Since the column name is the same in both tables we must state which table we are referring to using the construct *table.column-name*. Our query will then look like this:

```
select adrs1, town, bedroom_size, bedroom_no
    from houses, bedrooms
    where houses.ref_no = bedrooms.ref_no;
```

resulting in output of the form in Figure 5.8 below.

SQL :   New [Run] Modify Use-editor Output Choose Save Info Drop Exit
Run the current SQL statements.

---------------------- property ----------------------------- Press CTRL-W for Help --------

adrs1	town	bedroom_size	bedroom_no
82 Ash Lodge Drive	Ash	13' x 12' 6"	1
82 Ash Lodge Drive	Ash	12' 9" x 12'	2
82 Ash Lodge Drive	Ash	10' x 10' 6"	3
82 Ash Lodge Drive	Ash	10' x 10' 3"	4
Mon Choise	Woking	14' x 11'	1
Mon Choise	Woking	11' 6" x 10'	2
Mon Choise	Woking	8' 9" x 9'	3
.	.	.	.
.	.	.	.

Figure 5.8 The output from a join of the **houses** and **bedrooms** tables.

At this point it would be useful to introduce the idea of a *table alias*. A table alias is to a table what a display label is to a column. It gives us a shorthand name for a table which we can use in other parts of the query. The query above could be written using table aliases like so:

```
select adrs1, town, bedroom_size, bedroom_no
    from houses h, bedrooms b
    where h.ref_no = b.ref_no;
```

Table aliases are essential for *self-joins* which will be covered shortly. The simple two-table join can be easily extended to give a multi-table join. We would like now to display an agent's name, the addresses of houses on his books, and the bedroom details of those houses:

```
select a.agent, h.adrsl, bedroom_size, bedroom_no
   from agents a, houses h, bedrooms b
   where a.agent = h.agent
   and h.ref_no = b.ref_no;
```

We can of course combine other search conditions with the join conditions:

```
select a.agent, h.adrsl, bedroom_size
   from agents a, houses h, bedrooms b
   where a.agent = h.agent
   and h.ref_no = b.ref_no
   and h.price between 100000 and 120000;
```

A report generator is required here to format the output properly. **ACE** is covered in Chapter 8.

Self-joins
Consider the following. It is possible that an agent who is selling one house is also the owner of another. What we would like to do is take a copy of the **houses** table and join the **houses** table to this copy of itself, using the agent and owner columns as join fields. We can achieve this by using table aliases, as in the following example, which tells us which house owners are also agents:

```
select h1.owner, h1.adrsl
   from houses h1, houses h2
   where h1.owner = h2.agent;
```


Outer joins
In our property database, we may wish to list all the agents' names and the houses they have on their books. However, if an agent has no houses currently, then his name will not be listed, since the join condition

```
where agents.agent = houses.agent
```

is never met. We can force all agent names to be listed by use of an *outer join*, in which *all* the values from the *select-list* of *table1* are returned, even if there are no matching values in *table2*:

```
SELECT select-list
   FROM table1 OUTER table2
```

Where the join condition is not met, the columns from *table2* are set to null values for the purposes of this query. For example:

```
select a.agent, h.adrsl
   from agents a, outer houses h
   where a.agent = h.agent;
```

5.4.5 Subqueries

Consider the following question. What is the address of the most expensive house in the database? This is really two queries in one: what is the price of the most expensive house, and what is the address of the house with this price? We can use an *aggregate* (covered in Section 5.4.6) to find the highest price: max(price). Query 1 is then:

```
select max(price)
    from houses;
```

and query 2 is:

```
select adrs1, town
    from houses
    where price = (result of query 1);
```

The query can be written as one statement, where the query inside the parentheses is known as a *subquery*:

```
select adrs1, town
    from houses
    where price =
        (select max(price)
            from houses);
```

The subquery above returned a single value, but some subqueries return more than one value. You must specify how the returned values are to be used in the WHERE clause by use of the keywords ANY or ALL, and a comparison operator (such as =, >, etc.). The following query finds all the houses whose price is greater than *any* houses (i.e. the *lowest* price) in Woking:

```
select adrs1, town, price
    from houses
    where price > any
        (select price
            from houses
            where town = "Woking");
```

If you use ALL instead of ANY, the query will select rows in which **price** is greater than *all* the values returned by the subquery. In other words it will select houses with prices greater than the *highest* price in Woking:

```
select adrs1, town, price
    from houses
    where price > all
        (select price
            from houses
            where town = "Woking");
```

You may also use the keyword IN (or NOT IN) to select rows having values among (or not among) those returned by the subquery. The following query selects houses in Woking with the same owner's name as houses in Guildford:

```
select owner, adrs1, town
    from houses
    where town = "Woking"
    and owner in
            (select owner
                from houses
                where town = "Guildford";
```

Subquery conditions may be summarised as follows:

WHERE *expr rel-op* {ALL | ANY} (*SELECT-statement*)

WHERE *expr* [NOT] IN (*SELECT-statement*)

A final form of the subquery condition is:

WHERE [NOT] EXISTS (*SELECT-statement*)

in this case the main query is only executed when the subquery is true (or false if NOT is used). A particularly good use of this may be found at the end of the following section on correlated subqueries.

Correlated subqueries
A correlated subquery is one in which each execution of the subquery is correlated with the value of a field in the main query's currently selected row. For example, to find all the houses which are more expensive than the average price in their town, you need two queries. The main query selects houses from the **houses** table whose price is greater than the average for their town:

```
select adrs1, town, price
    from houses
    where price > (average price for this town);
```

and the subquery calculates the average house price for each house's town:

```
select avg(price)
    from houses
    where town = (town value from main query's
                        current row);
```

The complete solution requires a table alias and involves a sort of self-join to connect the **town** fields from the main query and the subquery:

```
select adrs1, town, price
    from houses x
    where price >
            (select avg(price)
                from houses h
                where x.town = h.town);
```

The following example displays the names and addresses of agents who do not have any houses on their books:

```
select a.agent, a.adrs1
    from agents a
    where not exists
            (select h.agent
                from houses h
                where a.agent = h.agent);
```

Exercise

1. Display the company name and first address column of all the agents, with the addresses and prices of houses on their books, joining **agents.agent** to **houses.agent**. Order the output by price within agent name.

2. Using an outer join, modify your query to also display agents who currently have no houses on their books.

3. Using a self-join, check if any agents are also owners of other houses.

4. Find the address and price of the cheapest house in the database using a subquery.

5. Using a correlated subquery, display the names and addresses of agents who have no houses on their books.

5.4.6 Aggregate or group functions

The type of SELECT statements we have seen so far returned a value for each row selected. But there are certain functions which allow you to obtain summary information about *groups* of rows in the database. For example, we may want to know:

- The average price of houses in the database

- The average price for each town

- The price of the most expensive house in the database

- How many houses there are in the database

The following aggregate functions are available in **INFORMIX-SQL**:

COUNT(*)

> The COUNT(*) function returns the number of rows which satisfy the WHERE clause, including NULL values. For example, to count the number of houses in the database with three bedrooms:

```
select count(*)
  from houses
  where no_bedrooms = 3;
```

COUNT(DISTINCT *col-name*)

> This function returns the number of unique values in column *col-name* from rows that satisfy the WHERE clause, excluding NULL values. If the column contains only NULLs, then zero is returned. For example, to count the number of different agents there are, without referring to the **agents** table, we could write:

```
select count(distinct agent)
  from houses;
```

SUM([DISTINCT] *expr*)

> The SUM function returns the sum of all the values in *expr* from rows that satisfy the WHERE clause, excluding NULL values. Use of the keyword DISTINCT allows you to sum just the unique values in the column. Obviously the column has to be a numeric column. For example, to find the total number of bedrooms in the database, we could write:

```
select sum(no_bedrooms)
  from houses;
```

AVG([DISTINCT] *expr*)

AVG returns the average of all the values in *expr* from rows that satisfy the WHERE clause, excluding NULL values. Use of the keyword DISTINCT allows you to take an average of just the unique values in the column or expression. To find the average price per bedroom of houses in Woking, we could write:

```
select avg(price/no_bedrooms)
   from houses
   where town = "Woking";
```

MAX(*expr*)

The MAX function returns the highest value in *expr* from rows that satisfy the WHERE clause, excluding NULL values. For example, to find the price of the most expensive house in the database, using a display label:

```
select max(price) max_price
   from houses;
```

MIN(*expr*)

The MIN function returns the lowest value in *expr* from rows that satisfy the WHERE clause, excluding NULL values. To find the price of the cheapest house in Guildford we could write:

```
select min(price)
   from houses
   where town = "Guildford";
```

Notes

(i)   *expr* may not contain another aggregate function.

(ii)   The DISTINCT keyword may only be used with columns, not with expressions.

(iii)   The DISTINCT keyword may only be used once within a *select-list*, either inside or outside an aggregate function, but not both.

(iv)   You may not mix aggregate functions and non-aggregate expressions in a *select-list* without using the GROUP BY clause (see Section 5.4.7). However you may have more than one aggregate, e.g.

```
select max(price), min(price)
   from houses;
```

(v)   NULL values are handled as follows:

Function	Rows containing NULL values are	Result if all NULL values
COUNT(*)	counted	number of rows
COUNT (DISTINCT *col*)	ignored	0
SUM(*expr*)	ignored	NULL
AVG(*expr*)	ignored	NULL
MAX(*expr*)	ignored	NULL
MIN(*expr*)	ignored	NULL

5.4.7 The GROUP BY clause

Within the same SELECT statement you may not mix aggregate functions (which return a value for a number of rows) with column names or other items that return a value for each row, unless you use either a subquery (see Section 5.4.5) or a GROUP BY clause. The following is therefore invalid:

```
select town, avg(price)
    from houses;
```

The GROUP BY clause divides a table into groups of rows so that the rows in each group have the same value in a specified column. A group function may then be applied to the rows in each group, e.g.

```
select town, avg(price)
    from houses
    group by town;
```

The following figure should help to explain:

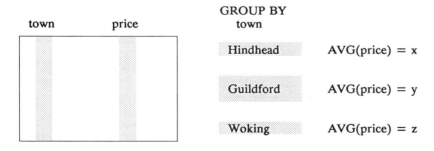

Figure 5.9   The steps involved in selecting an
AVG(price), grouping by town.

First the rows are grouped according to the column named in the GROUP BY clause, then the group function (AVG) is applied to the different groups in turn, with this result:

```
town                    (avg)

Ash                     #108900.00
Lindford                #100002.50
Hindhead                #108900.00
Guildford               #117916.67
Woking                  #127378.20
New Malden              #100000.00
```

If a WHERE clause is present it must come before the GROUP BY clause. Any ORDER BY clause must still be the last clause in the statement. This query lists the average price of 3-bedroomed houses, grouped by town (note the display label **avg_price**):

```
select town, avg(price) avg_price
    from houses
    where no_bedrooms = 3
    group by town
    order by town;
```

You may group by more than one column, as in:

```
select town, no_bedrooms, avg(price) avg_price
    from houses
    group by town, no_bedrooms
    order by town, no_bedrooms;
```

giving this result:

```
town            no_bedrooms         avg_price

Ash                  4              #108900.00
Guildford            3              #123750.00
Guildford            4              #115000.00
Hindhead             5              #108900.00
Lindford             4              #100002.50
New Malden           3              #100000.00
Woking               3              #114791.00
Woking               4              #130525.00
```

and you may use more than one aggregate function, as in:

```
select town, min(price), max(price)
    from houses
    group by town;
```

Notes

(i)   If you need to GROUP BY an expression which appears in the *select-list*, you may use an integer representing that expression's position in the *select-list*, as in:

```
select town, no_bedrooms/no_baths, avg(price)
   from houses
   group by town, 2
   order by 1, 2;
```

(ii) If an ORDER BY clause is present, it must be the last clause in the statement.

5.4.8 The HAVING clause

Just as the WHERE clause imposes conditions as to which individual rows are selected, the HAVING clause imposes conditions as to which *groups* are selected:

HAVING *condition*

For instance, the following query will only select those groups (towns) where the total value of houses in the town is greater than £250,000. It will display the average price and number of houses in each selected town:

```
select town, avg(price) avg_price,
                  count(*) no_houses
   from houses
   group by town
   having sum(price) > 250000
   order by 2;
```

Notes

(i) Since the HAVING clause is for selecting groups, the *condition* must be based on a group or aggregate function.

(ii) To select groups based on comparisons with other groups, you may include a subquery in the HAVING clause. The following query selects groups (towns) whose average house price is less than that of houses in Guildford:

```
select town, avg(price) avg_price
   from houses
   group by town
   having avg(price) <
               (select avg(price)
                  from houses
                  where town = "Guildford")
   order by 2;
```

5.4.9 The INTO TEMP clause

It is sometimes useful to be able to save the results of a query in a temporary table, allowing the results to be easily reviewed or to be the subject of new queries. This may be achieved through the use of the INTO TEMP clause:

INTO TEMP *table-name* [WITH NO LOG]

The temporary table created disappears automatically when you exit **INFORMIX-SQL** (alternatively you may drop it using the DROP TABLE statement; see Section 5.6.2). The column names of the temporary table will be those named in the original *select-list*, unless you specify a display label, in which case this is used instead. A display label is mandatory for an expression, date or aggregate function. For example:

```
select town, avg(price) avg_price
    from houses
    group by town
    into temp temp1;
```

Selecting all values from the temporary table **temp1** then gives us this output:

town	avg_price
Ash	#108900.00
Lindford	#100002.50
Hindhead	#108900.00
Guildford	#117916.67
Woking	#127378.20
New Malden	#100000.00

Notes

(i)   You may not use an ORDER BY clause if you are using an INTO TEMP clause. You are creating a new relational table, and by definition the order of the rows is not significant.

(ii)   Though by definition, a relational table does not contain duplicate rows, a table created with the INTO TEMP clause may do. It may be necessary therefore to use the DISTINCT keyword when creating the temporary table. Individual rows in *any* table are distinguished by the hidden column **rowid**, which is always present but must be explicitly specified in a SELECT statement.

(iii)   You may use the optional WITH NO LOG clause to suppress all transaction logging for the temporary table.

5.4.10 The UNION operator

Consider the situation where we have two tables of the same format and we need to combine the data from one table with the data from the other to form a third table, or possibly just to display the results. The UNION operator allows us to do this by combining two or more SELECT statements into a single query.

> *SELECT-statement* UNION [ALL] *SELECT-statement*
> [UNION [ALL] *SELECT-statement* . . .]

Example

```
select adrs1, town, county, price
   from houses1

union

select adrs1, town, county, price
   from houses2
   into temp shorthouses;
```

Notes

(i)   The keyword ALL may be used to leave duplicates.

(ii) The number of items in the *select-list* of each query must be the same, and corresponding items in each query must have identical data types.

(iii) You may use an ORDER BY clause in the last SELECT statement but it must refer to an item by integer, not by identifier.

(iv) UNION operators may not occur inside a subquery and may not be used in the definition of a view.

(v)   The column names of the resulting table are the same as those from the first SELECT statement, which may be display labels.

5.4.11 Summary of the SELECT statement

We are now in a position to review the full syntax of the SELECT statement:

```
SELECT [DISTINCT] select-list
   FROM {table-name [table-alias]
        | OUTER {table-name [table-alias]} [,...]
   [WHERE condition]
   [GROUP BY column-list]
   [HAVING condition]
   [ORDER BY column-name [ASC | DESC][,...]
   [INTO TEMP table-name [WITH NO LOG]]
```

The operation of the various clauses can best be summarised by considering their effects in the *logical* order in which they are applied (the query optimizer may well have other ideas!):

1.   The tables referred to in the FROM clause are reduced by the elimination of all rows not satisfying the *condition* specified in the WHERE clause.

2.   A Cartesian product is formed from the reduced tables resulting from Step 1. In other words, every row from one table is joined to every row from the other tables. (To see the effect of this, do a query including a join, but leave out the WHERE clause, i.e. the join condition.)

3.   The result of Step 2 is grouped by the values of the columns specified in the GROUP BY clause.

4.   The result of Step 3 is reduced by the elimination of all groups that do not satisfy the *condition* specified in the HAVING clause.

5.   The result of Step 4 is reduced by the elimination of duplicate rows if the DISTINCT keyword is specified in the SELECT clause.

6.   The result of Step 5 is sorted according to the column names specified in the ORDER BY clause *or*, if the INTO TEMP clause is present, the result of Step 5 is saved in the temporary table specified.

5.4.12 Variables in SQL statements

We conclude our discussion of the SELECT statement with some ideas on the use of prompt variables. The ideas are equally applicable to all SQL statements, but particularly useful for WHERE clauses.

There is no facility in **INFORMIX-SQL** to prompt the user for input to a variable contained in an SQL statement. This feature would be particularly useful where a pre-defined query needs to be run against different values in the WHERE clause, as in:

```
select * from houses
    where town = "&town" and price <= &price;
```

Here is a novel and user-friendly way of achieving this through the use of a UNIX (Bourne) shell program. DOS users will unfortunately have to resort to a programming language, unless you have DOS versions of the UNIX utilities mentioned below.

The program
The shell program (which I have called **sqlprompt**) takes an SQL command

file as a parameter on the command line. The command file contains variables of the form *&variable*. Each time **sqlprompt** sees one of these it prompts the user for input which it then substitutes for the variable in the command file, writing these changes back to the file unless the −s option is used, in which case the changed file is written to standard output leaving the original file intact. The program uses **tr, awk, sed** and **mv**, to which the user must have access.

There are a number of forward and backward quotes, as well as double quotes. These are all significant, and you must take care with them.

```
#
# Usage:   sqlprompt [-s] sqlfile.sql
#
if [ $1 = "-s" ]
then SAVE=y; shift
fi

VARLIST=`tr ",;\"" "   " < $1 | awk ' \
    { split ($0,x); \
      for (i in x) \
        { if (substr (x[i],1,1) == "&" ) \
      { print x[i] } \
          } \
    }'`

for v in $VARLIST
do
    echo "\nEnter value for $v ->\c" > /dev/tty
    read a
    SEDLIST=`echo "s/$v/$a/g;$SEDLIST"`
done

if [ "$SEDLIST" ]
then
    if [ "$SAVE" ]
    then
      sed -e $SEDLIST < $1
    else
      sed -e $SEDLIST < $1 > $1.t
      mv $1.t $1
    fi
fi
```

Running the program

There are two methods of running the program. The first method runs the program within the menu system and the second from the command line.

Method 1

1.   From the SQL (**Query-Language**) menu, select **Choose**.

2.   Choose an SQL command file (which contains some &variables) from the list displayed.

3.   Select **Use-editor** and enter **sqlprompt** as the editor.

4.   You will be prompted for each variable in the command file. After answering the last prompt you are brought back to the SQL menu and the command file is displayed, with substituted variables.

5.   Select **Run** to run the command file.

6.   To reinput the variables you must go from Step 1, not Step 3, as the modified command file is now in a temporary file.

Notes

(i)   You may set **DBEDIT = sqlprompt** if you wish. Either way after you have replied to the USE EDITOR >> prompt once, you are not prompted again in this **INFORMIX-SQL** session, which means that you cannot use **vi** as well as **sqlprompt**.

(ii)   The command file is not changed using this method, since **INFORMIX-SQL** provides a copy in a temporary file.

Method 2

1.   Type in the following line from the UNIX command line:

```
sqlprompt -s sqlfile.sql | isql dbname -
```

replacing *sqlfile.sql* with the name of your SQL command file, and *dbname* with the name of your database.

2.   Answer the prompts as they appear, just as in Method 1 above.

UNIX masters may like to include the above command line in a simple shell script.

Exercise

1. Find the average price per bedroom for houses in Guildford. Use a display label.

2. How many houses are there in Woking?

3. How many houses are there in the price range £100,000 to £120,000?

4. For each town in the database, display the number of houses with each number of bedrooms. Use a GROUP BY clause.

5. Display the town and average price of 3-bedroomed houses, but only for towns having more than one 3-bedroomed house. Order by the average price.

6. Modify the above query (or any query) to put the results into a temporary table, then display all the rows in the temporary table.

7. If you are happy with UNIX shell programming, type in the **sqlprompt** program (but take care with the quote marks – ′, ` and "). Run it using Method 1.

5.5 INSERT, UPDATE and DELETE Statements

Together with the SELECT statement, these complete the DML (Data Manipulation Language) statements and are as follows:

INSERT

Adds one or more rows to a table:

> INSERT INTO *table-name* [(*col-list*)]
> {VALUES (*value-list*) | *SELECT-statement*}

There are two main forms of the INSERT statement. The first is where you specify the VALUES keyword and a list of values to be inserted into a row, for example:

```
insert into houses (ref_no, owner, adrs1, adrs2,
                    town, county, no_bedrooms)
   values (0, "Thompson", "9, The Street", null,
           "Bagshot", "Surrey", 4);
```

The second is where the values are to be taken from rows from another table in the database according to the SELECT statement specified, for example:

```
insert into temph
   select * from houses
      where town = "Woking";
```

In either case you may either specify a list of column names to contain the values, the rest being set to NULL, or the list may be omitted in which case a value must be specified for every column in the row (the keyword NULL may be used as a value).

Notes

(i)   The keyword NULL may be used to insert a NULL value in a particular column.

(ii) If a serial column is being inserted, a zero must be used as the value. This will be replaced with the next appropriate serial value when the row is added.

UPDATE

Modifies data in one or more rows of a table:

UPDATE *table-name* SET *col-name* = *expr* [,...]
[WHERE *condition*]

UPDATE *table-name* {(*column-list*) | *} = (*expr-list*)
[WHERE condition]

See Section 5.4.2 for details of the WHERE clause.

Examples

This example increases the prices of all the houses in the **houses** table by 10%. Because no WHERE clause is specified and therefore all the rows are affected, **INFORMIX-SQL** gives a warning and a second chance (unless it is executed from within a command file):

```
update houses set price = price * 1.10;
```

This example changes all the **county** columns to Surrey, if the **town** column is Guildford, and sets the **notes** column to Modified:

```
update houses (county, notes) =
               ("Surrey", "Modified")
       where town = "Guildford";
```

Notes

(i) *expr* may be a SELECT statement subquery, returning a single value and enclosed in parentheses, e.g.

```
update houses set price =
       (select avg(price) from houses)
   where price is null;
```

(ii) You may not update a SERIAL column.

(iii) For databases with transactions, all statements within a BEGIN/COMMIT WORK block (see Section 5.8.2) are treated as a single transaction. All the rows affected by an UPDATE will thus be locked for the duration of the transaction.

DELETE

Deletes one or more rows from a table:

DELETE FROM *table-name* [WHERE *condition*]

See Section 5.4.2 for details of the WHERE clause.

Examples

In this example all houses costing less than £100,000 are deleted from the **houses** table:

```
delete from houses where price < 100000;
```

In the next example all houses which have been on the books for more than three months (ninety days) are archived to an operating system file using the UNLOAD statement (covered in Section 5.9) and then deleted from the database:

```
unload to "/usr/dbarchive"
        select * from houses
            where book_date < (today - 90);
    delete from houses
        where book_date < (today - 90);
```

5.6 Data Definition Statements

Data Definition Language (DDL) statements are used for the creation, modification and administration of the database, its tables and its views. There is a separate section on each of these subjects. Most of the statements may be executed from menu options on the DATABASE or TABLE menus and those that are not are summarised at the end of each section.

5.6.1 Database statements

CLOSE DATABASE

Closes the current database and leaves no database current. The syntax is simply:

CLOSE DATABASE

CREATE DATABASE

Creates a database dictionary, sets up the system catalogues and makes the new database the current database. You may optionally create a transaction log in which case your database is a database 'with transactions' (see Chapter 3).

CREATE DATABASE *database-name*
    [WITH LOG IN *"pathname"* [MODE ANSI]]

Note

The SQL statements needed to recreate a database and its tables can be produced using the utility **dbschema**, described at the end of Section 3.8, and in detail in an Appendix to the **INFORMIX-SQL** manual.

New for Version 4.0

You may create a database as MODE ANSI, in which case transactions are implicit and automatically initiated by any statement. They are terminated by the use of the statements COMMIT/ROLLBACK WORK. MODE ANSI cannot be dropped from a database.

DATABASE

Selects a database and makes it the current database. There can be no more than one current database per user at any time (except with **INFORMIX-STAR**, the distributed database product for **INFORMIX-OnLine**). The EXCLUSIVE option should only be used by the DBA to allow modifications to be made to the database without interference from other users, who may then not open the database until the DBA closes it.

DATABASE *database-name* [EXCLUSIVE]

DROP DATABASE

Deletes all tables, indexes, system catalogues and the database directory (unless there are files other than database files in it). You must own *all* the tables or have DBA status to drop the database, which may not be the current database.

DROP DATABASE *database-name*

With the exception of CLOSE DATABASE and the various optional clauses, all the above statements may be executed by selecting the appropriate option on the DATABASE menu.

5.6.2 Table statements

ALTER INDEX

Allows the table owner or DBA to cluster a table in the order of an existing index, or to release an index from the clustering attribute. Clustered indexes are covered more fully in Chapter 3, Section 3.5.

ALTER INDEX *index-name* TO [NOT] CLUSTER

When the database engine executes the ALTER INDEX TO CLUSTER command, it attempts to lock the table in EXCLUSIVE mode, i.e. no other users may have access to the table to which *index-name* belongs. The statement will fail if some other process is using the table.

ALTER TABLE

Used to add a column to a table, delete a column or modify the data type of a column:

```
ALTER TABLE table-name
    {ADD (newcol-name newcol-type [NOT NULL]
        [UNIQUE [CONSTRAINT constr-name]] [,...])
        [BEFORE oldcol-name]
    | DROP (oldcol-name [,...])
    | MODIFY (oldcol-name newcol-type)
        [NOT NULL] [,...])
    | ADD CONSTRAINT UNIQUE (oldcol-name [,...])
        [CONSTRAINT constr-name]
    | DROP CONSTRAINT (constr-name [,...])} [,...]
```

One or more ADD, DROP or MODIFY clauses may be specified, separated by commas. All the options in this statement are covered by the **Alter** option on the TABLE menu of the Interactive Schema Editor (see Chapter 3, Section 3.8), except for those dealing with CONSTRAINTS. You must be either the owner of the table, or DBA, or have ALTER permission on the table (see Section 5.7).

New for Version 4.0

You may use the ALTER TABLE statement to add or drop a unique constraint. (Constraints are covered below under the CREATE TABLE statement.)

CREATE INDEX

Used to create indexes for one or more columns in a table. By specifying a list of columns (maximum eight, but a total of 120 bytes, or sixteen columns and 255 bytes in **INFORMIX-OnLine**) one can create a **composite index**. Indexes and their creation (including clustered indexes) are covered in much more detail in Chapter 3, Section 3.5.

CREATE [UNIQUE] [CLUSTER] INDEX *index-name*
    ON *table-name* (*column-name* [ASC | DESC] [,...])

Example

```
create index i_bedrooms
on bedrooms (ref_no, bedroom_no);
```

CREATE SYNONYM

This statement allows a user to create an alternative name for a table or view. The new name is only valid for the user who creates it.

CREATE SYNONYM *synonym* FOR *table-name*

New for Version 4.0

In Version 4.0, synonyms are now available to all users on the system, although the creator of the synonym must grant them the necessary access permissions. This is particularly useful in a distributed database using **INFORMIX-OnLine** and **INFORMIX-STAR**, where a short synonym may be given for a long remote table name. It also ensures location transparency, as the actual table name or its location may change, but the synonym may remain unchanged.

CREATE TABLE

Creates a new table in the current database:

CREATE [TEMP] TABLE *table-name*
    (*column-name datatype* [NOT NULL]
    [UNIQUE [CONSTRAINT *constr-name*]] [,...]
    [UNIQUE (*unique-col-list*)
       [CONSTRAINT *constr-name*]] [,...]})
    [WITH NO LOG]
    [IN *"pathname"*]

Tables may be created much more easily using the Interactive Schema Editor (see Chapter 3), however the options to create a temporary table, to create a table in a directory other than the current database directory, or to create a table with a constraint (Version 4.0) are only available using this statement. The table may be created in any directory to which the user has access, including different disk volumes and remote network nodes.

New for Version 4.0

The keywords UNIQUE and UNIQUE CONSTRAINT may now be applied to a column or group of columns to create a unique index.

CONSTRAINT *constr-name* is optional and is only required if the generated *constr-name* conflicts with an existing identifier.

Example

```
create table bedrooms
   (ref_no integer not null,
    bedroom_no smallint not null,
    bedroom_size char(11),
    ensuite_bath char(1),
    unique (ref_no, bedroom_no) constraint uc1)
   in "/remote/usr1/dbdir";
```

DROP INDEX

Deletes an index from the current database:

DROP INDEX *index-name*

You may display the names of all the indexes associated with the current database by executing the INFO command (see Section 5.9) or through the **Info** option on the SQL or TABLE menu, as in Figure 5.10 below. However, you must use the ALTER TABLE statement to drop a constraint.

INFO - houses :   Columns Indexes Status Privileges Exit
Display information about indexes for the columns in a table.

-------------------- property ------------------------------ Press CTRL-W for Help --------

Index name	Owner	Type	Cluster	Columns
ix100_1	tony	unique	No	ref_no
ix100_13	tony	dupls	No	agent

Figure 5.10 Index information from the INFO menu.

DROP SYNONYM

Removes a previously created synonym, which *you* must have created:

DROP SYNONYM *synonym*

DROP TABLE

Deletes all the data and indexes for a table and erases its system catalogue entry:

> DROP TABLE *table-name*

You must be either the owner of the table, or DBA, or have ALTER permission on the table (see Section 5.7).

RENAME COLUMN

Used to change the name of a column in a specified table:

> RENAME COLUMN *table.oldcol* TO *newcol*

You must be either the owner of the table, or DBA, or have ALTER permission on the table (see Section 5.7). This statement may also be executed through the **Alter** option of the TABLE menu.

RENAME TABLE

Used to change the name of a table:

> RENAME TABLE *oldname* TO *newname*

You must be either the owner of the table, or DBA, or have ALTER permission on the table (see Section 5.7).

5.6.3 Views

Views are *dynamic* windows into the database and they differ in this respect from temporary tables. A temporary table can only show the state of the database at the time when the table was created, whereas views reflect the current state of the database. **INFORMIX-SQL** achieves this either by combining the SELECT from the CREATE VIEW statement with the query SELECT statement to form a new query, or by creating the view as a temporary table and applying the query to this table.

What you can do with a view:

• Provide different users with different views of the data in the database. A view may include columns from different tables or may show values derived from values in the tables (aggregates). A view has a name and to a user appears exactly as if it is a table.

• Limit access to sensitive data by allowing users to see only part of the information in a record. The accounts department need only see an employee's reference number and salary, not his full name and address.

- Permit users to update, insert and delete data in the database as though the data were organised as it appears in the view, though with a number of restrictions.

What you cannot do with a view:

- Although views appear to the user as tables, they may not be used in place of tables in a form specification unless they are based on only one table and contain no aggregate information.

- You cannot create an index on a view.

- Naturally, a column in a view which is derived from an expression or aggregate may not be updated.

- You may not update the data in a view if it is taken from more than one table.

The syntax of the view statements is as follows:

CREATE VIEW

Creates a new view based on existing tables and views in the database. If *col-list* is not specified to give new names to the columns in the view, the names are as in the underlying tables:

CREATE VIEW *view-name* [(*col-list*)]
    AS *SELECT-statement* [WITH CHECK OPTION]

The optional clause WITH CHECK OPTION prevents the user from inserting or updating data through the view which is inconsistent with the constraints of the view. For instance in the example below, a user could insert a row for a house in Woking into the **houses** table through the **guildford** view. The user would then not be able to select this row through the view. The WITH CHECK OPTION would prevent the user from inserting the row.

Examples

This example creates a view which only contains houses in Guildford. As it stands, a user could still input a house through the view which was in another town, but he would not be able to retrieve it through the view (but see the WITH CHECK OPTION above).

```
create view guildford
   as select * from houses
        where town = "Guildford";
```

Referential integrity is the ability of a database to hold rules and conditions about what can and cannot be done with its data, particularly when two tables have some form of logical connection.

A form of referential integrity can be imposed through the use of views. We want to make sure that no agent's details are ever removed while that agent still has houses in the **houses** table. We can do this by only allowing users to delete agents through the **delagents** view, which is created as follows. Note that we cannot revoke delete privilege on the **agents** table, since this will be reflected in the view:

```
create view delagents as
   select * from agents a
      where not exists
         (select h.agent from houses h
            where a.agent = h.agent);
```

Note

The SELECT statement on which the view is based may be displayed by querying the **sysviews** table as follows, where *viewname* is the name of the view for which the information is required. The subquery is required because there may be multiple rows relating to the same view definition:

```
select text from sysviews
   where tabid =
            (select tabid from sysviews
               where text like "%viewname%");
```

DROP VIEW

Used to remove a previously created view from the database:

DROP VIEW *view-name*

Exercise

1.   INSERT some new rows into the **houses** table with a **notes** column value of 'SQL test'.

2.   Increase the price of these houses by 10% and set the **notes** column to a value of 'SQL test2' (in one statement).

3.   DELETE the new rows.

4.   Create a composite index called **i_bedrooms** for the bedrooms table consisting of the columns **ref_no** and **bedroom_no**.

5.   If you have not done so already, explore the **Info** option on the SQL menu.

6.   Create a view on your database consisting of all the houses in Guildford. Prevent users from inserting houses that are not in Guildford.

7.   Try some SELECT statements using the name of your view as a table name. Attempt to INSERT a house which is in Woking.

8.   Remove your view from the database.

5.7 Data Access Control Statements

A user other than the DBA or the creator of the database only has access to the database and to specific columns within a table when the Database Administrator (DBA) or the owner of the table specifically grants these privileges. A user must have CONNECT permission before they can access the database at all. SQL provides the following statements to achieve access control.

New for Version 4.0

CREATE SCHEMA AUTHORIZATION

This statement, new with Version 4.0, allows you to issue a set of CREATE and/or GRANT statements as a single unit. Its syntax is:

CREATE SCHEMA AUTHORIZATION *username*
{set of create and/or grant statements}

where *username* is the name of the user issuing the statement.

The following statements may be used within a CREATE SCHEMA statement. The statements do not need any separators, the CREATE SCHEMA statement being terminated with a semi-colon or end-of-file.

CREATE INDEX
CREATE SYNONYM
CREATE TABLE
CREATE VIEW
GRANT *table-privilege*

For example:

```
create schema authorization tony
    create table five (id serial, lname char(30))
    create index i_id on five(id)
    grant all on five to claire;
```

GRANT

Allows the DBA (Database Administrator) to specify user access privileges to a database and for the DBA or table owner to specify user access privileges to a table. There are two forms, one for database-level privileges and one for table-level privileges.

GRANT *db-priv* TO {PUBLIC | *user-list*}
[WITH GRANT OPTION]

Where:

db-priv   is one of the following database-level access types:

CONNECT   allows access to database tables but without permission to create permanent tables and indexes.

RESOURCE   allows access to database tables with permission to create permanent tables and indexes.

DBA   allows full database administrator privileges.

If you additionally specify the WITH GRANT OPTION clause, you allow the user to whom you are granting the privilege the ability to grant that privilege to another user.

Example

```
grant connect to public;
```

would be the same as running:

```
grant all on table1 to public;
revoke alter on table1 from public;
```

on *every table* in the database.

Note

Database-level privileges are not displayed from the **Privileges** option on the INFO menu. However, they may be displayed by executing:

```
select * from sysusers;
```

The second form of the GRANT statement operates on table-level privileges, and so may be executed by the DBA or the table owner.

GRANT *table-priv* ON *table-name* TO {PUBLIC | *user-list*}
[WITH GRANT OPTION]

Where:

table-priv   is one or more of the following table-level access types, multiple privileges being separated by commas:

ALTER   add or delete columns or modify data types of columns

DELETE	delete rows
INDEX	create indexes
INSERT	insert rows
SELECT [(*cols*)]	retrieve data from specified columns
UPDATE [(*cols*)]	change values in specified columns
ALL	all of the above.

user-list   is a list of login names separated by commas, or the keyword PUBLIC may be used to denote all users.

If you additionally specify the WITH GRANT OPTION clause, you allow the user to whom you are granting the privilege the ability to grant that privilege to another user.

Example

```
grant update (price, notes) on houses
      to jack, jill;
```

Note

You can display the privileges for a particular table by selecting the **Privileges** option on the INFO menu, or by executing the INFO statement (see Section 5.9).

REVOKE

Removes another user's privileges for a table or the database:

REVOKE *table-priv* ON *table-name* FROM {PUBLIC | *user-list*}

REVOKE *db-priv* FROM {PUBLIC | *user-list*}

The privileges and syntax are the same as for the GRANT statement. To restrict access privileges at the table-level, you must first revoke *all* privileges and then grant those you want:

```
revoke all on houses from public;
grant all on houses to tom, dick, harry;
grant update (price) on houses to joan;
grant select (adrs1, price) on houses to public;
```

LOCK TABLE

Prohibits access to a table by other users. Can be used when making major changes to a table in a multi-user environment when simultaneous access by another user would interfere. **N.B.** Do not forget to UNLOCK the table afterwards!

> LOCK TABLE *table-name* IN {SHARE | EXCLUSIVE} MODE

Where:

table-name   is the name of the table to be locked.

SHARE   is the mode in which other users only have *read access* to the table.

EXCLUSIVE   is the mode in which other users have *no access at all* to the table.

Example

```
lock table houses in exclusive mode;
```

UNLOCK TABLE

Unlocks a table that was previously locked with the LOCK TABLE statement.

> UNLOCK TABLE *table-name*

SET LOCK MODE

When a row or table that you wish to alter or delete is locked for some reason, the database engine issues an error message but returns control to you; the lock mode is NOT WAIT. This statement allows you to change the lock mode to WAIT, and if a row that you wish to alter or delete is locked, the database engine will wait until it is unlocked. The syntax is:

> SET LOCK MODE TO [NOT] WAIT

This statement should be used *with extreme caution* (and preferably not at all) since if the statement that locked the row does not complete, your statement will wait *indefinitely*. If **user2** is waiting for a row that **user1** has locked, but **user1** is waiting for a row that **user2** has locked, *both* users wait indefinitely – a so-called *deadly embrace.*

New for Version 4.0

SET LOCK MODE TO WAIT [*seconds*]

In Version 4.0 you may optionally specify a number of seconds after which the database engine will return an error code equivalent to that obtained when the lock mode is set to NOT WAIT.

5.8 Data Integrity Statements

An **audit trail** is a file containing a history of all modifications to a single table, whereas a **transaction log** records all the modifications made to the whole database. A transaction log, once created, may not be dropped without some reworking of the database, whereas audit trails may be added and deleted as required.

- Use an audit trail when only one or two tables need protection.

- Use a transaction log when multiple tables must remain synchronised or when you must have the option to ROLLBACK and discard changes.

Four subjects are covered in this section: audit trails, transaction logs, backing up and restoring the database, and index maintenance.

5.8.1 Audit trails

CREATE AUDIT

Creates an audit trail file and starts writing to it. Note that you must have ownership of the table or DBA status for this statement, and that the directory in pathname must have search permission for those users accessing the database.

CREATE AUDIT FOR *table-name* IN *"pathname"*

You should make a backup copy of your table as soon as you run the CREATE AUDIT statement, but before you make any changes to the database, for example:

```
lock table houses;
create audit for houses in "/usr/common";
unload to "/usr/dbarchive/houses.unl"
   select * from houses;
unlock table houses;
```

The presence of an audit trail is indicated in the output from the **Status** option of the INFO menu which may be found through the SQL or TABLE menus.

DROP AUDIT

Use this statement to delete an audit trail file.

DROP AUDIT FOR *table-name*

RECOVER TABLE

In the event of a system failure, you can use the RECOVER TABLE statement to restore a database from a backup copy and an audit trail file.

RECOVER TABLE *table-name*

5.8.2 Transaction logs

See also Chapter 3 for a full explanation of transaction logs.

BEGIN WORK

This statement marks the beginning of a transaction, (except in a MODE ANSI database, in which each statement marks the beginning of a transaction) which must be terminated by the COMMIT WORK or ROLLBACK WORK statement. Note that each row affected by an UPDATE, DELETE or INSERT statement during a transaction is locked for the duration of the transaction. If your system runs out of locks, you may need to lock the entire table instead, using LOCK TABLE. The syntax for this statement is simply

BEGIN WORK

Example

In this example, we would like to remove all the bedroom rows and the house row associated with the owner 'Archer'. Since they are in different tables however, we do not want one to exist without the other. By enclosing the DELETE statements in a transaction we can ensure that both DELETE statements have been successful before we COMMIT the operations.

```
begin work;
   delete from bedrooms
      where ref_no =
                     (select ref_no from houses
                        where owner = "Archer");
   delete from houses
      where owner = "Archer";
```

The user may then decide whether to COMMIT or ROLLBACK WORK, depending on the success of both statements.

COMMIT WORK

Marks the end of a transaction by authorising all changes to the database since the last BEGIN WORK statement.

> COMMIT WORK

ROLLBACK WORK

Marks the end of a transaction by revoking all changes to the database since the last BEGIN WORK statement. Note that DDL statements such as CREATE, ALTER and DROP cannot be rolled back.

> ROLLBACK WORK

ROLLFORWARD DATABASE

Uses a transaction log file to restore a database from the last backup copy.

> ROLLFORWARD DATABASE

START DATABASE

This statement starts a new transaction log file allowing you to either change a database without transactions to one with transactions, or to change the location of a transaction log file. In Version 4.0 you may change the database to MODE ANSI, but *not back again.*

> START DATABASE *database-name*
> WITH LOG IN *"pathname"* [MODE ANSI]

For both security and efficiency it is wise to put the transaction log on a different disk to the database. The database must be closed to execute this statement.

5.8.3 Backing up and restoring the database

Backing up the database
To back up the database the DBA should perform the following steps:

1.   Execute a DATABASE EXCLUSIVE statement to prevent other users from modifying the database.

2.   Copy the transaction log file and the database directory on to a backup medium. A more secure backup can be achieved by using different media – the log file may fit on a diskette.

3.   Create an empty log file with the same name as the old file. The easiest way to do this is to use a shell command such as `>filename`.

4.   Execute a CLOSE DATABASE statement. This releases the database from its exclusive mode.

The database is now ready for use by other users.

Notes

(i)   If the database is too big to back up every day, you may wish to take interim backups of the log file only.

(ii) In two generations of backups, the following relationship applies:

dbase.bk2 = dbase.bk1 + logfile.bk2 + ROLLFORWARD

In other words, you can restore the current database by applying a ROLLFORWARD DATABASE statement to the current log file plus the previous database backup.

Restoring the database from a backup
To restore the complete database from a backup the DBA should perform the following tasks:

1.   Restore the database and log file from their backup media. The log file must have *exactly* the same pathname as it had previously.

2.   If you are restoring the database to a different Unix system, use the `chgrp` command to ensure that the log file, the database directory and the files under that directory belong to the group `informix`. A sample set of commands follows:

```
# chgrp informix /usr1/dblog
# chgrp informix /usr/tony/property.dbs
# chgrp informix /usr/tony/property.dbs/*
```

The database is now ready for use.

Crash situations

Consider the following backup scenario:

Day	DB backup	Log file backup
Monday	dbase.mon	logfile.mon
Tuesday	dbase.tue	logfile.tue
Wednesday	**CRASH !!**	

If the current log file (**logfile.wed**) is intact, then all the changes made to the database since the last backup (**dbase.tue**) are saved. Therefore we can return the database to its current state by following these steps:

1. Save the log file (as **logfile.wed**) to a backup medium.

2. Restore the last database backup (**dbase.tue**) only.

3. In DATABASE EXCLUSIVE mode, apply a ROLLFORWARD DATABASE statement.

4. Satisfy yourself that the database is correctly restored and save the database onto backup medium (as **dbase.wed**).

5. Clear out the log file with a command such as >filename.

6. Execute a CLOSE DATABASE statement to release the database from its exclusive mode.

5.8.4 Index maintenance

The utility program **bcheck** (see the Appendix to the **INFORMIX-SQL** manual) is a **C-ISAM** program that checks and repairs **C-ISAM** index files. It may be invoked from **INFORMIX-SQL** by use of the CHECK TABLE and REPAIR TABLE statements.

CHECK TABLE

Allows the DBA or table owner to compare a table with its indexes to see if they match. The statement effectively invokes **bcheck** with the −**n** option.

CHECK TABLE *table-name*

REPAIR TABLE

Allows the DBA or table owner to delete and rebuild damaged indexes for a table. The statement effectively invokes **bcheck** with the **−y** option.

REPAIR TABLE *table-name*

5.9 Auxiliary Statements

INFO

The INFO statement may be used to display a wealth of information on the tables in the current database, including column names, indexes and access privileges. You can print the results of this statement by selecting the **Output** option on the SQL menu.

INFO {TABLES
        | COLUMNS FOR *table-name*
        | INDEXES FOR *table-name*
        | PRIVILEGES FOR *table-name*
        | STATUS FOR *table-name*}

This statement gives the same output as the **Info** option on the SQL or TABLE menus. For database-level privileges you must execute the statement:

```
select * from sysusers;
```

LOAD

Reads an ASCII formatted system file into a database table. Note that if your database has transactions, you must execute the LOAD statement inside a transaction. The file may have variable length fields separated by the character specified in the environment variable **DBDELIMITER**, which by default is " | ". Records in the file must be separated by **NEWLINE** characters. LOAD is an SQL implementation of the utility program **dbload** which has many more useful features and is described in an Appendix of the **INFORMIX-SQL** manual.

LOAD FROM *"pathname"*
    INSERT INTO *table-name* [(*column-name* [,...])]

Example

```
load from "/usr/tony/upload"
    insert into houses;
```

Notes

(i)   The number of data fields in the load file must equal the number of columns in the table or in the optional list of column names.

(ii) LOAD appends to rather than overwrites data in the table.

(iii) The presence of indexes on the table has an effect on the speed of loading. You should consider dropping all indexes on the table and then restoring them after the load is completed.

(iv) If a field in the load file is to be loaded into a SERIAL column, each occurrence of this field must be unique in the load file.

(v)   Fields within the records to be loaded may be guaranteed to be unique by creating a unique index before the load is executed.

UNLOAD

Writes the contents of a database table in ASCII format to a system file, the fields being delimited by the character specified in the environment variable **DBDELIMITER** which defaults to " | ".

UNLOAD TO *"pathname" SELECT-statement*

Example

```
unload to "/usr/dbarchive/houses.unl"
   select * from houses;
```

UPDATE STATISTICS

Causes the number of rows in a table to be recorded in the **systables** catalogue file. The database engine uses the data generated to optimise its searching strategy. It thus improves the efficiency of queries after a table has been extensively modified. The statistics are not updated unless you execute this statement.

UPDATE STATISTICS [FOR TABLE *table-name*]

The statistics may be updated for the whole database or, using the FOR TABLE option, individual tables. In Version 4.0 the new optimiser makes extensive use of the statistics, so efficiency is improved if they are updated regularly. This statement will also take longer to execute in 4.0.

OUTPUT

The OUTPUT statement may be used to send the results of a query to an operating system file or through a pipe to another program. The same results may be achieved by using the **Output** option on the SQL menu.

> OUTPUT TO {*pathname* | PIPE *program*}
> [WITHOUT HEADINGS] *SELECT-statement*

The WITHOUT HEADINGS option allows you to display the results of the query without column name headings.

Example

```
output to /usr/tony/query.out
    select * from agents;
```

New for Version 4.0

SET EXPLAIN

The SET EXPLAIN statement records exactly how the query processor is accessing the database when executing a query. Although the user has no control over this process, he may be able to modify the query to increase its efficiency. The syntax is

> SET EXPLAIN {ON | OFF}

Once this statement has been issued, the query paths of all subsequent queries are appended to the file **sqexplain.out**, until SET EXPLAIN OFF is issued or the program exits.

Exercise

1.   Allow another user to access your database, but only allow them to insert and retrieve rows.

2.   Display another user's privileges on your database using the **Info** option from the SQL menu and also using the command

```
select * from sysusers;
```

3.   If you have a database with transactions, start a transaction which increases the prices of houses in Woking by 20%, but do not commit the changes. Now check the prices – have they changed?

4.   Execute a ROLLBACK WORK statement. You have now revoked all the changes since the last BEGIN WORK.

5.   If you are the DBA and you have the time, backup and restore your database, according to the instructions in Section 5.8.3.

6.   Unload the **houses** table to a system file and then reload from that file.

7.   Experiment with the INFO statement.

8.   Using the OUTPUT TO PIPE statement, output the addresses and prices of all the houses to your system printer, without printing any headings.

Chapter 6

Introducing PERFORM

6.1 Introduction

The use of data entry and retrieval forms in **INFORMIX-SQL** may be split into two parts:

1. The design and creation of forms, which are compiled using the **FORMBUILD** program, and

2. The use of these forms for data entry and retrieval, using the **PERFORM** program.

Both of these tasks may be performed through options on the **INFORMIX-SQL** FORM menu. In this chapter we shall consider the creation of simple default forms and the use of the **PERFORM** program. But first let us consider the FORM menu (Figure 6.1 below), which may be obtained by selecting **Form** from the main **INFORMIX-SQL** menu.

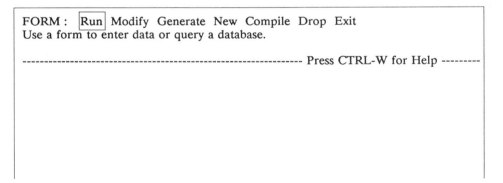

```
FORM :  Run  Modify Generate New Compile Drop Exit
Use a form to enter data or query a database.

----------------------------------------------------------- Press CTRL-W for Help ---------
```

Figure 6.1 The FORM menu.

These are the options on the FORM menu:

Run   Displays the RUN FORM screen from which a previously created form may be run by selecting it from the list displayed. Just move the cursor to the desired form name and press **RETURN**.

Modify   This option is used to modify the text of a form specification file using the system editor (or the one specified in the **DBEDIT** environment variable, see Chapter 1). The form specification file must be compiled before the form can be run.

Generate   The **Generate** option creates a default screen form. This option is covered in detail in Section 6.2.

New   Creates a new form specification from scratch, using the system editor.

Compile   The **Compile** option compiles a form specification file into a form that may be run.

Drop   Drops a form, selected from the list displayed, from the database.

Exit   Returns to the **INFORMIX-SQL** main menu.

6.2 Creating Default Forms

To create a default form, follow these steps:

1.   Select **Form** from the main menu.

2.   Select the **Generate** option from the FORM menu, and give your form a name.

3.   Select the main table on which your form will be based from the list of tables displayed on the CHOOSE TABLE menu (see Figure 6.2).

```
CHOOSE TABLE >>
Choose the table to be used in the default form.

------------------------------------------------------------ Press CTRL-W for Help ---------
houses

bedrooms

agents

sysmenuitems

sysmenus
```

Figure 6.2 The CHOOSE TABLE menu.

4.   You may then choose **Select-more-tables** up to a maximum of eight in one form (although you may later edit your form to include up to fourteen).

5.   Select the **Table-selection-complete** option and **FORMBUILD** will create and compile the default form specification.

A default form contains all the column names from the selected tables and validation is only at the data type level (i.e. CHARACTER, INTEGER, etc.). The default form may be customised to improve screen layout and add validation and control logic by using the **Modify** and **Compile** options. Forms customisation is covered in detail in the next chapter. Figure 6.3 shows a default form for the **agents** table.

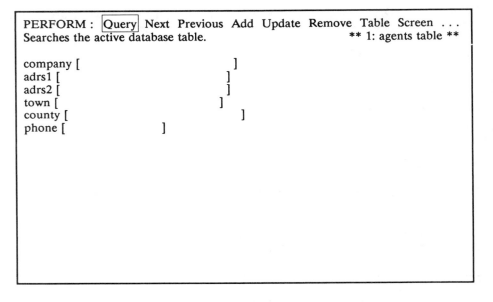

Figure 6.3 A default form for the **agents** table.

Notes

(i)   If you choose the **New** option on the menu, **INFORMIX-SQL** calls your system editor and allows you to create a form specification from scratch, however it is much easier to use the **Generate** option, followed by **Modify**.

(ii)   Default forms contain a separate screen for each table, activated by selecting the **Table** option (see Section 6.5, The Active Table).

(iii) The **sysmenuitems** and **sysmenus** tables are created when you create a User-menu (see Chapter 9).

6.3 Using PERFORM

A form may be run simply by selecting the **Run** option on the FORM menu and choosing the form name from the list displayed by moving the cursor to it and pressing **RETURN**. Forms may also be run directly from the command line (see the note below).

```
PERFORM :  Query  Next  Previous  Add  Update  Remove  Table  Screen  ...
Searches the active database table.                          ** 1: agents table **

company [                          ]
adrs1 [                          ]
adrs2 [                          ]
town [                          ]
county [                      ]
phone [                  ]




Field-specific comments may appear on this line.
The Status Line is for messages generated by PERFORM.
```

Figure 6.4 There are three areas in a PERFORM screen.

The **PERFORM** screen can be divided into three areas:

Information lines	the top line always displays a list of the currently available options and the second line a message describing the highlighted option, and the number and name of the currently active table.
Input area	the rest of the screen, apart from the last two lines, comprises the data entry/display area, each field surrounded by square bracket delimiters (these may be changed – see Chapter 7, Section 7.9.3).
Message lines	the last line, known as the Status Line, is reserved for **PERFORM** messages, and the line above it for comments specified in the form file.

Note

Forms may be run directly from the command line by using the **sperform** command or **isql** command as follows (the **–s** option suppresses the Informix copyright message on loading the form):

    sperform -s *formname*

or

    isql -s -fr *formname*

6.4 Function Keys

While entering data on the screen, for either insertion, updating, deleting or querying, a number of function keys are available. They may be split into three groups: special functions, cursor movement and field editing. We shall cover these individually.

6.4.1 Special functions

At any time during the execution of a form the following special functions are always available:

Help   Pressing **CTRL-W** (and also **F1** on DOS systems) displays a context-sensitive HELP screen containing a summary of function keys, special search characters and other useful information about **PERFORM**.

Execute   The **ESC** key confirms the information you have entered on the form, either for data entry or retrieval, and actually runs the option you have selected (e.g. after entering information in the form in **Add** mode, it actually adds the row).

Interrupt   You may cancel the option you are currently using by pressing the **DEL** key (on UNIX systems) or **CTRL-C** on DOS systems and some UNIX systems. The **Interrupt** key is determined by the **intr** setting of the **stty** command on your terminal, and may be changed by your system administrator. (Note that **CTRL-C** conflicts with the **Clear Screen** editing key).

6.4.2 Cursor movement

The order in which the cursor moves from one field to the next is determined by the order in which the field tags appear in the ATTRIBUTES section of the form specification file, unless modified by a NEXTFIELD instruction in the INSTRUCTIONS section (see Chapter 7, Section 7.10.3). With this in mind, the following keys may be used to position the cursor on the screen:

Next Field   The **RETURN** and **DOWN ARROW** keys move the cursor to the next field.

Back Field	The **BACKSPACE** and **LEFT ARROW** keys move the cursor backward one character at a time, but without erasing any text. Pressing either key at the beginning of a field moves the cursor to the previous field.
Forward	The **RIGHT ARROW** key moves the cursor forward one character at a time without erasing any text. Pressing **RIGHT ARROW** at the end of a field moves the cursor to the next field.
Fast Forward	Pressing **CTRL-F** (and also **F6** on DOS systems) moves the cursor down the screen rapidly, stopping at the first field on each line.
Fast Backward	Pressing **CTRL-B** (and also **F5** on DOS systems) moves the cursor up the screen rapidly, stopping at the last field on each line.

6.4.3 Field editing

The default editing mode for **PERFORM** is *typeover*. That means that when you first enter a field, anything you type will replace anything that is currently there. You may change to *insert* mode by pressing **CTRL-A** (see below). You will also note from the following that there is no *destructive* backspace, the **BACKSPACE** key always moving the cursor backwards without deleting any text.

Change Mode	Pressing **CTRL-A** (and also **Ins** on DOS systems) toggles between *insert* and *typeover* mode. The default mode for **PERFORM** is *typeover*.
Delete	Pressing **CTRL-X** (and also **Del** on DOS systems) deletes the character on which the cursor is currently positioned.
Delete Forward	**CTRL-D** (and also **F9** on DOS systems) deletes everything from the current cursor position to the end of the field.
Repeat Data	On UNIX systems pressing **CTRL-P** enters the most recently displayed value in a field. When you use the **Add** option to enter several rows in which one or more fields contain the same data, you can avoid retyping the data by pressing **CTRL-P**. When you use the **Update** option, **CTRL-P** restores the value that appeared in the field before you modified it. On DOS systems this key is also represented by **F3**.
Clear Screen	Pressing **CTRL-C** (and also **F10** on DOS systems) clears any search criteria you have entered with the **Query** option. (This key may be disabled if **CTRL-C** is used as the **Interrupt** key.)

New for Version 4.0

Multiline editor
By using the WORDWRAP attribute (see Chapter 7, Section 7.7.3) on long
character fields (data types CHAR, VARCHAR, and TEXT) you may split the
field over a number of lines on the form. This will also invoke the multiline
editor (though not for TEXT fields), which allows you to insert and edit the
text as if it was all one field. You can insert and delete text on one line, and
the words on the other lines will move to accommodate the changes.

The editor will insert *editor blanks* at the ends of lines to ensure that text
wraps on a word boundary (unless the optional COMPRESS keyword is also
used on this field).

Two keys behave differently in the multiline editor:

TAB   In typeover mode, moves the cursor to the next real tab stop
              (not an editor blank). In insert mode **TAB** inserts a tab
              character.

CTRL-N   Inserts a true **NEWLINE** character in the text, forcing subsequent
              text to move down through the screen fields.

6.5 The Active Table

A **PERFORM** screen usually includes columns from a number of tables in the
database tables (up to a maximum of fourteen). However, the columns from
only one of these tables can be accessed at any one time. This is known as the
active table.

The name of the active table is always displayed at the top right of the screen
on the second Information Line, and may be changed by selecting the **Table**
option. You can only access the fields on the screen belonging to the active
table, and only these fields will be enclosed in square brackets. Note that join
fields (join columns) will always have square brackets since they are common
to all the tables involved in the join.

6.6 Basic PERFORM Commands

The following **PERFORM** commands are the ones you will use most often and
they cover the four basic operations of adding, querying, updating and deleting
data. They all operate on the active table; you may use the **Table, Master** and
Detail commands (covered in Section 6.7) to change the active table.

6.6.1 Adding data

To add a new row to the active table, follow these steps:

1. Type **a** to select the **Add** option.

2. Enter the data for the new row by filling in the form, using the cursor movement and editing keys as described in Section 6.4. If you attempt to enter data which is inappropriate to the data type of the current field, **PERFORM** displays the error message **Error in field**, and will not allow you to move on to the next field until you correct the entry.

3. Press the **ESC** key to store the new row.

Note

The cursor will not stop on a SERIAL field, and a zero will appear instead. This is because the number in a SERIAL field is automatically generated by the database engine.

6.6.2 Querying data

To search for rows which have certain values, you may enter these search criteria into the fields in the form. The search criteria may also contain certain special query operators such as wildcards and range operators, detailed later in this section. All rows that are retrieved are put into the **current list** (see below), after which they may be viewed using the **Next** and **Previous** options. Follow these steps:

1. Type **q** to select the **Query** option. **PERFORM** clears the fields in the active table, except join fields without a QUERYCLEAR attribute.

2. Enter search values in one or more fields on the form.

   - If no values are entered, *all* the records in the table will be retrieved into the current list.

   - Certain wildcard characters and query operators (press **CTRL-W** to see a complete list) can be entered to search for a range of values. These are described below.

3. Press **ESC** to begin the search. Once started the search may not be interrupted. On completion of the search, the first matching row is displayed on the screen, and the Status Line contains the message

   n **row(s) found**

where *n* is the number of rows found. You may browse through this current list of records using the **Next** and **Previous** options. If no rows satisfy the search criteria, the message

There are no rows satisfying the conditions

is displayed on the Status Line.

The current list
The results of any query are stored by **PERFORM** in a temporary storage area called the current list, which may hold all the rows in the table if required. The **Next** and **Previous** options step through the current list in sequential order and the **Update** and **Remove** options only work with rows in the current list.

The Next and Previous options
You may step forwards and backwards through the records in the current list by means of the **Next** and **Previous** options. You may skip a number of rows in either direction by preceding the option letter with a number, e.g. **6p** would skip backwards six rows. When you have reached the last row in the current list and you select **Next** (or the first row and you select **Previous**) PERFORM displays the message

There are no more rows in the direction you are going

Query operators
The following operators may be used in form fields. If a field is too short on the screen to hold the search value, **PERFORM** creates a work space at the bottom of the screen which disappears when the query is executed.

= The equals sign on its own may be used to search for a row containing a NULL column; enter = * to find a row containing a column with an asterisk.

> Greater than means later in ASCII ordering (a>A>1), or later in time for DATE columns.

< Less than means earlier in ASCII ordering (1<A<a), and earlier in time for DATE columns.

| The pipe symbol represents the OR operator. For instance Smith|Jones would search for rows with Smith or Jones in the specified column.

: The colon operator signifies a range search, as in 120000:150000 to search for values between 120000 and 150000 inclusive.

.. DATETIME and INTERVAL data types in Version 4.0 may include colons, so the . . operator may be used in range searches to avoid ambiguity.

?   The question mark is a single character wildcard which matches any one character.

*   The asterisk is a wildcard character which represents zero or more characters, as in *son, to find any name ending in son.

\>\>   This operator may be entered to search for the highest value in a field.

\<\<   This operator may be entered to search for the lowest value in a field.

6.6.3 Updating data

You may only update data in the currently displayed row from the currently active table. Follow these steps:

1.   Find the row which needs to be updated by means of the **Query** option, followed by **Next** or **Previous** if necessary.

2.   Type **u** to select the **Update** option.

3.   Make the required changes to the fields.

4.   Press **ESC** to update the record, or **INTERRUPT** to abort the update and return to the menu.

If the row was updated, **PERFORM** will display the message

This row has been changed

6.6.4 Removing data

You may only remove the currently displayed row from the currently active table. Follow these steps:

1.   Find the row which needs to be removed by means of the **Query** option, followed by **Next** or **Previous** if necessary.

2.   Type **r** to select the **Remove** option.

3.   You are given the choice of removing or not removing the row. Select **Yes** or **No**, and the **PERFORM** menu returns.

If the row was removed, **PERFORM** will display the message

Row deleted

Exercise

1.   Create a default form with **houses** as the main table, but including the tables **bedrooms** and **agents**.

2.   Add some data to the **houses** table. Start with your own house, then use some of the sample data from Appendix 1.

3.   Now experiment with querying, updating and removing rows. When you have selected an option, press **CTRL-W** to examine the context-sensitive help.

6.7 Advanced PERFORM Commands

The following commands, apart from **Table** and **Screen** (or **View** in Version 4.0), may be found on the second screen of the **PERFORM** menu (see Figure 6.5). An option may be selected from the second screen without actually displaying it, by just typing its first letter, or the options may be displayed by spacing across to the ellipsis (. . .) on the first screen of the **PERFORM** menu.

6.7.1 The Table option

Screen forms may reference more than one table in the database, but only one table may be active at one time (the fields from the currently active table are denoted by the square bracket delimiters). The **Table** option may be used to select a new active table. The order in which tables may be made active depends on the order in which their columns are referred to in the form specification file. Each table in the form is assigned a number and this number, together with the table name is displayed on the right hand side of the second Information Line (see Figure 6.5). You may go directly to a table if you know its number by typing the number before the **t** option, e.g. 3t would immediately display the screen associated with table 3.

6.7.2 The Screen option

Use the **Screen** option to move to another display screen of the same form. Note that this option does not change the active table.

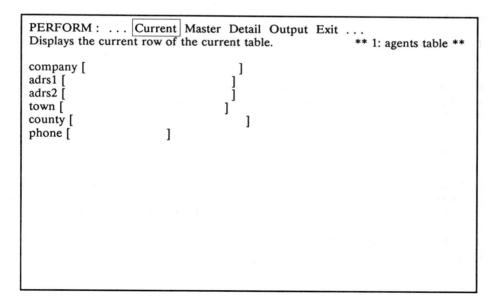

Figure 6.5 The second screen of the PERFORM menu.

6.7.3 Master and Detail

In the INSTRUCTIONS section of the form specification file, a table may be specified as being the *master* of another table. The other table is then the *detail* table in a master/detail relationship. This relationship typically refers to a one-to-many situation, and in our **property** database is exemplified by a single house having many bedrooms. The advantage of the **Detail** option is that by selecting it, you automatically change the active table and query the detail table using the join field as a search criterion, in one command. For example having displayed a particular house record, selecting **Detail** would change to the **bedrooms** table and query it, pulling into the current list all the bedroom records associated with that house. Selecting **Master** would make the **houses** table the active table again.

6.7.4 Current

The **Current** option rereads and redisplays the current row in the current list for the active table. Reading a row does not of course prevent other users from updating or removing that row, so the **Current** option may be used to display the most up-to-date information. Also, when a form includes a join field, each table contained in the form has its own current list. If you change tables by using either the **Table, Master** or **Detail** options, and then browse the current list of the new active table, you may lose your place in the other table. The **Current** option returns you to your original position in the active table's current list.

6.7.5 Output

The **Output** option may be used to write the displayed screen page to an operating system file, including all data, boxes and lines, etc. You may output either just the current row displayed, or all the rows in the current list. However, if a form has more than one screen associated with it, then each screen must be output separately. When outputting the current list, screen one must be output first for the whole list, followed by screen two, etc.

New for Version 4.0

In Version 4.0 you are now given the option to output the displayed screen pages to a file in UNLOAD format (ASCII). The order of the fields in each record output is the same as the order in which they appear in the ATTRIBUTES section of the form specification file. This output file may be used as input to the new READ statement of the **ACE** report generator (see Chapter 8).

New for Version 4.0

6.7.6 View

TEXT and BYTE type BLOB fields may be displayed using the **View** option. The cursor is positioned on the first TEXT field or the first BYTE field that uses the PROGRAM attribute (see Chapter 7, Section 7.7.3). To display the BLOB, type an exclamation mark (!). The BLOB will then be passed to the program specified in the PROGRAM attribute of that field. You may then type a **DOWN ARROW** or **UP ARROW** to move to the next or previous BLOB field that can be displayed. Press **ESC** to exit the **View** option and return to the PERFORM menu.

6.7.7 Exit

The **Exit** option returns you to the FORM menu, or if **PERFORM** was invoked from the command line, the operating system prompt.

Exercise

1.   Using your default form that you created in the previous exercise, select
      the **Screen** option a number of times and notice how the screens for the
      bedrooms and **agents** tables appear, followed by that for the **houses** table
      again. Notice how there are no square brackets around the fields on the
      screens containing the **bedrooms** and **agents** tables, meaning that they are
      inactive.

2.   Now use the **Table** option and see how the tables become active.

3.   We have not yet specified any master-detail relationships; these will be
      covered in Chapter 7, but try the **Output** option. You will need to
      examine the output file with an editor, or you may print it out.

Chapter 7

Forms Customisation

7.1 Introduction

PERFORM provides a sophisticated forms design language which allows you to customise default forms (as produced by the **Generate** option) by specifying, among other things:

- The format of the screen display

- Which columns are to be accessible through the form

- Joins between tables (including composite joins)

- Data entry validation

- Master/detail relationships

- On-screen arithmetic

There are two files associated with a form: a source file with the extension **.per**, and a compiled, runnable file with the extension **.frm**.

7.2 How to Customise a Form

1. To customise a default form or modify an existing form, first select the **Modify** option from the FORM menu, and **INFORMIX-SQL** will call your system editor (or the one specified in the **DBEDIT** environment variable, see Chapter 1, Section 1.4). You may then edit the various parts of the form according to the information given in the following sections of this module.

2. Having modified the form, exit from the editor, saving the changes; you are now in the MODIFY FORM menu, from which you must select **Compile**.

Note

Since your changes are made in a temporary file, selecting **Discard-and-exit** discards your *changes*, leaving the form as it was.

3.   If no errors are detected you may select **Save-and-exit**, which commits your changes to the source and runnable form files (*formname*.**per** and *formname*.**frm**) and returns you to the FORM menu from which you may run the form. If errors are detected, you will see the message

832: Error(s) detected in Form specifications.

and you should proceed to Step 4.

4.   You now find yourself on the COMPILE FORM menu, from which you should select **Correct** which will invoke the editor again. All error messages are included as comments in your source file, as in Figure 7.1 below. Errors have a number and an explanation, which may or may not be very helpful! Note that the error is often in the line *before* the one indicated. When correcting your errors, you need not delete the error messages, **FORMBUILD** will do that for you. Save your corrected form file and go back to Step 2.

```
atabase    property
£
£     The first line of the specification must be the keyword database
£ followed by the database name, or the FORMONLY keyword
£ (4GL only). An optional WITHOUT NULL INPUT may also follow.
£ See error number -2800.
£
screen
{
ref_no        [f000      ]
owner         [f001              ]
  .             .
  .             .
```

Figure 7.1   A form specification with errors.

7.3 Form Specification Structure

The form specification file has four sections, as shown in Figure 7.2 opposite:

database   in which the database to be used is specified

screen   each screen block (enclosed in curly brackets) defines a page of the form

attributes   this section defines the names of all the database columns to be used in the form, the order in which they are accessed, together with validation and join details

instructions   an optional section which specifies screen arithmetic, master/detail relationships and skip logic.

In all sections the keyword **end** is optional, but recommended for clarity.

```
database   property

screen
{
                          ---------------------------
                              PAGE 1 TITLE
                          ---------------------------


    First field      [f000     ]
    Field two        [f001       ]
    Third field      [a]
}
screen
{
                          ---------------------------
                              PAGE 2 TITLE
                          ---------------------------


    Another field [f002        ]
}
end

tables
tab1  tab2

attributes
f000 = tab1.col1, reverse, noupdate;
f001 = tab1.col2, reverse, default = today;
a = tab2.col1, reverse, upshift;
f002 = tab2.col2, reverse, include = (10, 20, 30);
end

instructions
before editadd of tab1.col1
                  comments 'You are about to enter col1'
end
```

Figure 7.2   The structure of a form specification file.

7.4 The DATABASE Section

The DATABASE section of the specification defines the database with which
the form is designed to work. A form may only access one database, but may
access all the tables within that database. There is an optional clause:

WITHOUT NULL INPUT

which forces **PERFORM** to display defaults of zeros for numeric fields and
spaces for character fields (those for which no defaults have already been
specified). No NULL values will be allowed in any fields on the form. For
example:

```
database property
          without null input
```

7.5 The SCREEN Section

The SCREEN section of the specification file describes how the form will
appear on the screen. Each page of the form must be preceded by the word
screen and enclosed in curly brackets. The page layout is a combination of text
– field labels, titles, etc. – and *display fields* which are usually data entry
fields, though they may also be *displayonly* fields. The data entry fields consist
of a field tag enclosed in square brackets. A sample SCREEN section is shown
in Figure 7.3 opposite.

7.5.1 Field tags

Each field tag must have an entry in either the ATTRIBUTES section of the
specification file, to associate the tag with a database column, or the
INSTRUCTIONS section, to define it as a displayonly field. When produced
by the **Generate** option, the length of a field tag is determined by the database
column with which it is associated, and the field tags are of the following
forms:

f000, f001, etc.   for fields of length four characters or more

a0, a1, etc.   for fields of length two or three characters

a, b, c, etc.   for fields of length one character

If numerical data to be displayed exceeds the length of the field on the
screen, the field will be displayed filled with asterisks.

Any table columns which do not appear on the form will be filled with
NULLs, unless the column does not permit them, or the form is defined as
WITHOUT NULL INPUT (see Section 7.4). Otherwise they will be filled with

spaces (for character columns) or zeros (for numeric columns) when the record is added.

```
screen
{
--------------------------------------------------------------
                 P R O P E R T Y    D A T A B A S E
--------------------------------------------------------------
      H O U S E  Reference [f000      ]   B E D R O O M S
      ---------                            ---------------
Owner      [f001            ] Bedroom no.   [f016   ]
Address    [f002            ] Bedroom size [f017       ]
           [f003            ] Ensuite bath [a]
Town       [f004            ]
County     [f005            ]              A G E N T
                                           ---------
No. of bedrooms  [f006   ]        [f119                 ]
No. of bathrooms [f007   ]        [f120                 ]
Lounge size      [f008        ]   [f121                 ]
Dining size      [f009        ]   [f122                 ]
Thru lounge size [f010        ]   [f123         ]
Notes            [f011                          ]
Price            [f012         ]  Max price [maxp       ]
Agent            [f013         ] Min price [minp       ]
Date booked      [f014      ]     Avg price [avgp       ]
}
screen
{
--------------------------------------------------------------
                      A G E N T S
--------------------------------------------------------------

            Name     [f013            ]
            Address  [f019            ]
                     [f020            ]
            Town     [f021            ]
            County   [f022            ]
            Phone    [f023       ]

--------------------------------------------------------------
}
end
```

Figure 7.3 A sample SCREEN section.

Notes

(i) You may create your own field tags. They must consist of from one to fifty characters, of which the first must be a letter. Field tags are case-insensitive (i.e. upper and lower case mean the same).

(ii)   The same field tag may be used more than once in a screen form to display the same information in different areas of the form, for instance on another page.

(iii) Character type fields may be shorter on the screen than the actual column width, in which case the data displayed will be truncated.

(iv)   The square bracket delimiters may be changed by use of the **DELIMITERS** statement in the INSTRUCTIONS section (see Section 7.9.3).

New for Version 4.0

7.5.2 Screen size

In Version 4.0 you may now specify a screen size other than the default of 24 lines by 80 columns. The first SCREEN section may have this syntax:

SCREEN [SIZE *lines* [BY *cols*]]

Remember that four lines are always reserved for system use.

New for Version 4.0

7.5.3 Graphics characters in forms

This was an undocumented feature in some earlier versions so it is worth trying even if you haven't got Version 4.0. The feature allows you to embed graphics characters within your form source to draw lines and boxes, if your terminal supports them. (However, you may need to change your **TERMCAP** environment variable to /usr/informix/etc/termcap.) All you need to do is insert the string \g to turn on the graphics escape mode. Until the end of the line, or another \g is encountered, whichever is the sooner, the following characters have special meanings:

Character	Meaning
p	Upper left corner.
q	Upper right corner.
b	Lower left corner.
d	Lower right corner.
–	Horizontal line.
|	Vertical line.

The \g characters take up space when you are designing your form, but not when you run it, so it is best to design your form *with* the special characters, but *without* the \g characters, and to add them when you have finished your form design. For example, the figure below shows the top part of the SCREEN section from Section 7.5 as it would look with embedded graphics characters, and underneath that, how the form would look when run.

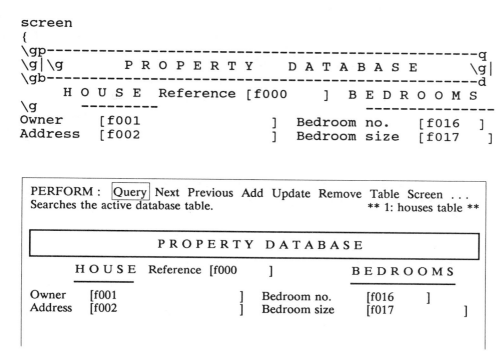

```
screen
{
\gp-------------------------------------------------q
\g|\g      P R O P E R T Y    D A T A B A S E      \g|
\gb-------------------------------------------------d
     H O U S E  Reference [f000    ] B E D R O O M S
\g      ---------                    ----------------
Owner     [f001             ]  Bedroom no.    [f016  ]
Address   [f002             ]  Bedroom size   [f017    ]
```

Figure 7.4   A PERFORM screen with graphics characters.

7.6 The TABLES Section

The TABLES section lists all the tables, table synonyms, or views from which columns will be drawn for this form. Table aliases may also be specified which operate just for this form. The maximum number of tables depends on your operating system, but is not usually less than twelve. Note that temporary tables may not be used, and only single-table views (views are covered in Chapter 5, Section 5.6.3) without aggregate information may be included. Here is an example of a TABLES section:

```
tables
h = houses          {alias for the houses table}
bedrooms agents
```

7.7 The ATTRIBUTES Section

The ATTRIBUTES section allows you to set validation and formatting criteria for the individual fields in a form, and also to associate each field tag with a particular database column (or joined columns). The order in which fields appear in the ATTRIBUTES section determines the order in which the cursor moves through them when the form is run (and also the order in which tables are made active through the **Table** command). The following is the ATTRIBUTES section relating to the SCREEN section example in Section 7.5. Note how each line ends with a semicolon:

```
attributes
f000 = *houses.ref_no = bedrooms.ref_no, queryclear;
f001 = houses.owner;
f002 = houses.adrs1;
f003 = houses.adrs2;
f004 = houses.town;
f005 = houses.county, default = "Surrey";
f006 = houses.no_bedrooms;
f007 = houses.no_baths;
f008 = houses.lounge_size;
f009 = houses.dining_size;
f010 = houses.thru_lounge_size;
f011 = houses.notes;
f012 = houses.price;

f013 = houses.agent = *agents.company,
                lookup f119 = agents.adrs1,
                       f120 = agents.adrs2,
                       f121 = agents.town,
                       f122 = agents.county,
                       f123 = agents.phone,
                joining agents.company;

f014 = houses.book_date,default = today;
f016 = bedrooms.bedroom_no;
f017 = bedrooms.bedroom_size,
        comments = "Format: 12'6 x 10'9";
a = bedrooms.ensuite_bath, default = "n", downshift;
f019 = agents.adrs1;
f020 = agents.adrs2;
f021 = agents.town,
        include = (Woking,Guildford,Weybridge,Hindhead),
        comments = "Woking, Guildford,
                        Weybridge or Hindhead";
f022 = agents.county, default = "Surrey";
f023 = agents.phone;
```

```
maxp = displayonly type money;
minp = displayonly type money;
avgp = displayonly type money;
```

end

Joins can be specified by allowing the join fields to share the same field tag, as in

```
f000 = houses.ref_no = bedrooms.ref_no;
```

Joins will be covered in greater detail in Section 7.8.

7.7.1 Displayonly fields

A *displayonly field* is a field in the form which is not associated with any database column. It exists to either display the results of some calculation, or to accept input, the value of which may be acted upon in the INSTRUCTIONS section (see Section 7.9). The syntax is as follows:

> *field-tag* = DISPLAYONLY [ALLOWING INPUT]
>   TYPE *datatype* [NOT NULL] [, *attr*];

For example:

```
maxp = displayonly type money;
```

For all the houses in the current list (i.e. those houses retrieved in the current query) the maximum price is calculated in the INSTRUCTIONS section and displayed at the field tag **maxp**.

Notes

(i)   The length of CHAR type displayonly fields is determined by the field length on the screen form; you do not need to specify it, as in

```
d120 = displayonly type char;
```

(ii) The optional ALLOWING INPUT clause permits the input of data to this field. The data is stored in a dummy table called **displaytable**, whose name may be referred to in the INSTRUCTIONS section.

(iii) *datatype* may be any of the **INFORMIX-SQL** data types except SERIAL, though there is little point using BYTE, since only the phrase **<BYTE value>** is displayed.

7.7.2 Subscripts

Character fields may be split by the use of subscripts, specified as follows (but see also the WORDWRAP attribute):

```
f008 = long_field[1,20];
f009 = long_field[21,40];
```

7.7.3 The attributes

Each individual field in a form may have its own set of validation and display attributes, specified as a list after the field name. The syntax is:

field-tag = [*table.*]*colname*[, *attr* [,...]];

Note that the table name is optional, and is only required if there is a *colname* of the same name in another table. However it does improve clarity.

Join fields may have separate attributes, for example:

field-tag = *col1, attr1, attr2;*
             = *col2, attr3, attr4;*

When the table containing *col1* is active, then *attr1* and *attr2* are effective, and when the table containing *col2* is active, *attr3* and *attr4* are in effect.

There is no limit to the number of attributes that may be specified for a field tag. They are listed here in alphabetical order.

autonext   allows the cursor to move to the start of the next field as soon as this field is filled, without the need for a carriage return. Particularly useful for fields which are split using subscripts (see Section 7.7.2). For example:

```
f008 = long_field[1,20], autonext;
f009 = long_field[21,40];
```

New for Version 4.0

color   (Sorry UK, that's how it's spelt!) Field text may now be displayed in one of eight colours, optionally combined with up to four screen attributes such as blink or underline.

The syntax is as follows:

field-tag = *colname,*
       COLOR = *dispmode-list* [WHERE *condition*];

dispmode-list is one of the following colours:

WHITE	CYAN
YELLOW	GREEN
MAGENTA	BLUE
RED	BLACK

and one or more intensities from this list:

REVERSE	BLINK	
UNDERLINE	LEFT	(left justified for number fields)

condition can be any of the conditions mentioned in the WHERE clause section of Chapter 5 (Section 5.4.2), including string matches, ranges and lists, and the logical operators AND and OR. For example:

```
f012 = houses.price,
       color = red where f012 < 100000;
f014 = houses.book_date,
       color = green blink
             where f014 < (today - 90);
```

comments   enables a message to be displayed on the Comments Line whenever the cursor is on a particular field. The message must appear on a single line of the form specification file:

```
f017 = bedrooms.bedroom_size,
       comments = "Format: 12'6 x 10'9";
```

default   if a certain field is more likely to contain one value in particular, this value can be specified as a default which will appear during an **Add** operation:

```
f005 = houses.county, default = "Surrey";
```

The system date may also be specified as a default using the keyword **today**:

```
f014 = houses.book_date, default = today;
```

For Version 4.0, you may also use the keyword **current** to specify the date *and time* for a DATETIME field.

downshift   causes any upper case letters entered into this field to be converted to lower case. This ensures that all the data in a particular column is in lower case, which is particularly useful when searching or ordering the output in a query or report. See also **upshift**.

format   used to specify (i) the precision and the position of the decimal point in the display of numeric fields of type DECIMAL, FLOAT or SMALLFLOAT, and (ii) the format of the display for fields of type DATE, overriding that in the environment variable **DBDATE**. The precision of numeric fields is specified by the use of hash signs:

```
f024 = decimalfield, format = "####.##";
```

For fields of type DATE (but not DATETIME or INTERVAL), the following characters may be used in the formatting string:

mm   displays the month as two digits, 01-12

mmm   displays a three-letter abbreviation of the month, as in Jan, Feb, etc.

dd   displays the day as two digits, 01-31

ddd   displays a three-letter abbreviation of the day, as in Mon, Tue, etc.

yy   displays the last two digits of the year

yyyy   displays the year as four digits.

Any other characters in the formatting string are displayed as literals. For instance:

format	Result
"mmm dd, yyyy"	Jun 26, 1990
"dd-mm-yy"	26-06-90

Note

It is not advisable to use complex date formats for anything but display fields, as adding and querying will be made more difficult by them.

include   allows you to specify acceptable values for the field. The values may be a list of discrete values:

```
f061 = table.numcol,
       include = (10, 20, 30, 40);
```

or a range of values:

```
f071 = table.ncol2, include = (1 to 100),
       comments = "Enter value 1 to 100";
```

Strings must be enclosed in quotes if they contain non-alphanumeric characters:

```
f016 = book_date,
     include = ("01/01/87" to "31/12/90")
     comments = "Any date in 1987-1990";
```

Note

It is always advisable to use a **comments** attribute with an **include** attribute, to inform the user of the allowable values.

lookup   lookup joins are covered in Section 7.8.2.

noentry   specifies that during an **Add** operation no data may be entered in this field.

noupdate   protects a field from change during an **Update** operation.

picture   specifies a pattern for the data to be entered. The pattern may consist of a combination of the following characters:

A   matches any alphabetic character

matches any numeric character

X   matches any character

For example:

```
f112 = postcode, picture = "AA#XX#AA";
```

would accept an entry such as "TW15 1TZ" and also "KT3 5PF" (with two spaces), but not "12W 7DB".

New for Version 4.0

program   INFORMIX-OnLine BLOBs may be accessed through **PERFORM** by using the **program** attribute to call an external program. TEXT fields may be displayed using the WORDWRAP attribute, but they may only be edited using **program**. BYTE fields are never displayed, instead the phrase **<BYTE value>** is shown, which is as long as the field tag needs to be. To invoke the program, you merely type an exclamation mark (!) when the cursor is on the first character of a BLOB field. On exit from the external program, the form screen is restored. The syntax for this attribute is:

> *field-tag* = *colname*, PROGRAM = "*command-string*";

For example, the following line will invoke the Q-ONE word processor with the document stored in the **full_descript** column of the current row. If the column for this row is empty, then Q-ONE will be invoked to create the document, which will be saved in the database.

```
f213 = full_descript, program = "Q1";
```

Note

For a TEXT field, the editor invoked when an exclamation mark is typed is taken from:

1. The program specified by the PROGRAM attribute, if any.

2. The program specified in the **DBEDIT** environment variable, if defined.

3. The default editor, **vi** for UNIX, and **edlin** for DOS.

queryclear   normally, when the user executes a query, all the fields on the screen are cleared, with the exception of the join fields. If the attribute **queryclear** is used, *all* fields, including join fields (but not displayonly fields) will be cleared:

```
f000 = houses.ref_no
     = bedrooms.ref_no, queryclear;
```

required   forces the operator to enter a value during an **Add** operation. If no value is entered, then when **ESC** is pressed, the cursor will move to the required field and this message is displayed on the Status Line:

This field requires an entered value

reverse   displays the contents of a field in reverse video.

right   right will right-justify a field. To search for a value in this field, you will have to begin your search string with an asterisk (*).

upshift   causes any lower case letters entered into this field to be converted to upper case. See also **downshift**.

verify   this attribute requires the operator to enter the data twice. If the two do not match, the data must be entered twice again.

New for Version 4.0

wordwrap   wraps a long character string (such as a VARCHAR or TEXT field in OnLine) to the next field that has *the same field tag*. For CHAR or VARCHAR fields, it also invokes the multiline editor (see Chapter 6, Section 6.4.3). The optional COMPRESS keyword tells **PERFORM** to discard any *editor blanks* (inserted by the editor when wrapping a word to the next line) which are not part of the data. The syntax is:

field-tag = *colname*, WORDWRAP [COMPRESS];

zerofill   right-justifies a field and fills it with zeros to the left.

Exercise

1.   Modify your default form as per the examples in the SCREEN and ATTRIBUTES sections (Sections 7.5 and 7.7). Compile and run your new form.

2.   Test your form in **Query, Add** and **Update** modes, using the sample data in Appendix 1.

7.8 Joins in PERFORM

There are four different kinds of join which may be specified in a form specification file, and they are:

- Joins

- Verify joins

- Lookup joins

- Composite joins

We saw briefly in Section 6.7 how columns from different tables may be joined in a form, by equating a single field tag to the database columns to be joined:

field-tag = col1 = col2[= colN][, attr [,...]];

For example, the **houses** and **bedrooms** tables may be joined on their **ref_no** columns:

```
f000 = houses.ref_no = bedrooms.ref_no;
```

Join fields may have separate attributes, for example:

field-tag = col1, attr1, attr2;
        = col2, attr3, attr4;

When the table containing *col1* is active, then *attr1* and *attr2* are effective, and when the table containing *col2* is active, *attr3* and *attr4* are in effect.

To retrieve all the bedrooms for a particular house the operator would:

1.   Find the required house using **Query** on the **houses** table

2.   Switch to the **bedrooms** table using the **Table** option

3.   Query the **bedrooms** table for all rows with the **ref_no** now displayed in the join field.

This process may be much simplified by use of the **master/detail** relationship, expressed in the INSTRUCTIONS section, and covered in Section 7.9.2.

Notes

(i)   When a query is executed, all the fields on the screen are cleared except the join fields. If the attribute **queryclear** is used, *all* fields including join fields (but excluding displayonly fields) will be cleared:

```
f000 = houses.ref_no = bedrooms.ref_no, queryclear;
```

(ii)   Any query involving a join will run faster if the columns in the join are indexed.

7.8.1 Verify joins

It is often the case that data should only be entered in a field if that data is already present in the corresponding column of another table. In our property database, we do not want a new house added unless we have that house's full agent details in the **agents** table. Similarly, we must prevent a bedroom row being added for a nonexistent house. We can achieve this verification by means of a *verify join*. In a verify join one of the columns is *dominant*, i.e. the value must exist in the dominant column before it can be entered into one of the subservient columns in the join. We denote a column as dominant by means of an asterisk, as in

```
f000 = *houses.ref_no = bedrooms.ref_no;
```

and

```
f013 = houses.agent = *agents.agent;
```

If an attempt is made to enter data in a field which is not present in the table containing the dominant column (e.g. the **agents** table), the following message is displayed:

This is an invalid value -- it does not exist in "agents" table

7.8.2 Lookup joins

When two tables are joined and the first table is queried, the join is executed automatically, displaying data from the second table where appropriate. However there is nothing to prevent the user making the second table active and entering or changing data in it (except the use of **noentry** and **noupdate** attributes, or table permissions). We can prevent the second table ever becoming active but still retain the ability to display data from it on a join by means of a *lookup join*. A lookup join is actually an attribute which allows us to display data on a join (or verify join) with another table, but without the ability to make the second table active. We could display an agent's details like this:

```
f013 = houses.agent,
            lookup f119 = agents.adrs1,
                   f120 = agents.adrs2,
                   f121 = agents.town,
                   f122 = agents.county,
                   f123 = agents.phone,
            joining agents.agent;
```

However, in the ATTRIBUTES section in Section 7.7, the first line is different:

```
f013 = houses.agent = *agents.agent,
             lookup f119 = agents.adrs1,
                    f120 = agents.adrs2,
                    f121 = agents.town,
                    f122 = agents.county,
                    f123 = agents.phone,
            joining agents.agent;
```

This is done so that on the first screen, lookup only is allowed, whereas on the second screen full **Add, Query, Update** and **Remove** facilities are permitted. Note the verify join.

Note

You may also have a *verify lookup join* which you specify by putting an asterisk on the joining column, as in

```
joining *agents.agent;
```

However, this will prevent the user from entering any new data in the table containing the dominant column.

7.8.3 Composite joins

When you need to specify the values of more than one column of a table to uniquely identify a row, and that table is to be involved in a join, you may need to use a *composite join*. Composite joins are specified in the INSTRUCTIONS section, and so are covered in detail in Section 7.9.1.

Exercise

1.   Make sure that you have included the verify join coding in your ATTRIBUTES section, as per the example in Section 7.7.

2.   Test out the verify joins by trying to enter a house with a nonexistent agent.

3.   Make sure that when you add a house with a correct agent that the agent's details appear in the display lookup fields.

4.   Try removing a house that has some bedroom rows. You should find that the verify join will not allow you to.

5.   Check that only valid house reference numbers can be entered when a new bedroom is added.

7.9 The INSTRUCTIONS Section

The optional INSTRUCTIONS section is the last section in a form specification file and is used to:

- Establish composite joins

- Specify master/detail relationships

- Perform on-screen arithmetic

- Define conditional control blocks and skip logic

Below is the INSTRUCTIONS section from our example form specification:

```
instructions
agents master of houses;
houses master of bedrooms;

before remove of agents
        abort

before editadd editupdate of houses
        nextfield = f013

after editadd editupdate of ensuite_bath
    nextfield = exitnow

after editadd editupdate of bedroom_no
        if f016 > f006
        then
            begin
            comments bell reverse "Too many bedrooms"
            nextfield = f016
            end

after query of houses
        begin
        let maxp = max of f012
        let minp = min of f012
        let avgp = average of f012
        end

after add of houses
        comments bell reverse
                "Please now add the bedroom details"

end
```

7.9.1 Composite joins

When you need to specify the values of more than one column of a table to uniquely identify a row, and that table is to be involved in a join, you may need to use a *composite join*. The **bedrooms** table requires the use of the **ref_no** and **bedroom_no** columns to identify a row uniquely. Let us suppose that another table called **furniture** exists, which details the pieces of furniture present in each bedroom. Each row in **furniture** must have as part of its primary key, the columns **ref_no** and **bedroom_no**, to identify which bedroom in which house the piece of furniture belongs. To join the **bedrooms** and **furniture** tables we would use the COMPOSITES statement, as below:

```
composites <bedrooms.ref_no, bedrooms.bedroom_no>
          <furniture.ref_no, furniture.bedroom_no>;
```

The full syntax of the COMPOSITES statement is as follows:

COMPOSITES < *table1.col1, table1.col2* [, *table1.col3* [,...]] >
    [*] < *table2.col1, table2.col2* [, *table2.col3* [,...]] >;

Notice that the two sets of column names are each enclosed in a pair of angle brackets < >, and also that an asterisk may be used to indicate a verify join as in Section 7.8.1.

Notes

(i)   Each column in a composite join must also be individually joined in the ATTRIBUTES section. In the example above, **bedrooms.ref_no** must be joined to **furniture.ref_no** and **bedrooms.bedroom_no** must be joined to **furniture.bedroom_no**. There must however be no other joins between columns of the two tables.

(ii)   Querying will be speeded up if the columns are individually and jointly indexed.

7.9.2 Master/detail relationships

In situations where there is a one-to-many relationship between two tables (for example one house has many bedrooms), cross-table querying is greatly simplified by the creation of a *master/detail* relationship. To retrieve all the bedroom rows for a particular house, you would normally have to perform these steps:

1.   Retrieve the required row from the **houses** table.

2.   Change to the **bedrooms** table using the **Table** option.

3.   Query the **bedrooms** table using the **ref_no** displayed from the house row.

If a master/detail relationship had been defined between the **houses** and **bedrooms** tables, then having retrieved the required house row, you would merely have to select the **Detail** option which would automatically change tables and query the **bedrooms** table using the join field. You may then return to the **houses** record using the **Master** option. Master/detail relationships are defined as in the examples below (note also that one agent has many houses):

```
agents master of houses;
houses master of bedrooms;
```

Master/detail relationships may also be used in the following way. Suppose we want to find all the houses having the same agent as one particular house. We would follow these steps:

1. **Query** for the particular house row.

2. Select **Master** to find the agent details.

3. Now select **Detail** to retrieve all the houses having that agent.

7.9.3 Delimiters

The default delimiters used to enclose fields on a screen form are square brackets [ ], but these may be changed for any other pair of printable characters, including spaces, by means of the DELIMITERS statement, which takes the form:

DELIMITERS "*ab*";

where *a* and *b* are the opening and closing delimiters respectively.

Notes

(i)   If you use spaces as your delimiters, you will not be able to tell which table is active if you have more than one table represented on the screen at the same time.

(ii) **FORMBUILD** requires that you use square brackets in the SCREEN section regardless of the delimiters specified with this statement. The one exception is where both opening and closing delimiters are to be the same, and you wish certain fields to butt against each other. You may then use a pipe symbol between the two butting fields, like this:

```
Combined code    [f210    |f211    ];
```

In this case, both the square brackets and the pipe symbol will be replaced by your chosen delimiter when the form is run.

Exercise

1.   Amend your form to include the master/detail relationships in the example of the previous section.

2.   Using the **Master** and **Detail** options, retrieve all of the houses which have the same agent as house number 5.

7.10 Control Blocks

The INSTRUCTIONS section may also contain *control blocks* which may be used to:

* Control cursor movement during an **Add** or **Update** operation

* Perform calculations on field values and enter the result in another field

* Display aggregate information such as averages and totals on columns in the current list

* Call C functions if you have **INFORMIX-ESQL/C**

Control blocks operate either *before* or *after* **PERFORM** operations are completed. Both BEFORE and AFTER blocks may be associated with **Add, Update** and **Remove** operations, whereas only AFTER blocks may be associated with a **Query** operation.

7.10.1 BEFORE blocks

The syntax of a BEFORE block is as follows:

> BEFORE *{option-list}* OF *table/column-list*
>
> > *action*
> > *action*
> > .
> > .
> > *action*

where:

option-list   is one or more of the following, separated by spaces:

EDITADD	during an **Add** operation, the *action* is executed when the cursor is on the field associated with any column name specified in *column-list*, but before any data is entered. If a table name is specified, the *action* is executed before data is entered into the first field associated with that table.
EDITUPDATE	during an **Update** operation, the *action* is executed when the cursor is on the field associated with any column name specified in *column-list*, but before any data is entered. If a table name is specified, the action is executed before data is entered into the first field associated with that table.

REMOVE   during a **Remove** operation, the *action* is executed before the row is removed. This option may only be used with a *table-list*.

table/
column-list   is a list of up to sixteen names of database tables and/or columns. Note that these must be database column names and not field tags.

action   is one of the five kinds of action described later in Section 7.10.3.

Examples

When a new house is added (or an old one updated), the agent's details must already be present in the **agents** table, and this is checked by the verify join set up between the **houses** and **agents** tables in the ATTRIBUTES section. It would be convenient therefore to start the **Add** operation at the Agent field, as in this example:

```
before editadd editupdate of houses
    nextfield = f013
```

This example prevents any **agents** rows from being removed:

```
before remove of agents
    abort
```

7.10.2 AFTER blocks

The syntax of an AFTER block is as follows:

AFTER {*option-list*} OF *table/column-list*

   action
   action
      .
      .
   action

where:

option-list   is one or more of the following, separated by spaces:

EDITADD   during an **Add** operation, the *action* is executed when data has been entered into the field associated with any column name specified in *column-list*, after you have pressed **RETURN**. If a table name is specified, the *action* is executed after **ESC** is pressed.

EDITUPDATE   during an **Update** operation, the *action* is executed when data has been entered into the field associated with any column name specified in *column-list*, after you have pressed **RETURN**. If a table name is specified, the *action* is executed after **ESC** is pressed.

ADD   may only be used with a *table-list*. The *action* is executed after the row is added to the table.

QUERY   may only be used with a *table-list*. The *action* is executed after the data has been retrieved.

UPDATE   may only be used with a *table-list*. The *action* is executed after the row has been updated.

REMOVE   may only be used with a *table-list*. The *action* is executed after the row has been removed.

DISPLAY   may only be used with a *table-list*. The *action* is executed after any **PERFORM** operation that causes data to be displayed on the screen (including **Next, Previous** etc.).

table/ column-list   is a list of up to sixteen names of database tables and/or columns. Note that these must be database column names and not field tags. The table names may include **displaytable**, which is the dummy table used to hold data from a displayonly field with input.

action   is one of the five kinds of action described later in Section 7.10.3.

Examples

While adding bedroom rows, the following AFTER block ensures that no more bedroom rows are added than have been specified in the corresponding house row:

```
after editadd editupdate of bedroom_no
   if f016 > f006
   then
      begin
      comments bell reverse
      "You have tried to add too many bedrooms"
      nextfield = f016
      end
```

Each time a **Query** is executed on the **houses** table, the following AFTER block displays the maximum, minimum and average prices of houses in the current list:

```
after query of houses
    let maxp = max of f012
    let minp = min of f012
    let avgp = avg of f012
```

When a house row has been added there is no way of automatically changing to the **bedrooms** table, but we can remind the operator to add bedroom details:

```
after add of houses
    comments reverse "Now add the bedroom details"
```

7.10.3 Control block actions

The following five actions may be used in BEFORE and AFTER blocks. They are presented alphabetically.

ABORT

Ends the current operation without altering the database, and returns control to the PERFORM menu. It is equivalent to pressing the **Interrupt** key. (Note that in contrast the NEXTFIELD = EXITNOW action is equivalent to pressing the **ESC** key.) For example the removal of **agents** rows may be prevented altogether:

```
before remove of agents
    abort
```

COMMENTS

Allows a comment to be displayed on the Status Line (the last line of the screen). In contrast, the **comments** attribute displays a message on the Comments Line, which is the last line but one. For example:

```
after update of houses
    comments "This house row has been updated"
```

Two options, BELL and REVERSE are also available with this action:

```
after remove of houses
    comments bell reverse
        "  Yet another house sold!   "
```

Note

As with the **comments** attribute, the message must be enclosed in quotes, must only be one line long and must be on one line of the form specification file (though the comments action itself may be broken over two lines, as in the example).

IF-THEN-ELSE

Performs actions based upon conditions involving field tags that can take on the values true or false. The full syntax is:

    IF *bool-expr* THEN *action(s)* [ELSE *action(s)*]

where:

bool-expr   is a combination of expressions involving field tags, comparison operators (=, < >, >, <, > =, < =), logical operators (AND, OR, NOT), and the operators IS NULL and IS NOT NULL. For field tags of type CHAR, the MATCHES operator may also be used, and the comparison string may then include the wildcards ? and * as previously defined in Chapter 5, Section 5.4.3.

action(s)   is either a single action as defined in this section or more than one action between the keywords BEGIN and END.

For example:

```
after editadd editupdate of bedroom_no
   if f016 > f006
   then
      begin
      comments bell reverse "Too many bedrooms"
      nextfield = f016
      end
```

LET

Assigns a value to a field tag. The field tag must be either a displayonly field, or a field tag associated with a column in the active table. This means that either the column's table or the column itself must be specified in the *table/column-list* of the BEFORE/AFTER statement. The syntax is as follows:

    LET *field-tag* = *expr*

where:

expr   is an expression consisting of a field tag, a constant, an aggregate function, the keyword TODAY (and CURRENT in Version 4.0), or any combination of these using the arithmetic operators +, −, * and /. Parentheses ( ) may also be used to change the precedence of the operators.

The aggregate functions take the following form:

agg-function OF *field-tag*

and are computed for all the values of *field-tag* in the current list. Note that *field-tag* must be associated with a database column and not a displayonly field. The aggregate functions are:

COUNT   the number of rows

TOTAL   the sum of the values of the field tag

AVG   the average of the values of the field tag

MAX   the maximum value of the field tag

MIN   the minimum value of the field tag

Examples

The following AFTER block computes and displays the maximum, minimum and average prices of houses in the current list after every **Query** operation:

```
after query of houses
    let maxp = max of f012
    let minp = min of f012
    let avgp = avg of f012
```

The following AFTER block computes the time in weeks that the house has been on the books:

```
after display of houses
    let h01 = (today - f014) / 7
```

NEXTFIELD

Overrides the default order of field access (i.e. the order in which the fields appear in the ATTRIBUTES section). For example:

```
before editadd of houses
    nextfield = f013
```

The keyword EXITNOW may be used in place of a field tag. This is then equivalent to pressing the **ESC** key, committing the current **Add, Update** or **Remove** operation. (By contrast, the ABORT action is equivalent to pressing the **Interrupt** key.) For example:

```
after editadd editupdate of ensuite_bath
    nextfield = exitnow
```

As soon as data has been entered into the field tag associated with the **ensuite_bath** column, in either **Add** or **Update** mode, the row is added or updated and the cursor returns to the PERFORM menu.

Exercise

1. On a query, display the maximum, minimum and average of the prices of the retrieved houses.

2. Ensure that when a new house is added and the bedroom details are added, that as far as possible, only details for the right number of bedrooms are allowed to be entered. There is a limit to what you can do here!

7.11 Example Form

The following is a full listing of the example form used in this Module. It includes most of the features of **PERFORM**, though not those introduced with Version 4.0. It does however use the graphics characters as discussed in Section 7.5.3, since many 2.10.03 versions contain this feature already.

The form has been compressed slightly to fit within the page.

```
database property end
screen
{
\gp-----------------------------------------------------q
\g|               P R O P E R T Y      D A T A B A S E           |
\gb-----------------------------------------------------d
    H O U S E   Reference [f000      ]  B E D R O O M S
\g        ---------                          ---------------
Owner       [f001            ]  Bedroom no.   [f016   ]
Address     [f002            ]  Bedroom size  [f017            ]
            [f003            ]  Ensuite bath  [a]
Town        [f004            ]
County      [f005            ]               A G E N T
\g                                            ---------
No. of bedrooms   [f006    ]         [f119                      ]
No. of bathrooms  [f007    ]         [f120                      ]
Lounge size       [f008        ]     [f121                      ]
Dining size       [f009        ]     [f122                      ]
Thru lounge size  [f010        ]     [f123          ]
Notes             [f011                             ]
Price             [f012            ]  Max price [maxp      ]
Agent             [f013            ]  Min price [minp      ]
Date booked       [f014 ] Wks [h14] Avg price [avgp      ]
}
screen
{
\gp-----------------------------------------------------q
\g|                     A G E N T S                             |
\gb-----------------------------------------------------d
              Name     [f013            ]
              Address  [f019            ]
                       [f020            ]
              Town     [f021            ]
              County   [f022            ]
              Phone    [f023       ]

\g--------------------------------------------------
}
end
```

```
tables houses bedrooms agents
end

attributes
f000 = *houses.ref_no = bedrooms.ref_no, queryclear;
f001 = houses.owner;
f002 = houses.adrs1;
f003 = houses.adrs2;
f004 = houses.town;
f005 = houses.county, default = "Surrey";
f006 = no_bedrooms;
f007 = no_baths;
f008 = lounge_size;
f009 = dining_size;
f010 = thru_lounge_size;
f011 = notes;
f012 = price;

f013 = houses.agent = *agents.agent,
       lookup f119 = agents.adrs1,
          f120 = agents.adrs2,
          f121 = agents.town,
          f122 = agents.county,
          f123 = agents.phone
       joining agents.agent;
f014 = book_date,default = today;

f016 = bedroom_no;
f017 = bedroom_size, comments = "Format: 12'6 x 10'9";
a = ensuite_bath, default = "n", downshift;

f019 = agents.adrs1;
f020 = agents.adrs2;
f021 = agents.town,
          include = (Woking, Guildford,
                          Weybridge, Hindhead),
          comments = "Woking, Guildford,
                          Weybridge or Hindhead";
f022 = agents.county, default = "Surrey";
f023 = agents.phone;

h14 = displayonly type smallint;
maxp = displayonly type money;
minp = displayonly type money;
avgp = displayonly type money;

instructions
agents master of houses;
houses master of bedrooms;
```

```
before remove of agents
    abort

before editadd editupdate of houses
    nextfield = f013

after display of houses
    let h14 = (today - f014) / 7

after editadd editupdate of ensuite_bath
    nextfield = exitnow

after editadd editupdate of bedroom_no
    if f016 > f006
    then
        begin
        comments bell reverse "Too many bedrooms"
        nextfield = f016
        end

after query of houses
    let maxp = max of f012
    let minp = min of f012
    let avgp = average of f012

after add of houses
    comments bell reverse "Now add the bedroom details"

end
```

Chapter 8

ACE Report Generator

8.1 Introduction

ACE is a report generator which combines the facilities of SQL for interrogating the database with powerful report formatting capabilities. It allows you to combine information from several tables in a database, add page and column headings, group and subtotal data and print the report on the screen or printer, or save it in a file. Reports can be anything from phone directories to mailing labels, standard letters to resource schedules. In this chapter we will see how to create and customise a variety of reports, taking the data from our **property** database.

But first let us examine the REPORT menu, shown in Figure 8.1, which may be obtained by selecting **Report** from the main **INFORMIX-SQL** menu.

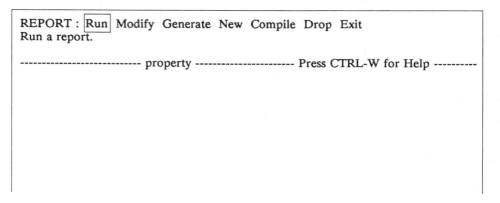

```
REPORT : Run  Modify  Generate  New  Compile  Drop  Exit
Run a report.

---------------------------- property ---------------------- Press CTRL-W for Help ----------
```

Figure 8.1 The REPORT menu.

These are the options on the REPORT menu:

Run   Displays the RUN REPORT screen from which a previously created report may be run by selecting it from the list displayed. Just move the cursor to the desired report name and press **RETURN**.

182

Modify	This option is used to modify the text of a report specification file using the system editor (or the one specified in the **DBEDIT** environment variable, see Chapter 1). The report specification file must be compiled before the report can be run.
Generate	The **Generate** option creates a default report. This option is covered in detail in Section 8.2.
New	Creates a new report specification from scratch, using the system editor.
Compile	The **Compile** option compiles a report specification file into a report that may be run.
Drop	Drops a report, selected from the list displayed, from the database.
Exit	Returns to the **INFORMIX-SQL** main menu.

8.2 Creating Default Reports

A default report takes information from one table in the database and provides a basic report layout including all the columns and all the rows in that table. It provides a good starting point for a fully customised report since it contains all of the mandatory sections required in a report specification file.

To create a default report specification, follow these steps:

1.   Select **Report** from the main menu, giving you access to the REPORT menu.

2.   Select the **Generate** option from the REPORT menu, and give your report a name (up to ten characters in UNIX, eight in DOS).

3.   Select the main table on which your report will be based from the list of tables displayed on the CHOOSE TABLE menu (see Figure 8.2).

```
CHOOSE TABLE >>
Choose the table to be used in the default report.

------------------------------------------------------- Press CTRL-W for Help --------

┌────────┐
│houses  │
└────────┘

bedrooms

agents
```

Figure 8.2 The CHOOSE TABLE menu.

4.   **INFORMIX-SQL** will then use the program **saceprep** to compile your
default report specification.

You may now select the **Run** option and run your report. It will be displayed
on the screen, since this is the default.

Figure 8.3 shows a default report specification for the **agents** table.

```
database   property   end


select
         agent,
         adrs1,
         adrs2,
         town,
         county,
         phone
from agents   end


format   every row   end
```

Figure 8.3   A default report specification
for the **agents** table.

The output from this default report will appear on the screen as below. Note
that the page width defaults to 132 characters (see Section 8.8, The OUTPUT
section) and so the output 'wraps around' on the screen.

```
agent                    adrs1                    adrs2
   town                  county                phone

Beasleys                 12 Bishopsmead Prde.
   East Horsley          Surrey                04865-1874
Ministers & Co           38 Commercial Way
   Woking                Surrey                04862-10707
Allen & Co               25 High Street
   Woking                Surrey                04862-11717
Thompson & Bayles        204 London Road          Burpham
   Guildford             Surrey                0483-727575
Granthams                3 Headley Road           Grayshott
   Hindhead              Surrey                Hind. 7474
Smiths & Co              29 Hemming Way
   Woking                Surrey                04862-54321
```

Notes

(i) If you choose the **New** option on the menu, **INFORMIX-SQL** calls your system editor and allows you to create a report specification from scratch. However it is much easier to use the **Generate** option, followed by **Modify**.

(ii) Using the **Generate** option, you may only specify one table to be used in the report, but more tables may be included during customisation.

(iii) There are two files associated with a report: a source file with the extension **.ace** (or **.ACE** on DOS), and a compiled, runnable file with the extension **.arc** (or **.ARC** on DOS).

8.3 Customising ACE Reports

A default report produces all the information from one table without any formatting, arithmetic, totalling or run time user input. To add these features, you must customise your default report using an editor. (At this point it is worth mentioning **INFORMIX-QuickStep**, a relatively new product from Informix which, being an *interactive* report generator, alleviates much of the drudgery of manual report customisation. A short overview of QuickStep is given in Appendix 3.)

Customising a report specification involves adding more instructions into the mandatory sections, and adding certain optional sections. All of the sections which may be included in a report specification are outlined shortly, and are then described in detail in the following sections. This section tells you how to edit and compile your customised report specification.

Follow these steps to customise a default or previously created report specification:

1. Select **Modify** from the REPORT menu. You are presented with the MODIFY REPORT menu, from which you may select a report from the list displayed, using the arrow keys followed by **RETURN**, or type in the name in full. This will call up the editor specified in the **DBEDIT** environment variable (see Chapter 1) or your system editor (such as **vi**).

2. Make the changes required to customise your report, according to the information contained in the following sections of this chapter, and save the file.

3. You are then presented with the second MODIFY REPORT menu (see Figure 8.4), from which you should select **Compile**.

4. If your report specification has compiled correctly, the message

Report compilation successful

will be displayed. Go to Step 6.

5.   If the compilation was unsuccessful and the report contained errors, you are presented with, and should select the **Correct** option from the COMPILE REPORT menu. Your editor is called again and the errors in your specification are highlighted with error messages. Correct the errors (you may leave the error messages, **ACE** will remove them for you), save your file and return to Step 3. Note that **ACE** often points to the line *after* where the error really occurred.

6.   When the compilation is successful, select the **Save-and-exit** option from the MODIFY REPORT menu. You may now run your report.

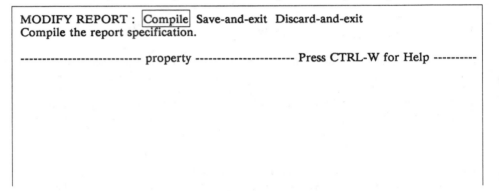

Figure 8.4   The MODIFY REPORT menu.

An example of a fully customised report specification appears in the next section.

Note

Comments may be included anywhere within a report by either enclosing them in curly brackets { }, or in Version 4.0, by preceding them with a double dash (--). Do not use a hash (#) to precede them since this kind of comment line is used by **ACE** to denote an error and is removed during compilation.

8.4 Report Specification Structure

The report specification file has up to six sections of which three are required and three are optional. The order in which the sections may appear is as set out opposite, and they are covered in detail in the following sections.

DATABASE   Required. The DATABASE section identifies the database on which the report is to operate.

DEFINE   Optional. This section is used to declare variables used in the report and also any command line parameters.

INPUT   Optional. Used to prompt the user at run time for parameters from the keyboard.

OUTPUT   Optional. Controls the overall page format, such as length and width, and also redirection of the output to a file, printer or (on UNIX systems) a pipe.

SELECT   Required. The SELECT section contains one or more SQL SELECT statements which specify the columns and rows on which the report is to based.

New for Version 4.0

READ   The SELECT section may be replaced by a READ section, which allows you to retrieve data from an ASCII file instead of from a database.

FORMAT   Required. The FORMAT section determines the final appearance of data in the report.

There follows an example of a fully customised report specification:

```
{ Example report number 1 }

database property end

define
    variable maxprice money
end

input
    prompt for maxprice using "Enter maximum price:"
end

output
    top margin 0
    bottom margin 0
    page length 23
end
```

```
select h.adrs1 hadrs1, h.town htown, agent, price
   from houses h
   where price <= $maxprice
   order by agent, price
end

format
   first page header
      print column 25, "HOUSES REPORT NO. 1"
      skip 3 lines

   on every row
      print hadrs1 clipped, ", ", htown clipped;
      print column 35, price using "$,$$$,$$$";
      print 3 spaces, agent

   after group of agent
      need 3 lines
      skip 1 line
      print col 5, "Total for ", agent, " = ",
         group count using "<<<&"
      skip 2 lines

   page trailer
      skip 1 line
      pause "Press <RETURN> to continue"
end
```

Note

Reports may be run directly from the command line by using the **ACEGO** program via the **sacego** command or the **isql** command as follows (the **−s** option suppresses the Informix copyright and system messages normally displayed at run time):

```
sacego -s reportname
```

or

```
isql -s -rr reportname
```

Exercise

1.   Create a default report for the **houses** table, and run the report.

2.   Customise your report adding some or all of the features from the customised report example in the previous section.

3.   Run your new customised report.

8.5 The DATABASE Section

This section must be the first and contains the name of the database from which the report will be generated:

DATABASE *database-name* END

For example:

```
database property end
```

New for Version 4.0

If you are using a READ section instead of a SELECT section, you may specify the keyword ASCII instead of the name of a database, as in:

```
database ascii end
```

8.6 The DEFINE Section

The DEFINE section (which if present must come directly after the DATABASE section) may be used to declare variables which can be used in the report, and parameters which can accept values from the command line.

8.6.1 The VARIABLE statement

The syntax of the VARIABLE statement is as follows:

VARIABLE *var-name datatype*

Here is an example of a DEFINE section with some VARIABLE statements:

```
define
    variable count1 type integer
    variable newdate type date
    variable string1 type char(20)
end
```

The variables are initially set to zero or spaces and may subsequently be assigned values using the LET statement (see Section 8.10.2). For example:

```
let count1 = count1 + 1
let string1 = "New text string"
```

8.6.2 The PARAM statement

Variables may also be used to accept values from the command line, when the report is run using **sacego** (or a **User-menu**, see Chapter 9) instead of from the REPORT menu. In this case the variables are defined as numbered parameters, the number referring to the position of the required argument on the command line. The syntax of the PARAM statement is as follows:

PARAM[*integer*] *var-name datatype*

Note that the square brackets are mandatory and do not refer to an optional argument. Let us look at an example. Here is an extract from a report which we shall call **proprep1**. The report will print the details of houses which are under a certain price and are in a particular town. The price limit and town name are entered on the command line:

```
define
    param[1] maxprice type integer
    param[2] reqtown type char(10)
end

select * from houses
    where price <= $maxprice
    and town = $reqtown
end
```

The report may then be invoked with a command line such as the following, which reports on houses in Guildford which cost less than £110,000:

```
sacego -s proprep1 110000 Guildford
```

Notes

(i)   A report which uses PARAM statements may not be run from the REPORT menu, only from the command line (or from a **User-menu**).

(ii)   A total of 100 variables may be declared in an **ACE** report using the VARIABLE and PARAM statements.

(iii) If a variable is to be used in a SELECT statement, then the variable name must be preceded by a dollar sign ($), as in the example above.

New for Version 4.0

8.6.3 The ASCII statement

The ASCII statement is used to specify the field names and data types of the records in an ASCII input file, when one has been specified in a READ section. The syntax is as follows:

ASCII *field-name data-type* [,...]

For example:

```
ascii name char(25), address1 char(25),
      town char(25), no_beds smallint, price money,
      agent char(25)
```

Notes

(i)   A MONEY data type must be specified simply as MONEY.

(ii)   Since the data is coming from an ASCII file and not from the database, the field names specified need have no correspondence to those in any table, even if the data was unloaded from that table.

8.7 The INPUT Section

Variables which have been declared in the DEFINE section may be prompted for at the start of the report using an INPUT section. Note the position in a report specification of the optional INPUT section:

DATABASE section
[DEFINE section]
[INPUT section]

There is only one type of statement that may appear in an INPUT statement – the PROMPT statement, the syntax of which is as follows:

PROMPT FOR *var-name* USING *"string"*

For example:

```
define
    variable start_date date
    variable end_date date
end

input
 prompt for start_date using "Houses booked after:"
 prompt for end_date using   "          but before:"
end

select * from houses
    where bookdate > $start_date
    and bookdate < $end_date
end
```

8.8 The OUTPUT Section

The optional OUTPUT section allows you to set page dimensions for the report and also to direct the output to a file, the printer or, on UNIX systems, via a pipe to another program. ACE assumes several default values for page dimensions as described in Figure 8.5 below.

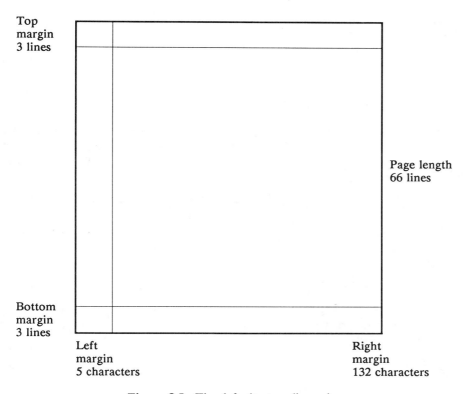

Figure 8.5   The default page dimensions of an ACE report.

These defaults may be changed in the OUTPUT section by a combination of any of the following statements:

```
LEFT MARGIN integer
RIGHT MARGIN integer
TOP MARGIN integer
BOTTOM MARGIN integer
PAGE LENGTH integer
REPORT TO { "file-name" | PIPE "program-name" | PRINTER }
```

For example the following OUTPUT section works well when sending a report to the screen:

```
    page length 22
    left margin 0
    bottom margin 0
end
```

Note the position of the OUTPUT section in a report specification:

    DATABASE section
    [DEFINE section]
    [INPUT section]
    [OUTPUT section]

8.8.1 The REPORT TO statement

The output from the report appears by default on the screen, but it may be redirected either to a file, to the printer or, on UNIX systems, to another command via a pipe using the REPORT TO statement, which has the following syntax:

    REPORT TO { "*file-name*" | PIPE "*program-name*" | PRINTER }

This OUTPUT section will save the output from the report in a file named **repout**:

```
output
    page length 22
    left margin 0
    bottom margin 0
    report to "repout"
end
```

If you use the statement

    REPORT TO PRINTER

the report output will be directed to the program named in the **DBPRINT** environment variable (see Chapter 1). If this is not set, then **ACE** will use **lp** on UNIX systems and **LPT1** on DOS systems.

There is no way of passing a printer name to the report at run time, but a choice of printers may be effected by use of a UNIX shell script and the REPORT TO PIPE statement. The shell script, which we shall call **acepr**, takes the following form:

```
#
#   Script to accept input from a pipeline and send
#   it to lp, but asking for the printer destination
#   first.
#
echo "Which printer? \c"
read DEST < /dev/tty
lp -d${DEST}
```

The OUTPUT section would then contain the line:

```
report to pipe "acepr"
```

The script may easily be extended to give the user a choice of redirecting the output to screen, file or printer:

```
#
#   Script to accept input from a pipeline and send
#   it to a choice of screen, file or printer.
#
echo "Output to (S)creen, (F)ile, or (P)rinter? \c"
read dest < /dev/tty
case $dest in
    s|S)  cat > /dev/tty ;;
    f|F)  echo "Enter file name->\c"
          read file < /dev/tty
          cat > $file ;;
    p|P)  lp ;;
esac
```

Notes

(i)   The RIGHT MARGIN statement is only effective when the FORMAT section consists solely of an EVERY ROW statement, and is independent of the LEFT MARGIN setting.

(i)   The PAGE LENGTH setting includes the TOP MARGIN and BOTTOM MARGIN.

(iii) The TOP MARGIN appears above any page header, and the BOTTOM MARGIN below any page trailer.

Exercise

1. Modify your report so that it prompts the user for a date. The houses retrieved by the report must all have been on the books before this date.

2. Modify the output section of your report to add a top and bottom margin of two lines. Run the report again. If you have a printer attached to your system, send the report to the printer (using REPORT TO PRINTER).

3. If you are confident with UNIX shell scripts, type in the **acepr** script (it must be in a directory which is in your **PATH** variable). Run the report.

4. If you know how to run a program from the command line, add a PARAM statement which requires the maximum price to be entered as a command line argument. Run the report using **sacego**, as explained at the end of Section 8.4. (You may escape temporarily to a shell by typing **!sh** for UNIX, or **!command.com** for DOS, followed by **RETURN**. To return to **INFORMIX-SQL** you must type *Ctrl-D* or **exit**).

8.9 The SELECT or READ Section

The SELECT or READ section is mandatory in a report specification, since it determines which data is retrieved for the report.

New for Version 4.0

The SELECT section may be replaced by a READ section, which allows you to take the data from an ASCII file instead of from a database. This option is covered in Section 8.9.4.

The SELECT or READ section is positioned relative to the other sections as follows:

    DATABASE section
    [DEFINE section]
    [INPUT section]
    [OUTPUT section]
    SELECT or READ section

A SELECT section starts with the keyword SELECT which also introduces the first SELECT statement. The section must still end with the END keyword, as in:

```
select owner, adrs1, town, price
    from houses
end
```

In **ACE**, SELECT statements have the same form as in SQL, but with certain conditions, covered in the following sections.

8.9.1 Non-unique column names

Where two columns in different tables have the same name, they can normally be distinguished from each other by use of the *table.column* construct. However in **ACE**, apart from in the *select-list* of the SELECT statement, this is not valid and instead a *display label* must be defined (see Chapter 5, Section 5.4.3). The display label can then be used in any of the following clauses:

    ORDER BY
    GROUP BY
    AFTER GROUP OF
    BEFORE GROUP OF
    PRINT statement

A display label may also be used to ORDER BY an expression, instead of using an integer.

Let us look at an example:

```
select a.agent agagent, a.adrs1 agadrs1,
    a.town agtown, h.adrs1 hadrs1, h.town htown
  from agents a, outer houses h
  where a.agent = h.agent
  order by agagent, htown
end

format
  before group of agagent
    print agagent, agadrs1, agtown
    print

  on every row
    print column 10, hadrs1, htown
end
```

Note the following points about this example:

1.   Table aliases **a** and **h** have been defined for the tables **agents** and **houses**, and an *outer join* which will return rows of the **agents** table which have no associated **houses** rows:

```
  from agents a, outer houses h
```

2.   Display aliases **agagent, agadrs1, agtown, hadrs1** and **htown** have been defined for the **agent, adrs1** and **town** columns of **agents** and **houses**:

```
select a.agent agagent, a.adrs1 agadrs1,
    a.town agtown, h.adrs1 hadrs1, h.town htown
```

3.   These display aliases have then been used in the ORDER BY clause and PRINT statements:

```
  order by agagent, htown

  print agagent, agadrs1, agtown

  print column 10, hadrs1, htown
```

This report specification will result in output of the following form:

```
Beasleys                12 Bishopsmead Prde.East Horsley

Ministers & Co      38 Commercial Way   Woking
        Mon Choise          Woking
        Highland Cottage    Woking
        17 Laurel Crescent  Woking

Allen & Co              25 High Street      Woking
        Holly Ridge House   Woking
                .                   .
                .                   .
```

8.9.2 Variables in SELECT statements

ACE variables may be used in SELECT statements, but they must be preceded by a dollar sign ($) to distinguish them from column names. For example, the following report fragment shows how the variable **reqtown** could be used in a SELECT section to give information on the houses in a particular town:

```
define
    variable reqtown char(20)
end

input
    prompt for reqtown using "Enter required town: "
end

select owner, adrs1, no_bedrooms, price
    from houses
    where town = $reqtown
end
```

8.9.3 Multiple SELECT statements

If there is more than one SELECT statement, the following conditions must be borne in mind:

- A semicolon must be used to separate each statement from the next.

- All but the last statement must have an INTO TEMP clause.

- Only the last statement may contain an ORDER BY clause.

- You may find that a UNION clause suits your needs better, particularly if you need to read the same table twice.

New for Version 4.0

8.9.4 The READ section

The READ section may optionally replace the SELECT section in an ACE report specification, and allows you to retrieve data from an ASCII file, such as an UNLOAD file, instead of from a database. By default, the field delimiter is taken to be the vertical bar (|), or whatever is in the environment variable **DBDELIMITER** (see Chapter 1). This may be overridden by specifying a delimiter in the READ statement. Note that the ASCII statement in the DEFINE section (see Section 8.6) is required when using a READ section. The syntax of the READ statement is as follows:

```
READ "filename" [DELIMITER "symbol"]
    ORDER [EXTERNAL] BY field-name [ASC | DESC] [,...]
```

where:

filename   is the pathname of the ASCII file, enclosed in quotes.

symbol   is the delimiter character, enclosed in quotes, that separates the fields in the ASCII file, and overrides that in the **DBDELIMITER** environment variable.

EXTERNAL   is an optional keyword indicating that the records in the ASCII file are already sorted.

field-name   is the name of a field, as defined in the ASCII statement of the DEFINE section, that is used as a sorting key.

For example:

```
read "/usr/db/agents.unl"
    order by company
end
```

Notes

(i)   If you are using an ORDER BY clause, you should specify an existing database in the DATABASE section, rather than the ASCII keyword.

(ii)   Use an ORDER EXTERNAL BY clause to specify the ordering where the file is already sorted and you wish to use AFTER or BEFORE GROUP OF control blocks on two or more fields.

8.10 The FORMAT Section

The FORMAT section is mandatory and consists of one or more *control blocks*, each consisting of one or more *statements*. Note the position of the FORMAT section relative to the other sections in an **ACE** report specification:

```
DATABASE section
[DEFINE section]
[INPUT section]
[OUTPUT section]
SELECT or READ section
FORMAT section
```

There is a special, default control block called EVERY ROW, which excludes all other control blocks and does not allow any statements (see Section 8.10.1 for a full explanation of all the control blocks). However, the layout of a non-default FORMAT section is as follows:

```
format
    control block 1
        statement(s)
        ...
    control block 2
        statement(s)
        ...
end
```

For example, to print a title page to a report, you might use the control block FIRST PAGE HEADER, like so:

```
first page header
    print "REPORT NUMBER 1"
    skip to top of page
```

Here is a sample FORMAT section:

```
format
    first page header
        print column 25, "HOUSES REPORT NO. 1"
        skip 3 lines

    on every row
        print hadrs1 clipped, ", ", htown clipped;
        print column 25, price using "$,$$$,$$$";
        print 3 spaces, agent

    after group of agent
        skip 1 line
        print "Total for ", agent, " = ",
            group count using "<<"
        skip 2 lines
end
```

This would produce a report of the form:

HOUSES REPORT NO. 1

Mon Choise, Woking	£114,791	Ministers & Co
Highland Cottage, Woking	£133,650	Ministers & Co
17 Laurel Crescent, Woking	£143,550	Ministers & Co

     Total for Ministers & Co   = 3

Holly Ridge House, Woking	£124,950	Allen & Co

     Total for Allen & Co   = 1

8.10.1 Control blocks

This section describes the control blocks which may be used in a report. The order of the control blocks in a FORMAT section is not important, though, with the exception of the AFTER and BEFORE GROUP OF blocks, each block may only appear once. As these particular blocks are probably the most powerful and have a number of properties in common, they are preceded by a short section on group processing.

Group processing
It is often required to separate the information lines in a report into groups, and to print a heading before, or a total after the group, based on information contained within the group. This is known as *group processing*.

A group of rows is defined as all rows that contain the same value for a given column. Using an ORDER BY clause in the SELECT section automatically groups the rows according to the columns specified in the ORDER BY clause. ACE processes the statements in an AFTER or BEFORE GROUP OF control block each time the column specified in the control block header changes value and each time a more significant column (one that precedes this column in the ORDER BY clause) changes value.

Notes

(i)   The construct *table.column* is not allowed in an AFTER or BEFORE GROUP OF clause. You must use a display label as specified in Section 8.9.1.

(ii)   You may include one AFTER and/or BEFORE GROUP OF control block for every column specified in the ORDER BY clause of the SELECT statement.

(iii)   The order in which AFTER and BEFORE GROUP OF control blocks are processed for an ORDER BY clause of the form:

```
order by a, b, c
```

is as follows:

```
before group of a
   before group of b
      before group of c
         on every row
      after group of c
   after group of b
after group of a
```

AFTER GROUP OF

ACE processes the statements in an AFTER GROUP OF control block each time the specified column changes value, each time a more significant column (one that precedes this column in the ORDER BY clause) changes value, and at the end of the report. The syntax for this control block is:

> AFTER GROUP OF *column-name*[*int1*[,*int2*]]
>   *statement(s)*

where:

int1, int2   are optional subscripts that you can use with a type CHAR column to refer to a subset of the column beginning at character position *int1* and ending at character position *int2*. If *int2* is not specified, the end of the column is used. You must enclose the subscripts in square brackets, and this construct must have been used in the ORDER BY clause. For example:

```
after group of owner[1,3]
```

The AFTER GROUP OF control block is particularly appropriate for the printing of sub-totals. For example:

```
after group of agent
    skip 1 line
    print "Total for ", agent, " = ",
        group count using "<<"
    skip 2 lines
```

Notes

(i) When the statements in an AFTER GROUP OF control block are processed, the columns that the report is currently processing will have the values from the last row of the group.

(ii) Group aggregates (GROUP TOTAL, GROUP COUNT, etc.) may only be used in AFTER GROUP OF control blocks.

BEFORE GROUP OF

ACE processes the statements in a BEFORE GROUP OF control block at the beginning of the report, each time the specified column changes value and each time a more significant column (one that precedes this column in the ORDER BY clause) changes value. The syntax for this control block is:

BEFORE GROUP OF *column-name*[*int1*[,*int2*]]
    statement(s)

where:

int1, int2   are optional subscripts that you can use with a type CHAR column to refer to a subset of the column beginning at character position *int1* and ending at character position *int2*. If *int2* is not specified, the end of the column is used. You must enclose the subscripts in square brackets. This construct must have been used in the ORDER BY section. For example:

```
before group of owner[1,3]
```

The BEFORE GROUP OF control block is most often used to print column headings. For example:

```
before group of county
    skip 1 line
    print "Houses for", county
```

Notes

(i)   When the statements in a BEFORE GROUP OF control block are processed, the columns that the report is currently processing will have the values from the first row of the group.

(ii)   Group aggregates (GROUP TOTAL, GROUP COUNT, etc.) may only be used in AFTER GROUP OF control blocks.

EVERY ROW

The EVERY ROW control block is special in that it allows no other statements or control blocks to be present in the FORMAT section. It outputs every row retrieved by the SELECT or READ section in a default format, using the column names from the database (or the ASCII statement for a READ section). The only control you have is over the width of the report, using the RIGHT MARGIN statement in the OUTPUT section.

FIRST PAGE HEADER

This control block defines the actions to be taken before rows are read from the database. The usual use for this control block is to print information on the first page of a report, but it may also be used to initialise variables declared earlier in the DEFINE section. For example:

```
first page header
   let land = ascii 27, "&k2S"
   let norm = ascii 27, "&k0S"
   print land;
   print column 40, "HOUSES REPORT 2"
   print column 40, "----------------"
```

Notes

(i) A FIRST PAGE HEADER control block overrides a PAGE
HEADER control block for the first page of a report. This means
that if you need a FIRST PAGE HEADER block to initialise
variables but you want the same page headings as the other pages,
you must include these page headings in the FIRST PAGE
HEADER block as well. One way to make this easier and to ensure
consistency is to put the headings into a variable, and then print the
variable in both blocks. For instance:

```
first page header
   let headings = column 6,  "ADDRESS",
                  column 25, "PRICE",
                  column 40, "AGENT"
   print headings

page header
   print headings
```

(ii) An IF THEN ELSE statement must not allow any variation in the
number of lines printed in a FIRST PAGE HEADER block. In
other words, the number of lines printed by the PRINT and SKIP
statements must be the same in both the THEN and ELSE clauses.

(iii) You cannot use the PRINT FILE statement in a FIRST PAGE
HEADER control block.

ON EVERY ROW

The ON EVERY ROW control block specifies the actions to be taken
on each row retrieved by the SELECT section. This block is used to
format the detail rows of a report and is where most of the work of the
report is done. For example:

```
on every row
   print hadrs1 clipped, ",", htown clipped;
   print column 25, price using "$,$$$,$$$";
   print 3 spaces, agent
```

Notes

(i) If a change in column value triggers a BEFORE GROUP OF
control block, it will be executed *before* the ON EVERY ROW
block.

(ii) If a change in column value triggers an AFTER GROUP OF control
block, it will be executed *after* the ON EVERY ROW block.

ON LAST ROW

This block specifies the actions to be taken after the last row is returned
by the SELECT section. It is most often used to display grand totals. For
example:

```
on last row
    print "Total of agents = ", count of agents
    print "Total of houses = ", count of houses
    print
    print column 30, "END OF REPORT"
```

Notes

(i) The statements in the ON LAST ROW block are executed after
those in the ON EVERY ROW and AFTER GROUP OF control
blocks.

(ii) The values from the last row processed are available for use in an
ON LAST ROW block.

PAGE HEADER

The PAGE HEADER control block specifies what processing is to be
done at the top of each page of the report. It can be used to print
column headings or, using the PAGENO expression, the page number. It
may also be used to initialise variables at the top of each page. For
example:

```
page header
    print column 70, "Page ", pageno using "<<"
    print column 6, "ADDRESS", column 25, "PRICE",
        column 40, "AGENT"
```

Notes

(i) A PAGE HEADER control block is overridden by a FIRST PAGE
HEADER control block. To get the same page headings at the top
of each page including the first, you must duplicate the headings in

the PAGE HEADER and FIRST PAGE HEADER blocks.

(ii) An IF THEN ELSE statement must not allow any variation in the number of lines printed in a PAGE HEADER block. In other words, the number of lines printed by the PRINT and SKIP statements must be the same in both the THEN and ELSE clauses.

(iii) You cannot use the PRINT FILE statement in a PAGE HEADER control block.

PAGE TRAILER

This block specifies what information will appear at the bottom of each page of the report. Among other things, it may be used to print the page number automatically. For example:

```
page trailer
    print today using "dd/mm/yy",
        column 60, pageno using "<<"
```

Notes

(i) An IF THEN ELSE statement must not allow any variation in the number of lines printed in a PAGE TRAILER block. In other words, the number of lines printed by the PRINT and SKIP statements must be the same in both the THEN and ELSE clauses.

(ii) You cannot use the PRINT FILE statement in a PAGE TRAILER control block.

Exercise

1. To your previously created report, add a BEFORE GROUP OF control block that prints column headings each time the **agent** column changes.

2. Add a PAGE HEADER block that prints the page number at the top of each page. (Beware of note (i) in the explanation of the FIRST PAGE HEADER block.)

3. At the end of the report, print out the total number of houses processed.

8.10.2 Statements

Each of the control blocks mentioned above must have associated with it one or more *statements*. A statement actually tells **ACE** *what* to do; a control block tells **ACE** *when* to do it. Statements are made up of *keywords*, such as LET or PRINT, and *expressions* such as **adrs1 clipped.**

Certain statements such as FOR and IF THEN ELSE will only allow single statements within their clauses. Multiple statements may be included by the use of a *compound statement*, which is a group of statements bracketed by the words BEGIN and END. For example:

```
if county = "Berks"
then
    begin
        print "Berkshire"
        skip 1 line
    end
else
    begin
        print county
        skip 1 line
    end
```

FOR

A FOR loop defines a statement or set of statements which are executed a set number of times, this number being the difference between the starting value and the ending value of the *loop-index*. The *loop-index* may be incremented by one, or by any other amount, determined by *expr3*. The syntax of the FOR statement is as follows:

FOR *loop-index* = *expr1* TO *expr2* [STEP *expr3*]
    DO *statement*

where:

loop-index   is the name of a variable declared in the DEFINE section.

expr1   is an expression that specifies the starting value of *loop-index*.

expr2   is an expression that specifies the ending value of *loop-index*, and therefore the termination condition for the loop.

expr3   is an optional expression that specifies the amount *loop-index* is incremented for each pass of the loop. In the absence of this expression, the STEP value will default to one. If present, this expression must evaluate to a positive value.

The FOR loop is useful for initialising arrays, as in:

```
for count = 1 to 10
   do
      begin
         let array1[count] = 0
         let array2[count] = " "
      end
```

IF THEN ELSE

This statement defines a conditional branch, where certain statements are executed based on the truth or otherwise of a particular expression. Note that in the following syntax, *statement1* and *statement2* may be compound statements (i.e. bracketed by the keywords BEGIN and END).

IF *expr* THEN *statement1*
[ELSE *statement2*]

For example:

```
if (owner is null)
then
   begin
      print "The Occupier"
      let noname = "y"
   end
else
   print owner
```

LET

The LET statement assigns a value to a variable which has been declared previously in the DEFINE section. Its syntax is:

LET *variable* [*num-expr* [,*num-expr*]] = *expr-list*

where:

variable　　is the variable to which a value is to be assigned.

num-expr　　the two optional numeric expressions allow a substring of a CHAR type variable to be specified. If just one *num-expr* is present, the substring is from that character position to the end of the string. If a second *num-expr* is present, the substring ends at that position. Note that the square brackets are mandatory. Since *num-expr* may be a numeric variable, this provides a mechanism for using a CHAR variable as a one-dimensional array, as in:

```
let array[counter] = value1
let counter = counter + 1
let array[counter] = value2
```

expr-list   is normally a single expression, however in the case of a CHAR variable it may be a list of one or more expressions, separated by commas, which are concatenated and the result assigned to *variable*. For example the escape sequence required to set compressed print on an HP LaserJet could be assigned to the variable *comp* (which has been declared in the DEFINE section) using the following statement:

```
let comp = ascii 27, "&k2S"
```

In fact *expr-list* may use any of the expressions allowed in a PRINT statement, such as COLUMN, USING, etc.

Some examples follow.

```
let headline = column 10, "--------------------"

let commission = price * 0.015

let shortadrs = adrs1[1,10]
```

NEED

This statement causes a page throw if the specified number of lines will not fit on the page at the current position. It may be used to keep groups of lines together on a page.

    NEED *num-expr* LINES

The following example ensures that the column headings and at least two detail lines are printed at the start of each new agent.

```
before group of agent
    need 4 lines
    print "ADDRESS", column 25 "PRICE",
        column 34 "AGENT"
    print
```

PAUSE

Causes the specified string to be displayed on the terminal and output to be suspended until **RETURN** is pressed.

PAUSE [*string*]

For example:

```
pause "Press <RETURN> to continue"
```

Notes

(i) The PAUSE statement is only effective if the output is displayed on the terminal.

(ii) If you do not supply a message in *string*, PAUSE will not display any message.

PRINT

The PRINT statement is the one statement that actually displays information on the screen or printer. The information displayed may be text or data from the database which may be specified directly or via variables. The full range of expressions (see Section 8.10.3), from ASCII to YEAR can, and often are, used within a PRINT statement.

PRINT [*expr-list*][;]

where:

expr-list   is an optional list of one or more expressions, separated by commas.

;   is an optional keyword that suppresses a **NEWLINE** at the end of the line.

For example:

```
on every row
    print hadrs1 clipped, ", ", htown clipped;
    print column 25, price using "$,$$$,$$$",
        3 spaces, agent
```

Note

Columns of the various data types take up a predetermined number of spaces (see opposite). This number may be modified by use of the keywords CLIPPED or USING (see Section 8.10.3).

Data type	Default size
CHAR	declared size
DATE	10
FLOAT	14 (including sign and decimal point)
SMALLINT	6 (including sign)
INTEGER	11 (including sign)
SMALLFLOAT	14 (including sign and decimal point)
DECIMAL	number of digits plus 2 (including sign and decimal point)
SERIAL	11
MONEY	number of digits plus 3 (including sign and decimal point)

PRINT FILE

This statement allows you to include the contents of a text file in a report. It is particularly useful for mailshot letters.

PRINT FILE "*filename*"

For example:

```
print file "/usr/tony/sell1"
```

Note

A PRINT FILE statement may not be used in a FIRST PAGE HEADER, PAGE HEADER or PAGE TRAILER control block.

SKIP

This statement skips lines in a report.

SKIP *int* LINE[S]

For example:

```
skip 3 lines
```

SKIP TO TOP OF PAGE

Causes a page to be thrown. The syntax is:

SKIP TO TOP OF PAGE

Note

A SKIP TO TOP OF PAGE statement may not be used in a FIRST PAGE HEADER, PAGE HEADER, or PAGE TRAILER control block.

WHILE

The WHILE statement allows a statement or compound statement (a group of statements bracketed by the keywords BEGIN and END) to be executed while an expression remains true.

WHILE *expr* DO
    statement

where:

expr   is an expression that is evaluated on each pass of the loop. While it is true, the statements within the loop are executed, and when it evaluates to false, control passes to the statement following the loop.

The following example skips the number of lines specified in the variable *count*:

```
while count <> 0
    do
       begin
          skip 1 line
          let count = count - 1
       end
```

8.10.3 Expressions

Expressions are used predominantly in the PRINT and LET statements, though they form mandatory parts of most of the other statements as well. There is a special set of expressions called *aggregates* which allow you to summarise numeric information. They are dealt with first.

Aggregates
There are two forms of aggregate expression:

[GROUP] {{TOTAL | AVG | MIN | MAX} OF *expr1*} [WHERE *expr2*]

and

[GROUP] {COUNT | PERCENT} [WHERE *expr2*]

where:

GROUP   is an optional keyword that causes the aggregate to reflect information for the current group only. This keyword may only be used in AFTER GROUP OF control blocks.

COUNT   evaluates to the total number of rows retrieved by the SELECT section and further qualified by the optional WHERE clause that can appear in an aggregate expression. For example:

```
on last row
    print "Total number of houses: ", count
```

PERCENT   evaluates COUNT as a percentage of the total number of rows returned by the SELECT section and qualified by the optional WHERE clause that can appear in an aggregate expression. This is particularly useful during GROUP processing to display the number of rows in a group as a percentage of the total number of rows, as in the following example:

```
after group of company
    print group percent, "% of total houses"
    skip 1 line
```

TOTAL   evaluates as the total of *expr1* in the rows qualified by the SELECT section and the optional WHERE clause that can appear in an aggregate expression.

AVG   evaluates as the average of *expr1* in the rows qualified by the SELECT section and the optional WHERE clause that can appear in an aggregate expression. For example:

```
after group of town
    print "Average price for ", town,
        "is ", group avg of price
```

MIN   evaluates as the minimum of *expr1* in the rows qualified by the SELECT section and the optional WHERE clause that can appear in an aggregate expression.

MAX   evaluates as the maximum of *expr1* in the rows qualified by the SELECT section and the optional WHERE clause that can appear in an aggregate expression. For example:

```
after group of company
    print "Top wack: ", max of price
```

expr1   is an expression, typically a numeric column or an expression involving one.

expr2   is an expression which further qualifies the rows returned by the SELECT section.

Having dealt with the aggregate expressions, we can now proceed with the other expressions. They are presented alphabetically.

ascii   evaluates its numeric expression as a character value. It can be used to print control characters for the printer or terminal. For example:

```
first page header
    let compressed = ASCII 27, "&k2S"
    let normal = ASCII 27, "&k0S"
    print compressed;
        .
        .
        .
on last row
    print normal;
```

clipped   forces the preceding field to be printed without trailing blanks. The following example prints the address and town of a house with a comma in between:

```
print adrs1 clipped, ", ", htown
```

column *n*   specifies in which column (relative to the LEFT MARGIN value) the next field is to be printed:

```
print column 25, price using "$,$$$,$$$"
```

New for Version 4.0

current   evaluates to a character string with the value of the current date and time as supplied by the operating system, similar to **date**, but with the option to specify the precision (see Chapter 5, Section 5.4.3):

CURRENT [*first* TO *last*]

For example:

```
print current year to day
```

date   evaluates to a character string containing today's date in the form

```
Fri Mar 09 1990
```

Since **date** evaluates as a CHAR type you may use subscripts. For example:

```
print "Report date: ", date[5,15]
```

will print a string of the form

```
Report date: Mar 09 1990
```

See also the **today** expression.

date(*expr*)　　converts *expr* to a value of type DATE. This allows a string or numeric expression to take part in arithmetic with another value of type DATE, which may be in a variable or have come from the database. For example:

```
let day_of_year = today - date("31/12/89")
```

day(*date-expr*)

returns the day of the month when called with an expression of type DATE or DATETIME. For example, the following will print a reminder about monthly backups on the 28th of each month:

```
if (day(today) = 28)
then
    print "Monthly backup due"
```

lineno　　contains the value of the current line, except within a PAGE HEADER, FIRST PAGE HEADER or PAGE TRAILER block.

mdy(*num-expr1, num-expr2, num-expr3*)

returns a value of type DATE when called with three expressions evaluating to integers representing the month, day and year. For example:

```
if mdy(reqmonth, reqday, year(today)) = today
then
    print "Happy Birthday!!"
```

month(*date-expr*)

returns an integer corresponding to the month (1-12) of its argument, which must be of type DATE or DATETIME.

pageno　　contains the value of the current page number. It may be used to best effect in PAGE HEADER and PAGE TRAILER control blocks to print the page number. For example:

```
page header
    print column 65, pageno using "Page <<<"
```

n **space**[s]　　used to separate print items on the same line. The trailing **s** is optional. For example:

```
print "price", 3 spaces, "agent"
```

time   evaluates as a character string containing the current time in the
               form *hh:mm:ss*.

today   evaluates as a DATE type containing the current date supplied
               by the operating system but modified by the **DBDATE** en-
               vironment variable. You can set the format in which the date is
               displayed with the USING expression.

using   has the syntax

               expr1 USING *expr2*

               and allows you to format the numeric or date expression in
               expr1 using the format string in *expr2*. Left and right
               justification, space filling etc., may be specified for numeric
               expressions, and various formats for date expressions.

               For example:

```
print price using "$$$,$$&.&&"
```

               Numeric expressions may be formatted by using any
               combination of the following characters to make up the format
               string:

```
* & # < ,.- + ( ) $.
```

               Their descriptions follow.

&   the zero-fill character. Leading zeros are displayed as zeros.
      For instance:

```
"$&&&,&&&.&&"    would give   £000,005.88
```

prints a leading zero as a blank. For instance:

```
"$###,###.##"    would give   $        5.88
```

<   left-justifies the numbers to be displayed, as in:

```
"<<<<<"          would give   25
                 or           5960
```

,.   are literals which are displayed according to where they are
      positioned in the format string.

–   is a literal, indicating a negative number. Note that without
      the minus in a format string, a negative number will not be
      displayed as such.

+   is a literal. It will be displayed for numbers greater than or equal to zero, and a minus sign will be displayed for negative numbers.

( )   literals used to indicate a negative number.

$ a literal which will be replaced on display or printing with the currency symbol defined in the environment variable **DBMONEY**.

Date expressions may be formatted using a format string consisting of a combination of the characters **d, m** and **y**. Some examples follow:

Format string	Result
`"ddd, dd mmm, yyyy"`	`Fri, 09 Mar, 1990`
`"dd/mm/yy"`	`09/03/90`
`"mmm dd, yyyy"`	`Mar 09, 1990`

Notes

(i) The characters can be mixed to give the desired results with different values. For instance it is usually essential that a zero money value be shown as such. This can be achieved by placing the zero-fill character, &, in the appropriate positions, as in:

   `"$$$,$$&.&&"`   which would give £0.00

(ii) The characters − + (and $ are *floating* literals. That is, if you group several together on the left, a single character will float to the rightmost position without interfering with the number being printed. For example:

   `print price using "$$$,$$&.&&"`

would display the price with a currency symbol on the left, no matter how big or small the number (within the bounds of the format string, in this case 999,999.99), e.g.

   £135,000.00
   £39.00
   £2,000.00
   £0.00

(iii) The USING expression is normally used in PRINT statements, but may also be used in IF and LET statements (see the example for YEAR later in this section).

(iv) Many more examples of format strings and their results may be found in the manual under the USING expression.

weekday(*date-expr***)**

returns an integer in the range 0-6 (0 being Sunday) representing the day of the week when called with an expression of type DATE or DATETIME

New for Version 4.0

wordwrap   displays the contents of the character expression that precedes it on multiple, wordwrapped lines (i.e. lines which break at the end of a word), optionally at a temporary right margin.

char-expr WORDWRAP [RIGHT MARGIN *col*]

The left margin is taken as the current printing column; the keywords RIGHT MARGIN allow the right margin specified in the report to be temporarily overridden. Note that this expression is particularly useful with the new TEXT data type available in **INFORMIX-OnLine**. For example:

```
print column 15,
          paral wordwrap right margin 65
```

year(*date-expr***)**

returns an integer representing the year, in the form *yyyy*, when called with an expression of type DATE or DATETIME. In the following example, the variable *x* is defined as SMALLFLOAT and *y* is defined as INTEGER. Note the use of USING in the LET statement to remove the decimal portion of *x*:

```
let x = (year(today))/4    # Year / 4
let y = x using "<<<"      # Lose decimal part
if (x - y) = 0             # Check for decimal
then
   print today using "yyyy", " is a leap year"
else
   print today using "yyyy",
                        " is not a leap year"
```

Exercise

1. Produce a report consisting of all the agents' names, with their houses and bedroom sizes, in the following form:

HOUSES REPORT NO. 2

Agent	Ref	Address	Book Date	Bed	Bedrm. Size
Ministers & Co	5	Mon Choise	26/06/90	1	12'6 x 12'2
				2	12'6 x 12'2
				3	8'3 x 7'3
	6	Highland Cottage	26/06/90	1	16'6 x 12'3
				2	13'6 x 10'3
				3	13'10 x 9'9
	7	17 Laurel Crescent	26/06/90	1	13'2 x 10'5
				2	13'2 x 12'5
				3	14' x 9'7
				4	9'5 x 8'8
Allen & Co	12	Holly Ridge House	29/04/90	1	12'2 x 12'
				2	11'10 x 9'
				3	10'5 x 7'3
				4	10' x 7'10
Thompson & Bayles	1	82 Ash Lodge Drive	26/06/90	1	13'2 x 10'5
				2	13'2 x 12'5
				3	14' x 9'7
				4	9'5 x 8'8
	4	Cliffe Cottage	26/06/90	1	10'7 x 10'2
				2	11'7 x 10'7
				3	9'5 x 6'2
	8	19 Old Malt Way	16/03/90	1	12'6 x 11'6
				2	11'6 x 10'
				3	11'4 x 9'3
				4	7'7 x 6'

8.11 Sample Reports

Three sample reports are presented here. They provide examples of many of the statements and expressions used in **ACE** reports.

Report No. 1 prompts the user for a maximum price and then displays the houses which are lower than that price, in order of price within agent. They are grouped by agent and the total number of houses with each agent is also displayed.

Report No. 2 displays all of the houses in the database together with their agents, and the details of each bedroom.

Report No. 3 is a report for mailing labels, based on a similar idea from the Appendix of the **INFORMIX-SQL** manual. The major difference is that this report includes the ability to 'squeeze' blank lines in an address, i.e. close up the gap left by a nonexistent address line.

```
{ Houses Report No. 1 }

{Prompts the user for a maximum price, then displays
the houses which are lower than that price, in order
of price within agent. They are grouped by agent and
the total number of houses with each agent is also
displayed.}

database property end

define
    variable maxprice money
end

input
    prompt for maxprice using "Enter maximum price: "
end

output
    top margin 0
    bottom margin 0
    page length 23
end

select h.adrs1 hadrs1, h.town htown, agent, price
    from houses h
    where price <= $maxprice
    order by agent, price
end

format
    first page header
        print column 25, "HOUSES REPORT NO. 1"
        skip 3 lines

    on every row
        print hadrs1 clipped, ", ", htown clipped;
        print column 35, price using "$,$$$,$$$";
        print 3 spaces, agent

    after group of agent
        need 3 lines
        skip 1 line
        print col 5, "Total for ", agent, " = ",
            group count using "<<<&"
        skip 2 lines

    page trailer
        skip 1 line
        pause "Press <RETURN> to continue"
end
```

```
{ Houses Report No. 2 }

{Displays all of the houses in the database together
with their agents, and the details of each bedroom.}

database property end

define
    variable headyn char(1)
end

output
    left margin 2
    report to "houserep2.out"
    page length 70
end

select h.ref_no href_no,
    h.adrs1 hadrs1,
    h.agent hagent,
    book_date,
    bedroom_no,
    bedroom_size,
    from houses h, bedrooms b
        where h.ref_no = b.ref_no
        order by hagent, href_no
end

format

    first page header
        print col 25, "HOUSES REPORT NO. 2"
        skip 3 lines
        print "Agent",
            column 20, "Ref",
            column 24, "Address",
            column 44, "Book Date",
            column 57, "Bed",
            column 61, "Bedrm. Size"
        print


    page header
        print "Agent",
            column 20, "Ref",
            column 24, "Address",
            column 44, "Book Date",
            column 57, "Bed",
            column 61, "Bedrm. Size"
```

```
        print
        let headyn = "y"
        print agent clipped;

    before group of hagent
        need 6 lines
        if headyn <> "y"
        then
            print hagent clipped;

    before group of href_no
        need 6 lines
        print column 20, href_no using "<<<<",
            column 24, hadrs1 clipped;
        print column 44, book_date using "dd/mm/yy";

    on every record
        print column 53, bedroom_no, 2 spaces,
                                        bedroom_size
        let headyn = "n"

    after group of href_no
        print

end
```

```
{ Houses Report No. 3 - Mailing Labels }

{This report prints 1-3 mailing labels across a page.
It stores the labels in character strings (array1,
array2, and array3) as it reads each row, and prints
the labels when it has read the proper number of rows.
At run time, you specify the number of labels (1-3)
that you want ACE to print across the page.
}


database
    property
end

define
    variable towncnty char(25)    {holds town and county}
    variable array1 char(80)      {array for owner line}
    variable array2 char(80)      {array for adrs1 line}
    variable array3 char(80)      {array for adrs2 line}
    variable array4 char(80)      {array for town/county}
    variable start smallint       {beg. of label in array}
    variable finish smallint      {end of label in array}
    variable l_size smallint      {label width}
    variable white smallint       {spaces between labels}
    variable count1 smallint      {no. labels across page}
    variable i smallint           {label counter}
end

input
    prompt for count1
        using "Number of labels across page? [1-3] "
end

output
    top margin 0
    bottom margin 0
    left margin 0
    report to "labels.out"
end

select owner, adrs1, adrs2, town, county
    from houses
    order by county, owner
end

format
    first page header
        let i = 1                 {Init label counter}
        let l_size = 75/count1    {Get label width}
        let white = 5/count1      {Inter-label width}
```

```
on every row
   let towncnty = town clipped, ", ", county
   let finish = i * (l_size + white)
   let start = finish - l_size + 1

{This section assigns names and addresses to arrays
1, 2, 3 and 4 until i = the number of labels across
a page. It 'squeezes' if adrs1 or adrs2 are blank}

   if (owner is null or owner = " ")
   then
      let array1[start, finish] = "The Occupier"
   else
      let array1[start, finish] = owner

   if (adrs1 is null or adrs1 = " ")
   then
      begin
         let array2[start, finish] = adrs2
         let array3[start, finish] = towncnty
      end
   else
      begin
         let array2[start, finish] = adrs1

         if (adrs2 is null or adrs2 = " ")
         then
            let array3[start, finish] = towncnty
         else
            begin
               let array3[start, finish] = adrs2
               let array4[start, finish] = towncnty
            end
      end

   if i = count1
   then
      begin
         print array1 clipped
         print array2 clipped
         print array3 clipped
         print array4 clipped
         skip 1 line
         let array1 = " "           {Clear the arrays}
         let array2 = " "
         let array3 = " "
         let array4 = " "
         let i   = 1
      end
   else
      let i = i + 1
```

```
on last row
   if i > 1              {Print last set of addresses}
   then                  { if any left}
      begin
         print array1 clipped
         print array2 clipped
         print array3 clipped
         print array4 clipped
      end
end
```

Chapter 9

User Menus

9.1 Introduction

The **User-menu** option on the main **INFORMIX-SQL** menu allows you to create and run your own customised menu system. Though they are not ring menus like **INFORMIX-SQL** itself, they do allow you to build a complete hierarchy of application menus from which you can call submenus, run forms and reports, **INFORMIX-SQL** programs, and other programs on your system that you would normally run from the command line.

Figure 9.1 shows a sample user menu for the **property** database.

```
┌──────────────────────────────────────────────────────────────────┐
│                                                                    │
│            BRICKS & MORTAR PROPERTY MANAGEMENT LTD                 │
│                                                                    │
│        1. Queries and data entry                                   │
│                                                                    │
│        2. Reports                                                  │
│                                                                    │
│        3. SQL queries                                              │
│                                                                    │
│        4. Utilities                                                │
│                                                                    │
│                                                                    │
│                                                                    │
│        Use space bar, arrow keys, or type number to make selection.│
│        Enter 'e' to return to previous menu or exit.               │
│        Enter carriage return to execute selection:  1              │
│                                                                    │
└──────────────────────────────────────────────────────────────────┘
```

Figure 9.1 A sample user menu for the **property** database.

User menus are created using a special **PERFORM** screen (shown in Figure 9.2) and the data for each menu structure is held in two tables within the database, namely:

- sysmenus

- sysmenuitems

Because the data for the menus themselves is held within the database, this means that a menu structure is always associated with a particular database, and cannot live outside one. You may however, refer to other databases from the same user menu structure. If many databases are to be accessed, it would be wise to allocate a database solely for the purpose of the user menu system.

9.2 Creating a Menu

A user menu is created by entering the menu data through a **PERFORM** screen that has been specially written for this purpose (see Figure 9.2 below).

To create a user menu, follow these steps:

1.   Select **User-menu** from the main **INFORMIX-SQL** menu.

2.   If you have not already done so, choose a database to work on from the CHOOSE DATABASE screen.

3.   Choose **Modify** from the USER-MENU menu.

4.   **INFORMIX-SQL** displays the PERFORM menu with the **menuform** form (see Figure 9.2 below). The form is in two halves, with the top half

```
PERFORM : Query  Next  Previous  Add  Update  Remove  Table  Screen ...
Searches the active database table.              ** 1: sysmenus table **

============MENU ENTRY FORM================

Menu Name:    [          ]

Menu Title:   [                                              ]

---------------------------------SELECTION SECTION---------------------------------

Selection Number:                          Selection Type:

Selection
Text:

Selection
Action:
```

Figure 9.2 The PERFORM menu with the **menuform** form.

accessing the **sysmenus** table, which holds the menu name and title, and the bottom half accessing the **sysmenuitems** table, which holds the menu options and the action associated with each option. In the form, **sysmenus** is master of **sysmenuitems**.

5. Select the **Add** option and enter a name and title for the menu, pressing **ESC** to complete the add. Repeat this step until you have entered the details for the main menu and all the required submenus. You may not refer later to a submenu name unless it has been entered here first.
    N.B. The first menu must be named **main**.

6. You now need to enter the details of all the options on the menu, and this you do in the SELECTION SECTION of the form, so select **Detail** to activate the **sysmenuitems** table. Since there are no rows in the table at this stage, **PERFORM** displays the message

    There are no rows satisfying the conditions.

7. Select the **Add** option and enter details in the SELECTION SECTION for the first option on the **main** menu, pressing **ESC** to complete the add. Refer to Section 9.4 for explanations of all the fields in this part of the form. Repeat this step for all the options on the **main** menu.

8. To enter option details for another menu, select **Master** to reactivate the **sysmenus** table. Using **Query**, locate the name and title of your next menu. Select **Detail** to activate the **sysmenuitems** table again.

9. Enter the option details for the options on this menu, selecting **Add** to add each new option, and pressing **ESC** to complete the add.

10. Repeat Steps 8 and 9 to enter the details for all of your submenus, and select **Exit** to return to the USER-MENU menu.

To run your menu, just select the **Run** option on the USER-MENU menu. Alternatively, you may run the menu from the command line, without entering **INFORMIX-SQL**, by typing:

    isql -s *dbname* -u *menuname*

For example:

    isql -s property -u main

9.3 Modifying a Menu

To modify a user menu, you simply select **Modify** from the USER-MENU menu and modify the required fields in **menuform**, using the **PERFORM** options **Query** and **Detail** to retrieve the rows required, and **Update** to modify them. However, see also Section 9.6, Reordering a Menu.

9.4 Data Entry Fields in menuform

In this section we discuss the meaning of all the data entry fields in menuform, the form used to build up a user menu, and what data can be entered.

Menu Name   The Menu Name field gives each menu or submenu a unique name by which **INFORMIX-SQL** can find it. The name is not displayed on the screen and follows the rules for identifiers: 1 to 18 characters long; first character must be a letter; instead of a space use an underscore (_). The first menu must be named **main.**

Menu Title   This field is the title of the menu which is displayed at the top of the screen when the menu is run.

Selection Number
              Each option on a menu has a number which is displayed to its left on the screen (see Figure 9.1). You may have up to a maximum of 28 options on a single menu, which may be displayed in one or two columns and either single- or double-spaced depending on the number of options. Each option may be up to 33 characters long.

Selection Type   The following options are available for the Selection Type field:

          F   runs a form

          R   runs a report

          M   calls a submenu

          Q   executes an SQL command file

          P   executes a program

          S   executes a script menu (see Section 9.5).

For example, to run the mailing labels report **labels**, see Figure 9.3 opposite.

Selection Text   This is the text of the option that will appear on the menu screen. The maximum length of the text is 33 characters, but the number of options which may be displayed on the screen, and the line spacing of those options is dependent on this length.

Selection Action   This field specifies the name of the form, report, program etc., that is to be executed, according to the entry in the Selection Type field, as in the following table:

Selection Type	Selection Action
M	Enter the name (but not the title) of the menu, e.g. **reports**. It must first have been entered in the **sysmenus** table.
P	Enter an operating system command or the name of a program that can be executed from the command line, as in **lpstat -t**.
F	Enter a form name without the **.frm** extension. If you do not enter a Selection Action, the **INFORMIX-SQL** FORM menu will be called.
R	Enter a report name without the **.arc** extension. If you do not enter a Selection Action, the **INFORMIX-SQL** REPORT menu will be called.
Q	Enter an SQL command filename without the **.sql** extension. If you do not enter a Selection Action, the **INFORMIX-SQL** RDSQL menu will be called.
S	Enter the name of a script menu (see Section 9.5).

```
PERFORM : Query  Next  Previous  Add  Update  Remove  Table  Screen ...
Searches the active database table.              ** 2: sysmenuitems table **

= = = = = = = = = = = = =MENU ENTRY FORM= = = = = = = = = = = = = =

Menu Name:   [ reports ]

Menu Title:    REPORTS

------------------------------SELECTION SECTION----------------------------------

Selection Number:    [ 1        ]          Selection Type:    [ R ]

Selection
Text:       [ Mailing labels                                             ]

Selection
Action:     [ labels                                                    ]
```

Figure 9.3 The SELECTION SECTION entries to run the **labels** report.

9.5 Script Menus

A script menu is one which executes a number of actions in sequence without displaying the intervening menu choices. At the end of each action, the user is prompted by the message

Press Return to continue

after which the next action is executed. After all the actions have been executed, the user is returned to the menu. This type of submenu is signified by the letter **S** in the Selection Type field. A script menu may contain any number of the different types of action: forms, reports, SQL command files or programs, each of which is executed in sequence.

To create a script menu, follow these steps:

1. In the Selection Type field of the calling menu, enter the letter **S**.

2. In the Selection Text field enter the text of the option which will appear on the menu screen.

3. In the Selection Action field enter the name of your script menu and press **ESC** to add the entry.

4. You must now return to the **sysmenus** table to enter the details for the script menu itself. Select **Master**.

5. Select **Add** and enter the name of the script menu (from Step 3) in the Menu Name field.

6. In the Menu Title field you may enter a comment line describing the script menu, since this line is not displayed in a script menu. Press **ESC** to add this entry to the **sysmenus** table.

7. You must now enter the details of the actions that are to be executed in this script menu, so select **Detail** to activate the **sysmenuitems** table.

8. Select **Add** to add an action to the script menu.

9. Enter the details of the required action. Remember, this may be any of the allowable actions: reports, forms, programs, even another script menu. You may use the Selection Text field as a comments field, as it will not be displayed on the screen when the menu is run. Press **ESC** to save the details of this action.

10. Repeat Steps 8 and 9 to add the details of all of the actions required for this script menu, and select **Exit** to return to the USER-MENU menu.

Exercise

1. Create a User menu for your **property** database, of the following form. The various reports, forms and SQL queries can be found in the relevant parts of this book.

```
              BRICKS & MORTAR PROPERTY MANAGEMENT LTD

        1. Queries and data entry by forms

        2. Reports
           1. Houses Report No. 1
           2. Houses Report No. 2
           3. Mailing labels and display output

        3. SQL queries
           1. Query-language menu
           2. Houses in Woking
           3. Agent-owners

        4. Utilities
           1. Unload houses to /tmp/h1.unl
           2. Line printer status
           3. Information on houses table
```

You will need a script menu for the mailing labels option. Use the program **pg** (or **more**) to display the output.

9.6 Reordering a Menu

Unfortunately, no thought seems to have been given to the reordering of User menus, either to accommodate new options or after deleting old ones. You can remove unwanted options through the **menuform** form and the remaining options will display correctly on the screen; however the Selection Number field will not now correspond with the option numbers displayed when the menu is run.

I have devised two SQL scripts which can be used to overcome the problems of reordering and inserting of new options in a User menu.

The first script will reorder the menu specified (**main** is used in the example) to account for deleted options:

```
unload to "/tmp/t1"
select imenuname, mtext, mtype, progname, nextmenu
from sysmenuitems
where imenuname = "main";          {Replace main with}
                                   {actual menu name}


delete from sysmenuitems
where imenuname = "main";          {Replace main with}
                                   {actual menu name}


alter table sysmenuitems
modify (itemnum serial);

begin work;
load from "/tmp/t1"
insert into sysmenuitems
     (imenuname, mtext, mtype, progname, nextmenu);
commit work;

alter table sysmenuitems
     modify (itemnum integer);
```

The second script allows for the insertion of a new option in the middle of an existing menu. The effect is to repeat the option number specified (option 5 in the example) which can then be modified to the required option details using **menuform**:

```
unload to "/tmp/t1"
select imenuname, mtext, mtype, progname, nextmenu
from sysmenuitems
where imenuname = "main"   {Replace main with actual}
and itemnum <= 5;          {menu name and 5 with}
                           {actual option num}
```

```
unload to "/tmp/t2"
select imenuname, mtext, mtype, progname, nextmenu
from sysmenuitems
where imenuname = "main"    {Replace main with}
and itemnum >= 5;                {actual menu name and 5}
                                 {with actual option num}


delete from sysmenuitems
where imenuname = "main";        {Replace main with}
                                 {actual menu name}

alter table sysmenuitems
    modify (itemnum serial);

begin work;
load from "/tmp/t1"
insert into sysmenuitems
    (imenuname, mtext, mtype, progname, nextmenu);
load from "/tmp/t2"
insert into sysmenuitems
    (imenuname, mtext, mtype, progname, nextmenu);
commit work;

alter table sysmenuitems
    modify (itemnum integer);
```

Chapter 10

Summary

We have now covered the five parts of **INFORMIX-SQL**, namely:

- Interactive Schema Editor

- SQL Editor

- **PERFORM** forms package

- **ACE** report generator

- Menu builder

In this chapter we will briefly review the function of each of the parts, and how they might fit together during the development of an application.

Creating the database
An application consists of data and operations, so it is appropriate to start by defining the structure of the data. This may be done interactively by using the interactive schema editor, which allows you to create a database and its tables, and define the column names and datatypes that make up the tables. You may also create indexes for the columns (though you will need SQL to create composite indexes), and decide whether a particular column will accept NULL values or not.

Defining composite indexes and user privileges
The interactive SQL editor may be used here to create composite or multi-column indexes (such as exists for the **ref_no** and **bedroom_no** columns of the **bedrooms** table). If other people will be working on the application, they will need at least CONNECT permission to the database and SELECT permission on the tables. These may be given using the GRANT and REVOKE statements of SQL.

Creating query and data entry screens
The **PERFORM** package may be used to generate default screen forms and to customise them to the requirements of the customer. These forms may be used

both for data entry and for query-by-example, and may extend over multiple tables (with restrictions) and multiple screens. On-screen arithmetic and control logic may also be included.

Creating new, ad hoc queries, and batch operations

The SQL editor may be used to experiment with queries outside those included in the screen forms. They may include complex subqueries, aggregate values (average, max, min, etc.), complex joins and in particular queries that return a number of rows. These may be displayed a screenful at a time, unlike in **PERFORM** where only one row may be displayed at a time.

The SQL queries required to retrieve data for reports may also be tried out, before being incorporated into a complete **ACE** report.

If any batch operations are required – the loading or unloading of data, mass deletes or updates – they can be done using the SQL editor.

Generating reports

The **ACE** report writer allows you to take the output from an SQL statement (embedded within the report code) and format it for presentation either on screen or paper. Page titles, column headings, totals, subtotals, grouping may all be included in an **ACE** report.

Pulling it all together as an application

So, we have created a database, screen forms, SQL queries, admin functions and reports, but how can the user get the best out of all the different parts of the application? How does he know they even exist? The answer is – through a menu system, in this case an **INFORMIX-SQL** User menu. The User menu function allows the developer to tie all of the different parts of the application into a cohesive whole, and can include any of the operations developed using **INFORMIX-SQL**, as well as any program that can be called from the command line.

Appendix 1

The property Database

The **property** database is made up of three tables:

- **houses**

- **bedrooms**

- **agents**

Figure A.1 below shows a map of the database, highlighting the columns on which the tables may be joined.

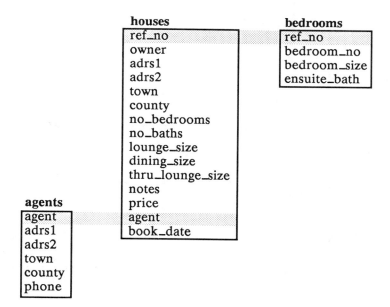

Figure A.1 Map of the **property** database.

The agents Table

The **agents** table contains details of each agent in the database. It may be joined to the **houses** table on the **agent** column.

agent	char(20)
adrs1	char(20)
adrs2	char(20)
town	char(20)
county	char(20)
phone	char(12)

A unique index exists on the **agent** column.

The houses Table

The **houses** table contains details of each house in the database, such as owner, address, price, etc. Each house has a unique identifier in the **ref_no** column.

ref_no	serial
owner	char(20)
adrs1	char(20)
adrs2	char(20)
town	char(20)
county	char(20)
no_bedrooms	smallint
no_baths	smallint
lounge_size	char(11)
dining_size	char(11)
thru_lounge_size	char(11)
notes	char(30)
price	money(11,0)
agent	char(20)
book_date	date

There is a unique index on the **ref_no** column and an index allowing duplicates on the **agent** column.

The bedrooms Table

Each bedroom for each house has a row in the **bedrooms** table and is uniquely identified by a combination of the **ref_no** and **bedroom_no** columns.

ref_no	integer
bedroom_no	smallint
bedroom_size	char(11)
ensuite_bath	char(11)

There is an index allowing duplicates on the **ref_no** column, and a unique composite index consisting of the **ref_no** and **bedroom_no** columns.

Data in the property Database

The agents table

```
agent     Beasleys
adrs1     12 Bishopsmead Prde.
adrs2
town      East Horsley
county    Surrey
phone     04865-1874

agent     Ministers & Co
adrs1     38 Commercial Way
adrs2
town      Woking
county    Surrey
phone     04862-10707

agent     Allen & Co
adrs1     25 High Street
adrs2
town      Woking
county    Surrey
phone     04862-11717

agent     Thompson & Bayles
adrs1     204 London Road
adrs2     Burpham
town      Guildford
county    Surrey
phone     0483-727575

agent     Granthams
adrs1     3 Headley Road
adrs2     Grayshott
town      Hindhead
county    Surrey
phone     Hind. 7474

agent     Smiths & Co
adrs1     29 Hemming Way
adrs2
town      Woking
county    Surrey
phone     04862-54321
```

The houses table

```
ref_no              1
owner               White
adrs1               82 Ash Lodge Drive
adrs2               Ashley Park
town                Ash
county              Surrey
no_bedrooms         4
no_baths            2
lounge_size
dining_size
thru_lounge_size    21'6 x 13'3
notes               Double garage, private gardens
price               £108900
agent               Thompson & Bayles
book_date           26/06/90

ref_no              2
owner               Black
adrs1               4 Bluebell Road
adrs2               The Meadows
town                Lindford
county              Hampshire
no_bedrooms         4
no_baths            2
lounge_size         17'  x 11'9
dining_size         13'3 x 9'10
thru_lounge_size
notes               Utility room, patio
price               £98005
agent               Granthams
book_date           26/06/90

ref_no              3
owner               Anderson
adrs1               Stoney Ridge
adrs2               Grayshott
town                Hindhead
county              Surrey
no_bedrooms         5
no_baths            2
lounge_size         18'8 x 8'2
dining_size         14'9 x 11'1
thru_lounge_size
notes               Interesting design, verandah
price               £108900
agent               Granthams
book_date           26/06/90
```

```
ref_no              4
owner               Aldridge
adrs1               Cliffe Cottage
adrs2               The Common, Shalford
town                Guildford
county              Surrey
no_bedrooms         3
no_baths            1
lounge_size         11'9 x 10'9
dining_size         10'2 x 10'2
thru_lounge_size
notes               Lovely views, garden shed
price               £123750
agent               Thompson & Bayles
book_date           26/06/90

ref_no              5
owner               Bailey
adrs1               Mon Choise
adrs2               Bagshot Road
town                Woking
county              Surrey
no_bedrooms         3
no_baths            1
lounge_size         27'5 x 15'4
dining_size         10'8 x 9'8
thru_lounge_size
notes               Cloaks, 80' garden, garage
price               £114791
agent               Ministers & Co
book_date           26/06/90

ref_no              6
owner               Nash
adrs1               Highland Cottage
adrs2               Blackbridge Road
town                Woking
county              Surrey
no_bedrooms         4
no_baths            2
lounge_size         19' x 12'
dining_size         10 x 9'8
thru_lounge_size
notes               Integral garage
price               £133650
agent               Ministers & Co
book_date           26/06/90
```

```
ref_no                7
owner                 Hipkiss
adrs1                 17 Laurel Crescent
adrs2
town                  Woking
county                Surrey
no_bedrooms           4
no_baths              2
lounge_size           21'3 x 12'6
dining_size           13'5 x 10'4
thru_lounge_size
notes                 Attractive open staircase
price                 £143550
agent                 Ministers & Co
book_date             26/06/90

ref_no                8
owner                 Harris
adrs1                 19 Old Malt Way
adrs2                 Horsell
town                  Woking
county                Surrey
no_bedrooms           4
no_baths              2
lounge_size
dining_size           11' x 9'
thru_lounge_size      23' x 12'
notes                 Full dble glzng, utility room
price                 £119950
agent                 Thompson & Bayles
book_date             16/03/90

ref_no                9
owner                 Bishop
adrs1                 19 Grayshott Laurels
adrs2
town                  Lindford
county                Hampshire
no_bedrooms           4
no_baths              2
lounge_size
dining_size           10'6 x 10'
thru_lounge_size      21'8 x 12'
notes                 NHBC wrnty, clks, stdy, gas ch
price                 £102000
agent                 Thompson & Bayles
book_date             16/03/90
```

```
ref_no              10
owner               Edwards
adrs1               1 Brittens Close
adrs2               Willow Park
town                Guildford
county              Surrey
no_bedrooms         4
no_baths            2
lounge_size
dining_size
thru_lounge_size    17'9 x 16'3
notes               Att. Garage, pleasant gardens
price               £105000
agent               Thompson & Bayles
book_date           29/04/90

ref_no              11
owner               Bayles
adrs1               Lancefield
adrs2               Clay Lane
town                Guildford
county              Surrey
no_bedrooms         4
no_baths            2
lounge_size         18'8 x 15'9
dining_size         10'2 x 9'
thru_lounge_size
notes               Dble garage, gdns, swimming pl
price               £125000
agent               Thompson & Bayles
book_date           29/04/90

ref_no              12
owner               Wilson
adrs1               Holly Ridge House
adrs2               Fenns Lane
town                Woking
county              Surrey
no_bedrooms         4
no_baths            1
lounge_size         16'2 x 13'3
dining_size         12'3 x 10'7
thru_lounge_size
notes               Integral garage, 80' garden
price               £124950
agent               Allen & Co
book_date           29/04/90
```

```
ref_no                13
owner                 Thompson
adrs1                 75 Sheephouse Way
adrs2
town                  New Malden
county                Surrey
no_bedrooms           3
no_baths              1
lounge_size
dining_size
thru_lounge_size      15'3 x 17'9
notes                 My house
price                 £100000
agent                 Thompson & Bayles
book_date             07/08/90

ref_no                14
owner                 Granthams
adrs1                 1 Adelaide Road
adrs2
town                  Walton-on-Thames
county                Surrey
no_bedrooms           3
no_baths              1
lounge_size
dining_size
thru_lounge_size      15'3 x 17'9
notes                 My old house
price                 £100000
agent                 Thompson & Bayles
book_date             07/08/90

ref_no                15
owner                 Jones
adrs1                 15 Haslemere Avenue
adrs2
town                  Hounslow
county                Middx
no_bedrooms           3
no_baths              1
lounge_size
dining_size
thru_lounge_size      15'3 x 17'9
notes                 Close to airport and shops
price                 £100000
agent                 Thompson & Bayles
book_date             07/08/90
```

The bedrooms table

ref_no	bedroom_no	bedroom_size	ensuite_bath
1	1	13'2 x 10'5	y
1	2	13'2 x 12'5	n
1	3	14' x 9'7	n
1	4	9'5 x 8'8	n
2	1	12'6 x 11'6	n
2	2	11'6 x 10'0	n
2	3	11'4 x 9'3	n
2	4	7'7' x 6'	n
3	1	15' x 10'	y
3	2	12'2 x 10'1	n
3	3	11'10 x 10'	n
3	4	9'10 x 7'10	n
4	1	10'7 x 10'2	n
4	2	11'7 x 10'7	n
4	3	9'5 x 6'2	n
5	1	12'6 x 12'2	n
5	2	12'6 x 12'2	n
5	3	8'3 x 7'3	n
6	1	16'6 x 12'3	n
6	2	13'6 x 10'3	n
6	3	13'10 x 9'9	n
7	1	13'2 x 10'5	y
7	2	13'2 x 12'5	n
7	3	14' x 9'7	n
7	4	9'5 x 8'8	n
8	1	12'6 x 11'6	n
8	2	11'6 x 10'	n
8	3	11'4 x 9'3	n
8	4	7'7 x 6'	n
9	1	15' x 10'	y
9	2	12 x 10'10	n
9	3	11'10 x 10'	n
9	4	9'10 x 7'10	n
10	1	11'10 x 11'	y
10	2	10'2 x 9'3	n
10	3	9'9 x 7'10	n
10	4	8'9 x 7'10	n

```
11        1 15'6 x 10'6      n
11        2 11'3 x 10'6      n
11        3 11'  x 10'2      n
11        4 8'9 x 6'9        n

12        1 12'2 x 12'       y
12        2 11'10 x 9'       n
12        3 10'5 x 7'3       n
12        4 10'  x 7'10      n

13        1 15' x 10'        y
13        2 12 x 10'10       n
13        3 11'10 x 10'      n
13        4 9'10 x 7'10      n

14        1 12'6 x 10'9      n
14        2 12'6 x 10'9      y
14        3 12'6 x 10'9      n

15        1 12'6 x 10'9      n
15        2 12'6 x 10'9      n
15        3 12'6 x 10'9      n
```

Appendix 2

Answers to Exercises

This Appendix contains answers to selected exercises, where the answers are not fully covered in the text.

Chapter 4, page 70

1.  ```
    select owner, adrs1
        from houses
        where town = "Woking";
    ```

2.  ```
    select adrs1, town, price
        from houses
        where no_bedrooms = 3
        order by price;
    ```

3.  ```
    select adrs1, town, price
        from houses
        where no_bedrooms = 3
        order by town, price;
    ```

4.  ```
    select ref_no, adrs1, town, price
        from houses
        where (no_bedrooms > 3 and price < 130000);
    ```

5.  ```
    select owner, h.adrs1, price, a.agent, a.adrs1
        from houses h, agents a
        where h.agent = a.agent
        and h.town = "Guildford"
        order by price desc;
    ```

6.  ```
    insert into houses
        values (0, "The Queen", "Buckingham Palace",
                "Buckingham Palace Road", "London", "",
                120, 20, "23' x 42", "17' x 21'", "",
                "Nice place, very large, suit royalty",
                50000000, "", "01/09/90");
    ```

```
7.  update houses
        set price = price * 1.1
        where owner = "The Queen";

8.  delete from houses
        where owner = "The Queen";
```

Chapter 5, page 90

```
1.  select owner, adrsl, town, price
        from houses
        where (no_bedrooms = 3 and price < 120000)
        order by town, price;

2.  select adrsl, town, county, agent
        from houses
        where weekday(book_date) = 0;

3.  select adrsl, town, price * 0.9 price_less_10
        where price * 0.9 < 115000;

4.  select distinct town
        from houses
        where no_bedrooms = 4;

5.  select owner, adrsl, town, price
        from houses
        where month(book_date) < 5;

6.  select adrsl, town, book_date
        from houses
        where book_date is null;

7.  select owner, adrsl, town, price
        from houses
        where (owner matches "[A-M]*
                and (town = "Woking"
                or town = "Guildford"))
                or price between 100000 and 140000;
```

Chapter 5, page 96

```
1.  select a.agent, a.adrsl, h,adrsl, h.price
        from agents a, houses h
        where a.agent = h.agent;

2.  select a.agent, a.adrsl, h,adrsl, h.price
        from agents a, outer houses h
        where a.agent = h.agent;
```

3.  ```
    select h1.owner, h1.adrs1
        from houses h1, houses h2
        where h1.owner = h2.owner;
    ```

4.  ```
    select adrs1, town, county, price
        from houses
        where price = (select min(price)
                            from houses);
    ```

5.  ```
    select a.agent, a.adrs1
        from agents a
        where not exists
            (select h.agent
                from houses h
                where a.agent = h.agent);
    ```

Chapter 5, page 107

1.  ```
    select avg(price/bedroom) avg_price_bed
        from houses
        where town = "Guildford";
    ```

2.  ```
    select count(*)
        from houses
        where town = "Woking";
    ```

3.  ```
    select count(*)
        from houses
        where price between 100000 and 120000;
    ```

4.  ```
    select town, no_bedrooms, count(*)
        from houses
        group by town, no_bedrooms
        order by no_bedrooms, town;
    ```

5.  ```
    select town, avg(price)
        from houses
        where no_bedrooms = 3
        group by town
        having count(*) > 1
        order by 2;
    ```

6.  ```
    select town, avg(price)
        from houses
        where no_bedrooms = 3
        group by town
        having count(*) > 1
        into temp temp1;
    ```
    ```

Appendix 3

Informix Database Products

Database Engines

INFORMIX-OnLine

INFORMIX-OnLine is Informix's offering for the UNIX online transaction processing (OLTP) market. It is the second generation of this offering, the first being **INFORMIX-TURBO** with which OnLine is upwardly compatible. OnLine offers very high, scalable performance, together with on-line archiving, software disk mirroring, support for multimedia datatypes (storing digitised images, sound, etc.) and distributed databases (using **INFORMIX-STAR**). It is available on most UNIX platforms, as well as Netware386 (by the end of 1990) and OS/2 Version 2 (sometime in 1991).

INFORMIX-SE

The Standard Engine was, until Version 4.0, bundled with the front-end tool products such as SQL and 4GL. It is a C-ISAM based engine which uses the UNIX file system – this makes it very easy to install and maintain, but limited in performance, though quite acceptable for a large proportion of database applications.

Application Development Tools

INFORMIX-SQL versus INFORMIX-4GL

Among existing and prospective users there is some confusion between these two products and the facilities they offer. I hope this section will clarify the situation.

INFORMIX-SQL is a powerful and user-friendly set of RDBMS tools in which many complete database applications have been written. However it does have limitations. In particular, **PERFORM** screens may not display more than one record on a single screen, screen processing is limited, and multi-table updates or inserts are not possible. These limitations may be overcome by moving to **INFORMIX-4GL**, but there are inevitable tradeoffs between power and flexibility, and ease of use. **INFORMIX-4GL** is very much for serious application developers; in contrast, **INFORMIX-SQL** can be grasped easily by end-users, and its ease of use makes it an ideal prototyping tool for serious developers. This is what you will lose in moving from **INFORMIX-SQL** to **INFORMIX-4GL**:

- The **PERFORM** transaction processing module. You must write a complete **4GL** program to process even the simplest of data entry or query screens.

- Although the **ACE** report writer remains largely unchanged, you must write a **4GL** program to *call* an **ACE** report.

- There is no SQL editor for interactive ad hoc SQL statements. (Although you could probably write a **4GL** program to do this!)

- You lose the interactive schema editor. All database table creation and modification requires a **4GL** program to be written.

- Note that in standard **INFORMIX-4GL** (as opposed to the Rapid Development System) programs are compiled in a four phase operation, of which the last phases are a standard 'C' language compilation and linking. This can take three to four minutes just for a program to say 'Hello World'.

- You lose the User-menu design system. However, much more powerful menu systems may be written in **4GL**.

And this is what you gain:

- The ability to display multiple rows from a table on a single screen, and to scroll them up and down.

- The ability to access multiple tables under program control. For example, when you insert a record into table 1, the program automatically inserts or updates a record in table 2.

- Complete and powerful control over all screen processing.

- The ability to create your own ring menu system.

- Powerful error/exception handling and help screen creation.

- The ability to call programs not written in **4GL**.

- A source code control system, helping you to keep track of all your source and linkable modules and libraries.

- Complete control over what menu options are available to the user.

- A means of tying program operations to terminal function keys.

- Pop-up windows.

In summary, if you need the power of the **INFORMIX-4GL** language, then, in the development environment the ideal is to have *both* **INFORMIX-SQL** (for rapid prototyping, the interactive schema editor and ad hoc SQL statements) *and* **INFORMIX-4GL** for its powerful multi-row, multi-table and **4GL** facilities. Remember that once a **4GL** program has been developed, all that is needed to run it on a user's machine is a *run-time* **4GL** licence, at a price much reduced from a full development licence.

RDS/ID Rapid Development System and Interactive Debugger

The Rapid Development System allows you to write **INFORMIX-4GL** code but to run it as an interpreted program, instead of a compiled one. The advantage of this is that no compilation or linking is required each time a change is made. There is a slight performance degradation of between zero and fifteen percent, depending on the type of application. The optional Interactive Debugger allows you to step through your source code, while the program is actually running. It also has a host of other features to aid the application developer.

ESQL/C, COBOL, Ada, FORTRAN

These products allow you to embed SQL statements and a relational database structure within a third generation language program. The advantages of this are that you may take an existing 3GL program and convert it to use an Informix database engine, or you may prefer to write an application from scratch in a 3GL because of the special facilities it offers, while retaining the power of Informix database engine.

QuickStep

QuickStep is a product that was released early in 1990 and is an SQL-based, *interactive* report generator. It allows the end-user or developer to generate an SQL query through a point-and-pick menu system (no knowledge of SQL required), and then to design the report layout itself through a WYSIWYG (what-you-see-is-what-you-get) layout facility – you can actually design your report on the screen. It can also export both the SQL statement generated and the **ACE** code (in the form of a 4GL module, which uses the same syntax as **ACE**) and use them as part of another application.

Decision Support Tools

Wingz-DataLink

Wingz was originally developed and sold as a standalone spreadsheet program operating on the Apple Macintosh. However its superb presentation graphics and powerful spreadsheet features, complemented by its own programming language, called HyperScript, make it ideal as an Executive Information System or EIS, particularly now that it is also available on all the major windowing environments such as Windows 3, Presentation Manager and OSF/Motif. DataLink is a bolt-on product which gives Wingz the ability to extract data from an Informix database.

SmartWareII-DataLink

This product will give Smart – the best-selling DOS integrated OA package in the UK – the ability to extract information from an Informix database.

Connectivity Products

INFORMIX-NET
Since Informix applications are built using a two-process or *client/server* architecture, it is possible to run the client part of the application – the part that the user sees – on a separate workstation, either DOS or UNIX, while running the database engine on a central, more powerful UNIX server. The product used to do this is **INFORMIX-NET**, which runs on the client workstation and connects to either another **INFORMIX-NET** on the server with the Standard Engine (**INFORMIX-SE**), or to **INFORMIX-STAR** on a server with the OnLine engine.

INFORMIX-STAR
This product has two functions. The first is to be the server connection to **INFORMIX-NET** when the database engine is **INFORMIX-OnLine**, and the second is to provide a distributed database function. With **INFORMIX-STAR** databases on multiple, separate servers may be accessed as if they were all on the local server. A distributed query may extract and join information from tables in remote databases, with no reliance on a central site. Distributed update across multiple remote database tables is expected to be part of Version 5.0 of OnLine and STAR, sometime in 1991.

Upgrading from INFORMIX 3.3 to INFORMIX-SQL

INFORMIX 3.3 was the last version of pre-SQL **INFORMIX**. It had many useful features, particularly the inclusion of 'C' routines within **PERFORM** and ACE programs. However, for those users who would like the power of SQL and the other benefits of **INFORMIX-SQL**, here is a simple comparison and upgrade guide.

- The database. The **sqlconv** utility is provided which will create an SQL database from an existing 3.3 database (**INFORMIX 3.3** does not need to be present).

- There is no composite data type in **INFORMIX-SQL** (it was a non-relational idea anyway!). Instead a composite index must be created and the columns making up the composite must be specified in a COMPOSITES instruction in any **PERFORM** program that needs to join on these composite columns.

- Permissions and locations are not transferred to the new database. Permissions are now handled by the GRANT and REVOKE statements in SQL, and locations by the CREATE TABLE statement.

- **PERFORM**. This is virtually unchanged except for the following:

    There is a new mandatory **tables** section to specify the tables in the form.

    There is a new optional COMPOSITES instruction in the INSTRUCTIONS section to specify any composite joins.

'C' routines may no longer be included or called; this facility is covered by a separate product called ESQL/C which may be used in conjunction with **INFORMIX-SQL**.

- **ACE.** Virtually unchanged apart from the following:

  READ statements are replaced by SELECT statements.

  The SORT BY clause is replaced by ORDER BY.

  Command line variable names are now preceded by a dollar sign (e.g. $variable$).

- **informer.** This is replaced entirely by SQL statements and the SQL editor.

- **dbstatus.** This is replaced by SQL statements and the SQL editor.

- **dbbuild.** This is replaced by SQL and the Interactive Schema Editor.

If you have no 'C' routines or calls in your **PERFORM** and **ACE** programs, then the conversion to **INFORMIX-SQL** is relatively painless. If you do then you must also purchase ESQL/C, or convert to 4GL.

The major advantages of **INFORMIX-SQL** over **INFORMIX 3.3** are:

- The provision of an SQL interface, the schema editor and the ability to progress to **INFORMIX-4GL** if required at a later date.

- The ability to use *transactions* (see Chapter 3).

- The extra functionality offered by the optional OnLine database engine, such as high performance, distributed database, fault tolerance and multimedia.

Index